The Stranahans of Fort Lauderdale

THE FLORIDA HISTORY AND CULTURE SERIES

UNIVERSITY PRESS OF FLORIDA

Florida A&M University, Tallahassee
Florida Atlantic University, Boca Raton
Florida Gulf Coast University, Ft. Myers
Florida International University, Miami
Florida State University, Tallahassee
New College of Florida, Sarasota
University of Central Florida, Orlando
University of Florida, Gainesville
University of North Florida, Jacksonville
University of South Florida, Tampa
University of West Florida, Pensacola

Map of the New River Area c. 1893

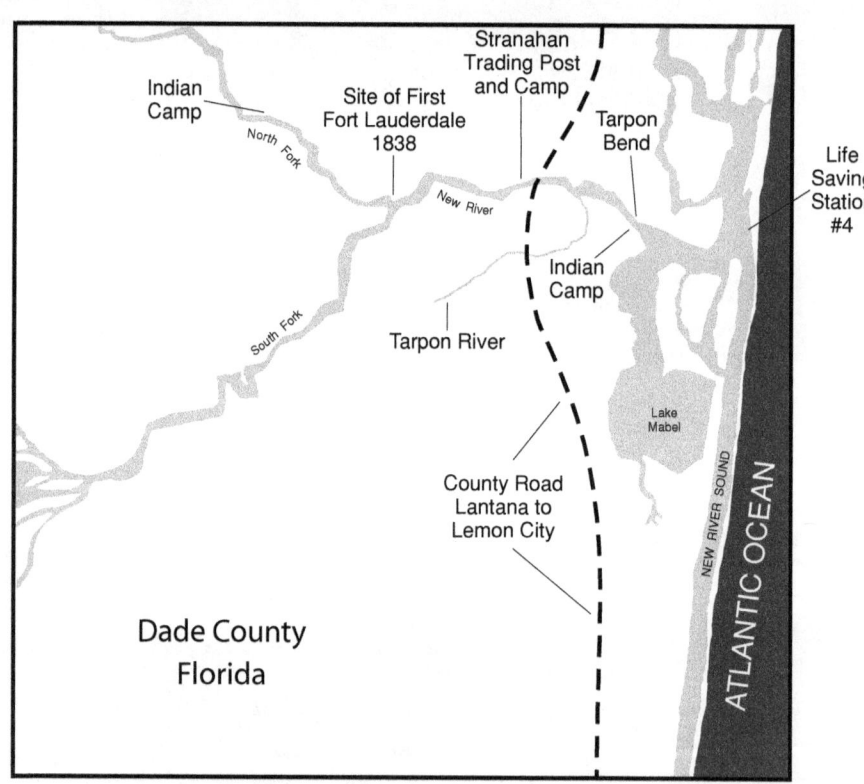

The Stranahans of Fort Lauderdale

A Pioneer Family of New River

HARRY A. KERSEY, JR.

Foreword by Raymond Arsenault and Gary R. Mormino

University Press of Florida
Gainesville · Tallahassee · Tampa · Boca Raton
Pensacola · Orlando · Miami · Jacksonville · Ft. Myers · Sarasota

Copyright 2003 by Harry A. Kersey, Jr.
Published in the United States of America
All rights reserved

First cloth printing, 2003
First paperback printing, 2022

27 26 25 24 23 22   6 5 4 3 2 1

Library of Congress Cataloging-in-Publication Data
Kersey, Harry A., 1935–
The Stranahans of Fort Lauderdale: a pioneer family of New River /
Harry A. Kersey, Jr.; foreword by Raymond Arsenault and Gary R. Mormino.
p. cm. — (The Florida history and culture series)
Includes bibliographical references (p.) and index.
ISBN 978-0-8130-2666-4 (cloth) | ISBN 978-0-8130-6891-6 (pbk.)
1. Stranahan, Frank, 1864–1929. 2. Stranahan, Ivy Cromartie, 1879?–1970.
3. Pioneers—Florida—Fort Lauderdale—Biography. 4. Businessmen—Florida—
Fort Lauderdale—Biography. 5. Politicians—Florida—Fort Lauderdale—Biography.
6. Women social reformers—Florida—Fort Lauderdale—Biography. 7. Fort Lauderdale
Region (Fla.)—Biography. 8. Frontier and pioneer life—Florida—Fort Lauderdale
Region. 9. Fort Lauderdale Region (Fla.)—History—20th century. I. Title. II. Series.
F319.F7K47 2003
975.9'35—dc21   2003050401
[B]

The University Press of Florida is the scholarly publishing agency for the State University
System of Florida, comprising Florida A&M University, Florida Atlantic University,
Florida Gulf Coast University, Florida International University, Florida State University,
New College of Florida, University of Central Florida, University of Florida, University
of North Florida, University of South Florida, and University of West Florida.

University Press of Florida
2046 NE Waldo Road
Suite 2100
Gainesville, FL 32609
http://upress.ufl.edu

For Marjorie Dickey Parson

During her term as executive director of the Fort Lauderdale Historical Society, in the years 1975–80, Marjorie initiated the idea for a Stranahan family history. We both admired the role that the Stranahan family had played in the development of Fort Lauderdale and were privileged to know Mrs. Stranahan in her later years. Marjorie took responsibility for the initial research for the book while I was engaged in other projects. Without her encouragement, tenacity, and unwavering enthusiasm, this book would have never been completed.

Contents

Series Foreword by Raymond Arsenault
and Gary R. Mormino   xi

Preface   xv

1. The New River Mystique   1

2. The Buckeye Connection   18

3. The New River Camp   33

4. Stranahan & Co., 1894–1911   65

5. Stranahan: Land Agent, Banker, and Promoter   83

6. Stranahan: Civic Leader and Politician   100

7. Ivy Stranahan, Civic Activist   115

8. Ivy Stranahan and the Indian Reform Movement   130

9. Public Lives, Private People   146

10. Epilogue   165

Appendixes   169

Notes   175

Bibliography   185

Index   191

Photographs follow page 49

Series Foreword

The Stranahans of Fort Lauderdale: A Pioneer Family of New River is the twenty-sixth volume of a series devoted to the study of *Florida History and Culture*. During the past half-century, the burgeoning population and increased national and international visibility of Florida have sparked a great deal of popular interest in the state's past, present, and future. As the favorite destination of countless tourists and as the new home for millions of retirees and other migrants, modern Florida has become a demographic, political, and cultural bellwether. Unfortunately, the quantity and quality of the literature on Florida's distinctive heritage and character have not kept pace with the Sunshine State's enhanced status. In an effort to remedy this situation—to provide an accessible and attractive format for the publication of Florida-related books—the University Press of Florida has established the Florida History and Culture series.

As coeditors of the series, we are committed to the creation of an eclectic but carefully crafted set of books that will provide the field of Florida studies with a new focus and that will encourage Florida researchers and writers to consider the broader implications and context of their work. The series includes standard academic monographs, works of synthesis, memoirs, and anthologies. And, while the series features books of historical interest, we encourage authors researching Florida's environment, politics, literature, and popular or material culture to submit their manuscripts as well. We want each book to retain a distinct personality and voice, but at the same time we hope to foster a sense of community and collaboration among Florida scholars.

The Stranahans of Fort Lauderdale offers a richly textured portrait of one of twentieth-century Florida's most remarkable couples, Frank and Ivy Stranahan. Their story, which begins in the pioneer era of the late nineteenth century, spans nine decades of historical change, encompassing a range of experiences and influences that defies easy description or explanation. As the most influential family in the small but growing community of Fort Lauderdale, the Stranahans presided over the social and economic transformation of an important segment of southeast Florida. But their saga involves much more than the standard story of economic success, urban boosterism, and regional development.

As Harry Kersey, a leading historian of twentieth-century Native American culture, demonstrates in this carefully crafted study, the Stranahans' accomplishments were inextricably linked to the fate of the Seminole Indians. Following his 1893 migration from Ohio to the Florida settlement then known as New River, Frank Stranahan first achieved economic success by developing an extensive pelt, hide, and plume trade with local Indian leaders. The contacts and trust established during these early years served him well throughout his life, and he remained a friend and supporter of the Seminoles until his untimely death in 1929. Ivy Cromartie Stranahan, who first came to New River as a young school teacher in 1899 and who married Frank a year later, became even more closely connected to the Seminoles than her husband, especially after she founded the Friends of the Seminoles, an education and social welfare organization, in the 1930s. A strong advocate of Indian rights, she never wavered in her commitment to Native American causes during the last four decades of her life.

The Stranahans' story, as told by Kersey, is a complex tale of success and failure. Economic reverses in the late 1920s led Frank Stranahan to take his own life and all but destroyed the family's banking and real estate empire. And the widowed Ivy traveled a hard road to recovery during and after the Great Depression. But, on balance, the dual legacy of tolerance and hard work left by these two individuals represented an important contribution to Fort Lauderdale's social and economic evolution. As local philanthropists and civic activists, they fought for a more humane and cosmopolitan vision of community life. Regrettably, they, like most of their contemporaries, did relatively little to mitigate the strictures of the Jim Crow system that kept Fort Lauderdale's black community from achieving social and economic progress. But the Stranahans' tolerant attitude toward Native Americans served as an instructive, if imperfect, model for the civil rights advances of later generations. Fortunately, Ivy lived long enough to see Fort Lauderdale grow into a modern metropolis, a city with all the problems and prospects of a place where historical burdens and grand dreams collide. Now, thanks to Harry Kersey, the chance to explore the origins of this ongoing collision is available to anyone who reads this fine book.

Raymond Arsenault and Gary R. Mormino, Series Editors

Preface

Simply put, this is a tale of one south Florida family—the Stranahans—and their pioneering spirit, economic enterprise, and facile adaptation to changing conditions along the New River. They were extraordinary people from very ordinary backgrounds, thrown together on the Florida frontier at the turn of the nineteenth century. Their lives became inextricably linked with the Seminole Indians, white settlers, venture capitalists, and other colorful entrepreneurs who frequented the New River. The couple never held high office or gained great fame during their lifetimes, yet they left an indelible mark on the history of their region and the state of Florida.

Frank Stranahan was not a young man when he came from Ohio seeking his fortune on a raw frontier. Through a combination of family connections, astute management, hard work, and some good luck, he was able to establish a thriving mercantile business. In the early years his success depended heavily on a lucrative trade in pelts, plumes, and hides with Seminole Indians who remained his lifelong friends.

As the Fort Lauderdale community grew, so did Stranahan's business interests. Profits from the store enabled him to move into real estate, where he built a small fortune. He became a partner in numerous commercial ventures, including the establishment of the first local bank. Stranahan's prominence as one of the first permanent residents, as well as a reputation for honesty, almost assured his emergence as a local political figure; he was regularly chosen to serve on the town's governing body. However, he had no political aspirations beyond serving the New River community. Following devastating hurricanes in 1926 and 1928 and collapse of the land boom, Florida and Fort Lauderdale endured economic hard times even before the start of the Great Depression. The bank's closure and the unraveling of Stranahan's other affairs took a physical and psychological toll, leading him to take his own life.

Ivy Julia Cromartie, a native Floridian, was eighteen years old when she arrived at the New River settlement in 1899 as its first schoolteacher. Sixteen years Frank's junior when they married the following year, she outlived him by more than four decades. The couple remained childless and enjoyed a degree of affluence, so the energetic and articulate Ivy Stranahan focused her activities outside the home. She was a prototypical southern club woman. Working through the state and national federation of women's clubs, she became an outspoken social activist who took a leading role in the women's suffrage movement and crusaded for Indian rights. This advocacy brought her into contact with a number of prominent state and national figures and established a network that she continued to use throughout her life.

Left nearly destitute following her husband's death, Ivy Stranahan proved resilient and resourceful. She regained financial stability by renting rooms in her home to winter visitors, and later leasing part of it as a restaurant during the tourist season. Eventually, land sales were negotiated with the municipality and school board that recouped part of the lost fortune. Before her death at age ninety, Ivy Stranahan was acknowledged as the "Mother of Fort Lauderdale" and a prominent civic benefactor who actively supported a broad range of causes. But she is best known for her work with Indian issues—especially the education and welfare of Indian children—primarily through the Friends of the Seminoles society, which she established in the 1930s. For nearly six decades Ivy Stranahan was a strong advocate for Indian rights in Florida.

Although Frank and Ivy were noted for their involvement with both Indians and African Americans, many of their activities could be viewed as paternalistic or even patronizing by contemporary social standards. Certainly they made no overt efforts to break down the segregationist racial and political barriers that prevented minorities from full participation in Fort Lauderdale community life. Nevertheless, the Stranahans far outpaced their fellow white citizens in striving to improve the health, education, and housing conditions of minorities.

South Florida is one of those unique locations in the nation where, because it remained an unsettled frontier for so long, some members of early pioneer families lived well into the twentieth century. Certainly it is our good fortune that Ivy Cromartie Stranahan lived such a long and full life, was a keen observer of events, and freely spoke of these experiences with numerous journalists and historians. Equally important, her sense of history ensured that her family's papers and photographs would be left to the Fort Lauderdale Historical Society, where they remain available to researchers. Eventually, through the foundation that Ivy Stranahan established for the society, funds became available to purchase the historical Stranahan House and restore it as a living memorial to the family.

A special note of appreciation is due Susan Gillis, former archivist at the Fort Lauderdale Historical Society, as well as executive director Joan Mikus and director of research Marilyn Rathburn, for their contributions to this project. Likewise, Barbara Keith, executive director of Stranahan House, Inc., was consistently supportive of the research. My colleagues in the Department of History at Florida Atlantic University, Sandra Norman and Donald Curl, contributed rigorous critiques of the manuscript; their incisive comments immensely improved the final product. My wife, Ruth Dyer Kersey, like myself a native Floridian, raised many issues that helped shape the book's perspective on a unique lifestyle that families such as the Stranahans—and our own—enjoyed here in a simpler time.

1

The New River Mystique

As rivers go, the New River is most unpretentious, a placid waterway with two branches that meander eastward from their source in the Everglades to converge at a point about three miles from the Atlantic Ocean. Yet the name still conjures up numerous colorful and contrasting images: pristine tropical beauty and savage bloodshed, Indian traders and northern tourists, pirate ships and sleek racing yachts. To the river over time came explorers, soldiers, adventurers, and energetic, sturdy souls hoping to carve out a future in the subtropical wilderness. The New River has wielded a magnetic, sometimes mystical, influence over residents and visitors to south Florida for centuries. Its image remains a powerful one that is not likely to diminish.

No one knows the origin of the river's name or that of its first visitor. A number of geographers have identified as the New River the Río Salado on the Freducci map of 1514–15, which drew upon the Ponce de León expedition for its data.[1] This led one historian to conclude that the famous Spanish explorer may have skirted or actually entered the New River inlet as it existed in 1513.[2] As early as 1631 the map *America Septemtrionalis* located R. Nova above the Bay of Biscayne.[3] Spanish explorer Antonio de Arredondo, who identified the coastal rivers and inlets of Florida, labeled the river "R Neubo" on his 1742 map.[4] Thus the name was clearly established on European maps by the mid-eighteenth century.

One local tradition attributes the name to an Indian legend that New River appeared overnight, during torrential rains "when the earth was trembling." Perhaps such an eruption did occur in prehistory, and the river may have existed as an underground stream eons ago. There were also tales that the river was "bottomless" in some parts. Late-nineteenth-century accounts do confirm the existence of strong whirlpools that sucked objects into subterranean passages, the flow from which was discharged ultimately as springs along the shore or in the Atlantic Ocean. Geologically, the river is a nonalluvial effluent of that unique natural phenomenon, the Florida Everglades. Prior to state drainage programs begun early in the twentieth century, the rocky base of the Everglades formed a huge holding basin that filled with rainfall, and the flowage moved slowly southward from Lake Okeechobee to the Florida Straits. The basin was higher than sea level, and over time the accumulating waters cut through the soft limestone of the coastal ridge at points, forming "rivers" that drained to the sea.

One surveyor, Marcellus Williams, wrote in his 1870 field notes, "New River both forks is a very deep Stream and Navigable to the rim of the Everglades. As you ascend the River towards the Everglades, there are deep Caverns in the Coral Rock from which the Water makes with great force, so much so as nearly to prevent propelling a Boat with oars. The rim of the Everglades are shallow and so is the water after getting into it until you get out some 4 to 6 miles, New River Sound and Middle River are deep."[5] Charles Pierce, son of a pioneer south Florida family, also traveled to the river's source and observed, "All the land hereabout was solid rock, and it became evident to me as I looked at it that at some time in the remote past there had been an earthquake that had opened this fissure from the Glades to the coast, making the channel now called New River. . . . Just at sundown we arrived at the end of the river. Here the water was pouring from the Everglades through a narrow channel and running so swiftly it taxed our strength to the utmost to paddle the old canoe through. When we reached the still water of the Glades we paused to eat."[6]

The waters of the New River always sought an opening on south Florida's ever-shifting coastline. Over the centuries natural forces opened and closed inlets along the coast in random fashion.[7] Littoral drift along the lower east coast transported sand southward, depositing it in the inlets. Tropical storms and nor'easters also battered and weakened the shoreline, closing inlets and opening others where none existed previously. Torrential rains piled up water in the Glades that had to find an outlet. Thus the New River inlet has been changed frequently by the whims of nature, as numerous maps attest. In the past such occurrences were viewed as acts of God; now they are attributed to hydrostatic pressure, littoral drift, beach erosion, and other environmental factors.

Following the French and Indian War (1756–63), Great Britain took possession of East and West Florida, and William Gerard De Brahm, surveyor-general for the southern colonies, was directed to make a survey of the coastline south of Saint Augustine. In 1765 he witnessed the creation of "a new inlet" along the present-day shoreline of Broward County. His notes reported that the great rains of May "filled this River and its Marshes with so much water that its weight within and the Sea without by Force of the N. E. gales demolished the Bank and made this Inlet between 25th and 30th May 1765. 17 common miles to the No. of this Inlet is a fine fresh water Spring issuing out of a Rock upon the Beach."[8] Accompanying De Brahm on his survey of the Florida coastline as a deputy surveyor was Bernard Romans, who became so enthralled with "The Floridas" that he subsequently spent several years conducting more detailed explorations on his own. Although De Brahm's notes were not compiled for publication until many years later, in 1775 the Dutch-born Romans reported, "5 miles to the south of Rio Seco is another point of rocks, and south of it a small bite, and a half a mile further is the mouth of the *Rio Nuevo*, which is about G of a mile wide and generally open but shallow, here Jew-fish are very abundant both within and without the river."[9] No early observer was more lavish in his appraisal of Florida than Romans. He described in detail its climate, flora, fauna, and possibilities for development, especially in agriculture. He forecast that Florida could become a "seat of trade" on the North American continent despite the presence of mosquitoes, the discomfort of heat and humidity, and its flooded conditions during the rainy seasons. Despite the enthusiasm of Romans and others who viewed the New River and south Florida as having great potential, the region suffered from its wild and lawless reputation. Francis Fatio, writing an economic report in 1790 to be used by the Spanish government for establishing commercial policy, found that the whole East Florida province was good for the growing of sugarcane and cotton; but he cautioned, "no people settled in those localities, no one ventures to risk his negroes and property to the inroad of the Indians, pirates, and rogues from the Bahamas who infest all these coasts."[10]

The transfer of Florida from Great Britain to Spain at the end of the American Revolution failed to usher in an era of tranquility. Some British subjects were not eager to be uprooted from their homes or submit to Spanish rule. They faced financial losses in disposing of their property and moving to areas under British control. A number of English sympathizers adopted disruptive tactics, including William August Bowles, a former Loyalist officer from Maryland with business ties in the Bahamas. In 1788 Bowles attempted to foment an insurrection by Florida Indians, which the Spaniards quickly quelled.[11] The knowledge that English sympathizers in Florida were a potential source of trouble prompted the Spanish government to send a secret mission to New River in 1793. Under the pretext of seeking fresh water at New River for a ship ostensibly en route to Havana, the mission sought information on the activities of another Englishman, Surla (sometimes called Charles) Lewis, and his four grown sons. Formerly associated with Bowles, Lewis was reportedly living in Florida and possibly serving as a foreign agent to the Indians.

Sebastian Verezaluze, an emissary of the Spanish governor of East Florida, commanded the mission to New River aboard the schooner *Juan Nepomuceno* and wrote a detailed account of the river's depth and navigability.[12] The Lewis family did indeed live there but was away on a month's trip to the Bahamas. Instead, the Spaniards found Joseph Robbins, a known confidant of Bowles, staying on New River and seeing to the Lewises' interests during the family's absence. "Robbins said that he had been there for five or six months, and that Mr. Lewis had lived in that house for several years, and that the latter had a plantation two miles to the west of this house. He also reported that Mr. Lewis had five horses which a certain Bowles had given him."[13] Nothing further is known of Surla Lewis, whom the Spanish sought to spy on; nevertheless, the Verezaluze report provided the first written account of non-Indian occupation on New River.

Although the Lewis family subsequently moved to the Miami River region, they continued to claim landownership on New River for many years. By 1825 only six south Florida land claims from the Spanish period had been validated. Jonathan Lewis and his sister, Polly, held tracts on the south side of the Miami River, while their mother secured a section on New River. Jonathan Lewis became justice of the peace at Cape Florida but later moved to Key West, where he resided for many years. His mother, Surla's widow Frankee Lewis, was at Cape Florida with her son on January 10, 1825, when she signed a deed selling the "Lewis Place" on New River to Solomon Snyder of New York, "with the buildings, orange, lime and coconut trees thereon."[14] Snyder inexplicably began action on behalf of Frankee Lewis to acquire title to the 640-acre tract on New River, signing the necessary claim as "Agent for Frankee Lewis."[15] An affidavit dated May 5, 1825, supporting the claim for the land grant, states "that he [Snyder] has known Frankee Lewis, the widow of Surla Lewis deceased to cultivate, occupy and possess for four years previous to the twenty second day of February in the year of our Lord One thousand eight Hundred and nineteen, the place known by the name of the 'Lewis Place' on New River."[16] The claim was confirmed on December 31, 1825.

Apparently Snyder had no opportunity to exercise his ownership rights on New River, for he died around 1825 in Saint Augustine. His deed from Frankee Lewis was never recorded in Monroe County records, and it first came to light in 1870 in the files of the U.S. General Land Office in Washington. Despite having sold the property to Solomon Snyder in 1825, Frankee Lewis resold it five years later, on September 8, 1830, to Richard Fitzpatrick. The widow Lewis, who died sometime before 1835, thus created a tangle in the legal ownership of the property that remained unsettled until 1895.[17]

Other early settlers came to the New River, such as the colorful Odet Philippe. His background, like that of the Lewis family, is obscure. He claimed a personal friendship with Napoleon Bonaparte dating from their student days at a boarding school in Lyons, and he later received an appointment as a surgeon in the Napoleonic navy. Captured at the Battle of Trafalgar, he spent time in an English prison before making his way to the Bahamas, and ultimately settling in Charleston, South Carolina.[18] Financial misfortunes in Charleston then reportedly led to Philippe's sojourn on New River, where he attempted the commercial production of salt from ocean water. The Frenchman arrived aboard his ship *The Ney* (named for Napoleon's marshal) in 1828, seven years after ratification of the Adams-Onís Treaty transferring Florida from Spain to the United States. Philippe's wife reportedly preferred an active social life, finding

Key West more to her liking. Census records reveal that Phillippe maintained a residence in Key West in 1830, and he served for a time as justice of the peace for Monroe County. Ties between Key West and the New River region were strong and contacts frequent, as Key West was the seat of federal government in south Florida. Philippe maintained contact with the New River community for a number of years before moving to Tampa, where he died in 1869.

William Cooley from Maryland took up residence on New River in 1824, moving there from north Florida, where he first settled in about 1813.[19] Cooley made his living primarily by processing arrowroot starch from the wild zamia root that grew abundantly in the region. He had perfected the Indian method of making the flour product, which they called *coontie*, at his water-powered mill on New River, and this profitable business is considered Broward County's first industry. He also lent an aura of legitimacy to the highly publicized "wrecking" business that flourished along the southeast Florida coastline. Wreckers made their living by salvaging the cargoes of merchant ships that foundered along the Florida coast. Many wreckers were accused of setting misleading signal fires to lure vessels onto reefs, where they could be exploited for salvage. Cooley, who made frequent trips to Key West, gained the respect of many, including Richard Fitzpatrick, a powerful territorial legislator. Fitzpatrick helped him secure appointment as justice of the peace for the New River settlement, serving the area from Cape Florida northward from 1831 to 1836. Fitzpatrick also exercised his considerable political clout to help bring about the creation of Dade County in 1836.

Richard Fitzpatrick, a forceful and influential figure, envisioned south Florida's future in terms of a flourishing plantation-based economy, and he promoted a system of connecting canals making inland navigation possible from the Saint Johns River south to Biscayne Bay. With a view toward bringing his dream to reality, Fitzpatrick purchased 2,600 acres—all of the privately owned property in southeast Florida save one small parcel on Key Biscayne. One of his holdings was the "Lewis Place" on New River, which he purchased in 1830. His friend William Cooley already lived on this tract but did not hold title. In 1832 Fitzpatrick described his new holdings: "The lands on the South Atlantic Coast of Florida consists of high Hammock, low Hammock, high marsh, low marsh, and pine barren. The growth of the high Hammock is principally live oak, Mulberry, red

Bay, Stopper, Mastic Ironwood, Wild fig, and palmetto; and produces Corn, Sugar and Cotton in great perfection. The low Hammock is covered with Red Bay Maple, Custard Apple, cocoa plumbs, and palmetto and is decidedly the richest land I ever saw."[20] In the same letter Fitzpatrick outlined his idea for cutting a canal connecting the different bays, sounds, and rivers from Cape Florida to the Saint Johns River. Using his political acumen, Fitzpatrick secured passage of a bill in the 1837 Florida legislature establishing the East and South Florida Canal Company. Naturally, he was one of many prominent Floridians who formed the company.

Fitzpatrick also introduced black slavery to the area and installed James Wright as overseer of his plantations. In 1830 Wright brought Stephen R. Mallory from Cape Florida to help develop the New River operation. Mallory found life quite congenial while working and living at Fitzpatrick's plantation. His diary records that he "not only hunted and fished but learned woodcraft from Indian companions." The outdoor life and sunshine improved his health, which had become weakened through violent attacks of fever. Days and even weeks were spent in the open hunting deer. There was also an abundance of turkeys, bears, ducks, partridges, and fish, both salt- and freshwater. He writes that their number was so great that neither labor nor skill was needed to get them. Besides Colonel Fitzpatrick and a Mr. Cooley and family, there were few other frontier people in the region, but Stephen declares that he was so enchanted with the wild life of a hunter and the genial climate that he seriously debated with himself the question of remaining there forever.[21] Mallory spent only a year there, however. (Many years later he became Confederate Secretary of the Navy and is known as the "father" of the iron-clad *Merrimack*.) By the time of the 1830 census, some sixty or seventy persons lived in a widely dispersed community along the New River. Cooley employed many of the able-bodied men in his salvage operations.

Despite William Cooley's connections and affluence, he is best remembered because an Indian attack on January 6, 1836, at the start of the Second Seminole War, resulted in the death of his wife, three children, and the children's tutor. Ironically, Cooley had always befriended the Indians, welcomed them into his home, and often took their side in quarrels with white settlers. The Seminoles wreaked their vengeance on Cooley because in the year before, as justice of the peace, he had imprisoned a white man accused of killing the local Seminole chief. Later the Monroe County Court in Key West released the prisoner for lack of evidence, and the Indians evidently believed Cooley had withheld information that would have led to a conviction.

There are contradictory reports surrounding Cooley's whereabouts when the Indians sacked his home. One source reports that Cooley was at Hillsboro Inlet with his crew, engaged in salvaging the Spanish brigantine *Gil Blas*, wrecked there during a severe storm. But Cooley later claimed that, for reasons unexplained, he had gone to the Cape Florida Lighthouse and heard of the tragedy from fleeing settlers.[22] Historian George Buker states that Cooley was at the Cape Florida Lighthouse, acting as temporary keeper, when he learned of his family's fate.[23] Odet Philippe was known to be a resident of Key West when the Cooley family members were killed; however, it has been reported that Philippe was on New River at the time and had been warned by the Indians to flee. Philippe claimed to have met Cooley as he fled southward in his boat and told him the tragic news. Of all those known to be living on New River at that time, the Indians killed only Cooley's family. Nonetheless, panic instantly gripped the region, and all the settlers fled south to the relative safety of Cape Florida and beyond, abandoning the flourishing New River settlement.

The Cooley family tragedy occurred before news of the Dade Massacre in central Florida reached the New River. The Indian ambush of December 26, 1835, in which Maj. Francis L. Dade and over a hundred members of his command were killed, ignited the Second Seminole War of 1835–42.[24] The Seminoles violently rejected federal efforts to remove the tribe from Florida and to resettle it in Indian Territory west of the Mississippi River. Hostilities raged across the peninsula, and by 1838 the New River area became a center of military operations. By order of Gen. Thomas Jesup, a fortification was built where the two forks of the river came together. Shortly thereafter Jesup directed the installation be designated "Fort Lauderdale," in honor of Maj. William Lauderdale, who recruited a unit of Tennessee Volunteers to serve in the Seminole campaign at the request of his close friend, President Andrew Jackson.[25] The unit was stationed on New River only about thirty days; then, as the period of their enlistment neared expiration, the Tennesseans under Lauderdale were ordered to depart. Although their commander died in Baton Rouge on May 18, 1838, the name Fort Lauderdale remains his legacy. Newspapers and periodicals in the Northeast that had previously carried items with a New River dateline now reported events from Fort Lauderdale.

A chronicle of events occurring along New River during the Second Seminole War is found in military records. One of the few significant engagements of the war took place on March 22, 1838, at an island a few miles west of the point where the river emerged from the Everglades.[26] Although the battle was inconclusive, it was the first time American forces had assaulted the Seminoles in their previously unreachable Everglades camps. No longer could the Indians visit their major source of food without fear of military interdiction. The marshes and waterways of the New River region provided ideal conditions for the Seminole Indians to pole or sail their canoes great distances in search of the plentiful marine life. Not only were fish, shellfish, manatee, and other aquatic fauna available to augment the Indian diet, but the river also served as a highway by which the Indians could come to the area for their most important food—the wild tuber *Zamia integrifolia*, from which they made the starch *coontie*. So important was the New River that the Seminoles called it *coontie hatchee—coontie river*.[27]

Many naturalists and botanists visited south Florida, and the New River area in particular, even during the period of conflict with the Seminoles. Dr. Benjamin B. Strobel was one who came with the U.S. forces in the winter of 1836 and observed, "As we approached New River, the land upon our right consisted of the same pine sandy barren as I have already described. The Indian arrow root called *coontie* is found here in great quantities. We landed, and collected several roots which were very large, weighing several pounds. This is the Indian's principal bread stuff. It is met with in most of the pine barrens in this section of Florida, but it grows in such a profusion in their neighborhood, that they come from considerable distance to procure it."[28] The superabundance of zamia along New River and its importance to the Indians for food at a time when the army was destroying their villages, field crops, and other supplies was one reason for building the first Fort Lauderdale. Its location on the major *coontie* grounds denied the Indians access and became a key element of army strategy.

Military personnel serving in the region kept diaries and wrote letters that found their way into publication. Among these reluctant visitors were a few individuals of outstanding literary ability, who later published journals describing the area and aspects of the conflict. Some of these writings contain lengthy and eloquent descriptions of the area's natural resources, although a few of the soldiers viewed Florida with great distaste and chose to dwell on its undesirable aspects. These reports constitute the greater part of what is known about the New River region between the 1836 Cooley massacre, which scattered the residents to areas of greater safety, and the time when the army abandoned Fort Lauderdale in 1842.

One of the most prolific observers was an army surgeon, Jacob Rhett Motte, who expressed his views in vivid and unambiguous terms. He wrote,

> Florida is certainly the poorest country that ever two people quarreled for. The climate in the first place is objectionable; for even in winter, while persons further north were freezing, we were melting with heat. In the next place, the larger portion of Florida is a poor, sandy country in the north; and in the southern portions nearly all wet prairies and swamp; healthy in winter but sickly in summer; and in the south even the Indians said they could not live a month without suffering, and in the summer not at all. It is in fact a most hideous region to live in; a perfect paradise for Indians, alligators, serpents, frogs, and every other kind of loathsome reptile . . . and offers but feeble allurements to an agricultural population, the only land fit for cultivation being on the margin of the rivers, and inconsiderable as to extent, and barely sufficient to raise the ordinary subsistence for small families.[29]

By contrast, Lt. Christopher Tompkins wrote, "Moreover, this must be a perfectly healthy place and its extraneous advantages such as fish and salt water bathing are not trifling considerations."[30] It was Tompkins who proved prophetic. By the mid-nineteenth century doctors began to recognize and recommend the healthful aspects of Florida's climate, especially during the winter months.

These officers also commented on the considerable logistical problems that the shifting location and varying depth of New River inlet created for the military. In 1839 Lieutenant Tompkins wrote his commanding officer concerning the relocation of Fort Lauderdale from the fork of New River: "Our removal to the beach has proved a most fortunate circumstance.

The bar at the Inlet has been gradually increasing and under the most favorable circumstances could scarcely have been crossed at high water by Steamboats of the lightest drought. It measured today 4'5" at high water which is a greater depth than I expected or have known for two months. But you must recollect this tide is the highest of the lunar month."[31] The inlet's shallowness created many navigational problems and caused delays in crossing from the sound into the ocean. As surgeon Motte reported, "On reaching the mouth of New River, we did not find sufficient water on the bar to permit our crossing, so dropping anchor, we remained stationary all night, waiting for high tide next morning."[32]

Notwithstanding frequent changes in the river's depth and the navigational difficulties posed by a sometimes impassable inlet, New River continued to attract mariners. At certain points along the shoreline, although no actual inlet existed, crossings from the sound into the ocean could be made at high tide by dragging small boats a short distance across the beach. One such location was designated as the "Indian Haulover" on the military's 1856 Ives map from the Third Seminole War (1855–58). It was here that Seminole Indians could shift their canoes from the sound into the ocean at high tides.[33] This is the same location where an artificial inlet for New River was excavated in 1923. A hurricane closed this inlet in the 1930s following the dredging of Port Everglades. The port channel then served as the New River inlet.

The Second Seminole War proved to be the death knell for Richard Fitzpatrick's dream of a plantation-based society in south Florida. In 1842 he borrowed $21,000 from his sister, Harriet English of Charleston, South Carolina, mortgaging all of his lands along both New River and the Miami River. Unable to repay the debt, a year later he deeded the property to William F. English, his nephew and Harriet's son. Fitzpatrick then moved to Texas, where an old friend from New River days, U.S. Senator Stephen Mallory of Florida, obtained several diplomatic appointments for him. With the start of the Civil War, Fitzpatrick became a commercial agent for the Confederacy in Matamoros, Mexico, where he died a poor man in 1865. However, Fitzpatrick's speculation in south Florida real estate seems to have set a pattern that persists to the present day. Young William English attempted to operate his uncle's plantations as soon as hostilities with the Seminoles ended. He, too, abandoned the effort in 1843, and later answered the call of the California Gold Rush, telling a friend he intended "to make a million dollars" and return to south Florida. Instead he died in Grass Valley, California, around 1855.

With the cessation of hostilities and Florida's admission to the Union in 1845, an uneasy peace prevailed. It is estimated that fewer than 500 Seminoles remained in Florida, and they were content to stay in the remote precincts of the Everglades and Big Cypress Swamp, well away from even sparsely settled areas. A survey of southern Florida, which Richard Fitzpatrick had first sought in 1832, became a necessity if commercial development were to take place. Accordingly, the state surveyor, George McKay, conducted a survey in 1845, and his work enabled Florida to identify and convey state lands. And, for the first time, boundaries of the "Lewis Place" on New River were fixed.

A final conflict with the Seminoles brought the first road development in the New River region. The Third Seminole War began in 1855, and after three years virtually all Seminoles were removed from Florida. Capt. Abner Doubleday, who commanded Company E at Fort Monroe, Virginia, was dispatched with his troops to Fort Dallas on the Miami River on October 25, 1856. Soon his unit, along with Company B of the First Artillery, was ordered "to build a road from Arch Creek, north to New River, a distance of fifteen miles. Preliminary surveys were made in January 1857, and the road was completed the following month. It was built on a ridge, and later the Florida East Coast [Railway] used the same route for the railroad from Fort Lauderdale to Miami."[34] On October 13, 1857, Doubleday and his command were reassigned to Fort Capron on the Indian River. He described the first part of the journey northward this way:

> The first 25 miles were easy traveling for Brannan & myself had made a good road but after that my ingenuity was taxed to the utmost for I had to make my way with a train of 12 wagons across large rivers great swamps and areas of the sea. The first obstacle I encountered was at New River some 30 miles from the post. The problem was to cross a wide stream with a train of twelve wagons & about 80 animals without a boat of any kind. I sent a man to swim over with a small cord tied to his waist the other end being fastened to a larger rope. The alligators were pretty thick but I have never known them to attack a man while swimming & the soldier was not afraid of them. When he was on the other side he pulled the large rope & fastened one end to the trunk of a tree the other end was

tied to a tree on our side. I then took a wagon body covered it with a canvass tent and thus made it nearly water tight. Having done this I used my improvised boat to take my wife & her maid over... I was much relieved in mind when I had passed these obstacles and found myself in the endless pine forest once more.[35]

The Third Seminole war ended in 1858, and Doubleday's company was soon transferred to Fort Moultrie at Charleston, South Carolina, where he remained as second in command until the firing on Fort Sumter in April 1861. Of his departure from Florida, the putative inventor of baseball wrote, "At last the welcome order came for us to leave the solitudes of Fla for the refinement of Charleston, S.C."[36] The second Fort Lauderdale site used briefly by Doubleday was again abandoned, never to be reactivated. The wooden structure on the beach was left to weather and rot.

The New River region did not immediately rebound to its pre-1836 activity level following the war. The Seminole conflict of 1855–58 had no doubt dampened enthusiasm for further settlement in the southern part of the peninsula. Then in 1861 the Civil War erupted, and the nation was torn apart. Following the war many individuals, especially Southerners from devastated areas, sought to rebuild their lives in a new environment. People began to trickle into the region again, slowly at first. The 1870 census showed a small number of families living along New River. Three Jenkins brothers from South Carolina—Washington, Josiah, and Joseph—were farming there, and their housekeeper was May Knight. The families of Isaiah Hall, John Addison, and Francis Infinger had migrated from Georgia; John Brown's family arrived from Virginia and Georgia. Edward Baseley of Massachusetts was a seventy-year-old farmer who returned to New River where he had been at the time of the 1836 Cooley massacre. To the south along the Miami River, the population had also increased.

Several events provided an impetus to opening the area for development. In 1870 Marcellus Williams was commissioned to make a second survey of southern Florida. His work corrected many inaccuracies in the 1845 McKay survey, and the number of land transactions increased. The era of peace that descended on south Florida was no small factor in attracting newcomers. In 1871 a couple from Ohio, William B. Brickell, Sr., and his wife, Mary, took up residence on the Miami River.[37] They engaged in a lucrative trade with the Seminole Indians and began acquiring land. Three years later Mary Brickell purchased from Harriet English the 640 acres on New River "known as the grant to Frankee Lewis."[38] Although the Brickells never lived on New River, they exerted a strong influence there for many years. The family's name is memorialized today by Brickell Drive in Fort Lauderdale, located within the bounds of the original Lewis property. A number of subdivision names reflect the Brickell interests.

Brickell's purchase of the "Lewis Place" began another cycle of land speculation in properties in the New River region as a growing population created demand. With the increased freight and passenger traffic along Florida's coast there were frequent shipwrecks, so in 1875 Washington officials authorized construction of a series of life-saving stations, five in all, starting about thirteen miles north of the Indian River Inlet. Station No. 4, built on Fort Lauderdale beach, was completed April 24, 1876. The first "keeper" was a New River resident, the farmer Washington Jenkins. The keepers were more than transient government employees; several of these men and their families purchased property, thus adding some stability to the area. Ultimately, the Lifesaving Service became part of the U.S. Coast Guard, which continues to have a presence in Fort Lauderdale.

The 1880 census revealed continuing population growth, and the pace of life in the New River region was quickening. In some states interim censuses are made; such was the case in Florida in 1885. The census for the New River area was made by Charles Peacock of Miami, whose brother J. T. Peacock became the keeper at Life Saving Station No. 4 in 1893. Because the 1890 federal census records were destroyed by fire the 1885 Dade County census is a particularly valuable source of New River history. It revealed a population of diverse backgrounds. For example, there were white planters from the Bahamas, with a number from England or of English parentage; others were native Floridians of Florida-born parents. There was one German farm family with a black servant from Virginia. New York, Ohio, and Michigan were also represented, as were several southern states. The inhabitants' occupations were generally agricultural or maritime in nature. Large tracts of land had been acquired by individuals and organizations with considerable resources, and this reflected the widespread interest in southeast Florida. A group of British investors purchased two million Florida acres in 1881, including large holdings in present-day Broward County. The state issued deeds as early as 1876 for property that had been seized for nonpayment of taxes. Citizens from Miami and Palm Beach acquired property, both small and large tracts. Ocean frontage became attractive in 1885 when two Chicago investors purchased Government Lot 6 along the beach. The Florida Tropical Fruit Propagating and Land Improvement Company purchased 1,067 acres in 1886. The following year "Palm City" was platted by Arthur T. Williams of Fernandina, and covered two sections of land. Although a number of lots were sold, it appears no structures were erected, and the venture failed. Nevertheless, it focused attention on New River.

In the 1870s, the New River began to be frequented by outdoorsmen who publicized their exploits widely, thereby attracting other visitors. At the same time, the medical profession touted the healthful aspects of Florida's climate, particularly during the winter months. One prominent visitor, Dr. James A. Henshall of Kentucky, brought his wife to Florida in an effort to improve her health. In 1884 Henshall wrote a popular book detailing his travels during 1879 and 1882, *Camping and Cruising in Florida*. He described New River in glowing terms:

> New River, for six miles above its mouth, is the straightest, deepest, and finest river I have seen in Florida, although a narrow one. It is famous for its sharks (regular man-eaters, some of them), and for the immense number and variety of its fishes.... Rushing in and out with the tide, at New River, fishes can be seen by thousands, which snap at any thing, even of rag tied to the hook and thrown to them by a strong hand line. We took crevalle from ten to thirty pounds, always large ones here, never less than ten pounds. By anchoring a boat in midstream they can be speared or gained as they swim rapidly by, often pursued by sharks and porpoises.[39]

Other works, such as Charles B. Cory's *Hunting and Fishing in Florida* (1896), also trumpeted New River as a sportsman's paradise.[40]

In time the uneasy peace that followed the Third Seminole War became a lasting one. The remaining Seminoles slowly emerged from their wilderness fastness to trade with the whites who now lived in south Florida in ever-increasing numbers. Some Indian groups that had retreated into the Everglades returned to the New River region for its abundance of *coontie* and marine life. By the 1890s a number of Seminole families had reestablished their camps at Pine Island in the Everglades west of the river's source. Henshall and Cory both traveled up the river to visit the large Pine Island settlement and left written observations of the people and their way of life. In their works one can identify many of the Seminole families that remain in Broward County to this day.[41]

Pine Island was a complex of several associated islands containing extended family camps; it was also a major ceremonial center and site of the annual busk ritual known as the Green Corn Dance. Henshall described a typical Indian camp, noting, "The houses are formed of upright posts set in the ground thatched roof of palmetto leaves, and a floor about three feet from the ground, the sides being open. They sit on the floor during the day, and sleep on them at night, their beds being rolled up in the daytime. They all sleep under mosquito bars, which are tucked up during the day. The store houses are A-shaped and are closely thatched all around, with a door in one end."[42]

Cory detailed the Seminoles' method of hunting and trapping game. He left this particularly vivid account of how they took manatees, which were valuable for meat and oil:

> New River is very deep in places and is one of the best localities on the coast for manatee. It is a favorite hunting ground of the Indians when they desire to kill one of these animals.... These animals come to the surface every few minutes to breathe, and their heads may be seen as they appear for a moment above the surface of the water.... [The hunters] harpoon them as they rise to the surface, using a steel point barbed on one side, attached to a long pole. To the steel point is fastened a strong cord, which in turn is attached to a float. Upon being struck the manatee sinks at once, but the direction in which he moves is indicated by the float. The Indians follow the float as closely as possible and watch for him to rise to the surface, when they shoot him through the head and the huge animal is towed to shore.[43]

Cory also described the Seminole practice of hunting alligators at night by torchlight, and of setting fire to the scrub to drive out game such as deer and bear. These traditional practices would occasionally place them at odds with white settlers, but for the most part the two cultures coexisted peacefully in the sparsely populated wilderness.

However, rapid development and population growth were in the offing. By 1890 William and Mary Brickell controlled over three thousand acres in the vicinity of the Miami River and along New River. That same year the Florida Coast Line Canal and Transportation Company acquired enormous tracts of land in connection with its plan to dredge a navigable inland waterway from Jacksonville to Miami by connecting the existing waterways. James L. Colee, a civil engineer, was for a number of years connected with the Florida Coast Line Canal and Transportation Company. The company established a work camp in Fort Lauderdale with Colee in charge, and he purchased property along New River in 1891. Today a residential area in Fort Lauderdale is platted as Colee Hammock, and is often erroneously identified as the site of the 1836 Cooley massacre. Also in 1891, the Florida Fiber Company purchased 1,300 acres of land a short distance north of New River on which it intended to produce sisal hemp, but this became another ill-fated venture.

The New River region, with its enormous capacity for contrasts, became many things to many people. Explorers and naturalists viewed it with excitement as they discovered and cataloged its varied fauna and flora, and their praise was lavish. There seems to have been no middle ground in how visitors reacted to the south Florida wilderness. Although some military personnel sent into the region wrote in glowing terms of its natural attractions, others reviled its climate, physical hazards, isolation, and other undesirable features. Adventurers engaged in shady activities viewed the New River region as ideal for it offered concealment and anonymity. The lawless came in the beginning; the entrepreneurs, speculators, and sportsmen arrived later. Those with an eye for business and commerce saw the area's great potential. Indeed, the New River and its environs offered opportunities to diverse individuals with varying purposes. It was to this region of incredible beauty that had seen so much turmoil, a placid river of mosquitoes, manatees, and Seminole Indians, that Frank Stranahan came seeking his fortune during the last week of January 1893.

2

The Buckeye Connection

In 1865 Florida had been a state for only two decades. The devastating Civil War had ended, and in its aftermath many individuals began migrating to an area of the country that appeared to offer social stability and economic promise. Among the Old South states, only sparsely settled Florida had escaped the worst ravages of war and its aftermath. Publications with a national distribution were extolling the healthfulness of Florida's climate, increasing its allure for winter tourists, while sportsmen found unsurpassed hunting and fishing on the peninsula. Certainly the state seemed to have strong economic potential. All of these features would attract members of two Ohio families, the Stranahans and Metcalfs.

At Civil War's end the Reverend Robert Stranahan and his second wife, Sarah McFadden Stranahan, were living in Vienna, in Trumbull County, Ohio. Both were Pennsylvania born. Robert, a Presbyterian clergyman, had resided in Ohio for a number of years. In 1860 his first wife, Rachel, died and was buried in Trumbull County; two years later an infant son from his second marriage, John, was also buried there. And it was here that the second son of Robert and Sarah Stranahan was born August 21, 1865. The child was named Frank after Robert's father.

Jennie Leah McFadden, the sister of Frank Stranahan's mother, was living in nearby Liberty Township, Ohio. When Frank was about fifteen months old, his aunt Jennie and her British-born husband, William Irwin Metcalf, had a son, whom they named Guy Irwin Metcalf. The lives of these two cousins were to be intertwined over the years, in both Ohio and

Florida. Each was to have an impact on the New River region through his business associations.

Young Frank Stranahan grew to adulthood in Ohio, attending public schools in Trumbull County. Two references contained in family records and correspondence attest to young Frank's scholarship. On February 27, 1876, W. R. Hawkins wrote from Dowagiac, Michigan, to "Franklin Benjamin Stranahan." The letter includes a reference to Frank's grades: "Glad to hear you were getting along so well at school. Tell Willie he will have to study his grammar a little to catch up with you. Fourty percent to one hundred is quite a difference I think."[1] It is primarily through such letters that we are able to glimpse Frank Stranahan's life prior to his arrival in Florida.

When Frank Stranahan was eighteen, his half-brother, Will, four years his senior, left home to seek his fortune in the West; he would lead a nomadic existence for the remainder of his life. Despite the distance between them, it appears that Will and Frank enjoyed a close relationship. During Will's long absences, his letters to Frank, written in a beautiful Spenserian penmanship, tell of restless wanderings, frequent job-hopping, and the search for elusive riches. More important for our purposes, Will's letters provide at least a sketchy record of Frank's activities.

As a young man Frank Stranahan reportedly went to work in the steel mills located near his Vienna home. By 1883, at age eighteen, he was working in Hazelton, Mahoning County, Ohio. In June of that year Will wrote to Frank from Ainslie, Montana Territory, and his letter includes the sentence, "I also have rec'd the Daily News Register and saw about the fire."[2] The length of time Frank worked in Hazelton is unknown. There is an often-repeated but undocumented tale that he was involved in an industrial accident at the mills that injured his lungs and left his health impaired. Will's reference to a fire may have been the source of this story, but no other details are known. In any event, by July 1883 Frank was again receiving mail addressed to his Vienna home. Will wrote describing the fertile farming lands and prices of choice properties in the Dakota and Montana territories. He mentioned Yellowstone Park, new towns springing up, jobs on railroad gangs—enough to excite the imagination of any younger brother.[3] Will's letters may have given Frank the idea of following his older brother westward.

Early in 1884 Frank Stranahan went to Sigourney in Keokuk County,

Iowa, to visit his paternal grandparents. Will wrote to him there, saying in part, "I was surprised this morning to receive a letter from you in Iowa. I hope you may do well and like the country well enough to stay there for a while and not get to running around like me." But he closed the letter on a discouraging note: "If you can get any thing to do hold it down for this country is no good. I will go east as soon as I can get fixed. Don't think for a minute of comming out here for there are 10 men to every job now."[4] Before the end of the year Frank returned east and took a job in Lindenville, Ohio, where he remained throughout much of 1885.

His correspondence suggests that young Stranahan was not satisfied with his Lindenville employment. By 1886 he was living in Elmdale, Kansas, home of his sister Lucy and her husband, Charles Dunlap. Frank's younger brother, Allen, wrote to him there in February, "We got your letter a week or so ago and ought to have written before but have not done it yet. I was glad to hear that you got there all safe and found them all well."[5] Ten days later Robert Stranahan wrote his son Frank:

> Excuse the delay in answering your letter which I received sometime ago. I had waited hoping to hear from you something about the country, how you liked it.... We got a letter from Lucy day before yesterday. We're glad to hear that you were all well. I would like to have been there when you unpacked your trunk. I think I can see Grace's [Lucy's daughter, who would later move to Fort Lauderdale] eyes sparkle as she beheld the little broom and dusting pan which I sent her. I suppose she makes the dust fly in all directions.... We were at Metcalfs a couple of weeks ago but they were not at home.[6]

The following day Robert again wrote to tell Frank the position in Hazelton he had left two years earlier was open again. Robert advised that he forget his differences with a former employer and write to say he was interested in the job, but despite this sound fatherly advice, Frank chose to remain in Kansas.

In April 1886 brother Will, back in Montana after a trip to California and Arizona, wrote Frank, "I ought to have went home last summer when I quit here. I never will be any better fixed to go home and have a good time and I could have paid you too, but I thought I would be all right untill I left California. I found I had been trying to be a Vanderbilt on Stranahan's money and that did not work surely.... I hope you will not get discouraged for I will make your money a good investment for you some day yet."⁷ A letter from Frank's father, written in June of that year, conveys disappointment that Frank failed to return to Ohio to take what appeared to be a sound job offer. It also asks, "How are Lucy and Charlie and the little folks. . . . Give them our love when you see them and tell them we are going West if possible this fall."⁸ This comment implies that Frank had found living quarters outside the Dunlap's home.

Economically, things were not going well for the Stranahan young men, but Will remained optimistic. On February 5, 1887, he wrote, "Am sorry that I have put you to so much trouble about sending you that money you asked for. . . . I am sorry that you have had such a streak of hard luck but you can just put yourself in my place and it is just the same. I think that times will be better in the northwest than they were next spring so don't give up for I will send for you to come and stay with me next summer sure. I think that business will be rushing everywhere next spring and I will get you a job out here and if you like the country we can make a barrel of money in jig time." He went on to confess that he had become a "hard case" for the last few years, but had turned over a new leaf and intended to stay that way until he could return home. He concluded, "I wish I could be at home and sit down around the grate in the front room. I think that a story of my life for the past four years would be as good as a first class romance. Give my best respects to all the Boys and Girls and Cousins and family in general and write soon."⁹ In this letter Will failed to follow his normal practice of including the addressee's name and address above the salutation. Yet the concluding request that Frank convey greetings to "all the Boys and Girls and Cousins and family in general" indicates that by early 1887 Frank had returned from Kansas to his home in Ohio.

The year 1887 became a turning point for Frank Stranahan. At age twenty-two he would make the journey to Florida. Perhaps it began as another of his youthful wanderings in search of purpose, or his health may have demanded a more congenial climate; in any case, in Florida he found permanency, achievement, influence, a degree of financial success, and recognition. Frank's younger cousin, Guy Metcalf, also had health problems. He was evidently a sickly child, and when Guy was ten years old his parents moved to Florida in hopes of rearing a more robust youngster. The family settled in Melbourne. Guy returned to Ohio for his secondary education and trained to be a teacher, graduating from the Girard Normal

School. Eschewing the field of education, young Metcalf then returned to Melbourne to engage in business. His health had improved, and he was active on the local scene. By the age of twenty-one, Guy appeared to have a promising future.

The Metcalf business interests were apparently prospering. Frank Stranahan's uncle, Will Metcalf, was a lawyer and also owned a lumber business in Melbourne. The *Florida Star*, published in Titusville, reported, "The demand for lumber is so great that Mr. Metcalf cannot secure it fast enough to supply the purchasers."[10] In 1887 he was about to embark on a new venture. The *Star* announced on January 19, "Messrs. Metcalf and Stout expect to publish the *Indian River News* in Melbourne in a short time. The material has been ordered from the foundry, and is expected to arrive shortly." Likewise, when he built a home, the *East Coast Advocate* noted, "The new residence of Mr. W. I. Metcalf, on the bluff near Bleak House, presents a fine appearance from the river."[11]

The Metcalfs, father and son, maintained a high profile in the community. Because of their varied business ventures both men traveled frequently on the river steamers plying the Indian River between Melbourne and Titusville, and the newspapers kept a running account of their coming and going. The *Star* carried several items during 1887 reporting on the progress of the new Metcalf newspaper. The first of these noted, "Several received the first issue of the *Melbourne News*, published by Messrs. Metcalf and Stout. It is a very creditable sheet with a good display of local advertising. The editorial pledges their devotion to the improvement of the great Indian river country and her local interests. We gladly enter on our list and hope it will meet with the success it deserves."[12] The following month the editors reported, "We received a call from Mr. G. I. Metcalf, of Melbourne, last Saturday, who is visiting Titusville in the interest of his paper, *Melbourne News*. This being our first acquaintance with Mr. Metcalf, we were quite well impressed with the zeal and energy he displayed in the interest of his new venture."[13] The younger Metcalf also received prominent mention: "Mr. Guy Metcalf, the lively editor of the Melbourne *News*, returned from a trip to Jacksonville last Friday, and started for his editorial home on Saturday on the steamer Rockledge."[14] And again in October, "Mr. Guy Metcalf, of Melbourne, the junior editor of the *News*, was in Titusville the first of the week. He said he came up to see the municipal election."[15] From the recurring mention of his efforts to promote the newspaper, it appears that Guy was taking an ever more prominent role in the publishing enterprise.

Initially, Frank Stranahan settled in Melbourne, where his aunt and her family lived. Years later Stranahan and his wife both indicated that more than health problems had brought him to Florida. His spirit of adventure and need for employment played a large part in luring him into the new frontier country with its real and imagined opportunities. But Stranahan did not make the journey alone; he came in company with other young Ohioans, the majority of whom presumably were seeking a broader range of opportunities. They arrived in connection with another facet of the Metcalfs' promotional activities, revealed by a notice appearing in the *Star:* "A party of forty Ohioans, who are visiting now in Melbourne with the prospects of settling, stopped at Titusville last Thursday and Friday, accompanied by Mr. W. I. Metcalf, who is largely interested in Melbourne, and Mr. Guy Metcalf, the editor of the *News.*"[16]

Frank Stranahan had no difficulty obtaining employment in Melbourne. He worked there for five years, gaining valuable experience in the mercantile business. The Florida climate seems to have agreed with him. An 1889 letter written to his parents revealed that he was achieving a mature outlook, had stayed in the same job, and was helping promote Metcalf interests. The letter also remarked on the slow-paced life of frontier south Florida before the railroad arrived:

Mch. 20, 1889

Dear Father & Mother:

Having a little spare time today I will try and scribble off a few lines. This afternoon will be a dull one. Trade was good this morning but the wind has shifted and we are getting a Norther. People would live by water and mostly on sail boats. We can come pretty near telling in the morning whether there is going to be much business or not for the day. Most everybody predicts a dull summer. These seasons for it is ——— [illegible] that everybody is going away that can possibly get away. They haven't got over the fever scare of last summer. There will be a couple of families more here for good this summer. Next month will see quite a number away. The travel is not near what it was last winter what are on the river are going on south to Jupiter and Lake Worth. It is getting to late to expect any here, I expect to hold this town down for another year. Can't say whether I will be in the store or not . . . [if nothing] turns up different from what I see now I probably will. I think I can get other work if I want it. I wouldn't advise any one to come here for work. I have had a streak of luck in getting work, if I ain't growing rich. I am looking out for myself down here, so have had no trouble about work or anything else, so I am still able to "paddle my own canoe."

Our "house" took a trip to Eau Gaillie last Sunday to help dedicate a church wind played out got there to late. So we crossed to Tropic. The finest land on the river for garden muck & flowers no end to them all year around. The land is held at one thousand dollars per acre. It's been cleared up within the last four years. You can see all kinds of tropical fruit and plenty of it. It's a strip of land between Banana & Indian Rivers and is fifty yards to half a mile wide runs that way for fifteen or twenty miles. It's a sight to see. I wrote Al a couple of weeks ago. Haven't heard from him yet. Is he still in Youngstown. I suppose Will is at home this time as I haven't heard from him lately. If not and you have his address I would like to hear from him someway. I hear from the rest occasionally. Suppose they are busy like myself. Do you get the paper all right. I sent half a dozen copies to help the thing along. It has a very good circulation at present, with the job press it keeps three of them busy in the office. Their lumber business is played out. I can't think of any thing more this time so hoping this will find you all well will close.

Yours,

Frank Stranahan[17]

Meanwhile, in the southern part of the state, Dade County residents were embroiled in controversy over a proposal to move the county seat from Miami northward to a more central location in the sparsely populated region. The matter was settled by an election in February 1889, and the following year a courthouse was built in Juno, at the north end of Lake Worth. This would provide new business opportunities for Guy Metcalf that required him to move from Melbourne to Juno. According to historian Donald Curl, "Many people on the lake wanted a newspaper to promote their community, so when Melville Spencer (an early resident) offered to erect a new building for Metcalf, he agreed to move the newspaper to Juno. The two-story, twenty-by-forty-foot frame building contained a printing room, with solid cement bases for the presses, a room for the editors and reporters, and a small private office for Metcalf, all on the first floor. The editor and his staff lived on the second floor."[18] Metcalf needed a new name for his newspaper, and county judge A. E. Heyser suggested the *Tropical Sun*, though some readers insisted on calling it the "Prodigal Sun."[19]

Early in 1891 the *East Coast Advocate* reported, "*The Tropical Sun* is located at Juno, and is the first newspaper ever published in Dade County. It is 8 pages of 6 columns, all home print, and the quality of the paper is away ahead of anything ever used in this section. . . . The rapid development of the field in which the new journal is located is bound to insure its success; especially when it is remembered that in the future all the legal advertisements and tax sales, section notices, etc. will go to the only paper in the county as a matter of course."[20] Whether by long-term design or happenstance, the *Tropical Sun* proved invaluable for promoting the various ventures in which the Metcalfs were engaged, or would ultimately become involved with. Another Metcalf business interest was the Tropical Real Estate Exchange, and the *Tropical Sun* became the major vehicle for advertising properties handled by that Juno company.

As early as 1888 the Dade County Commission committed to build a county road from the Lake Worth area southward, thereby providing a land route into the Biscayne Bay region. Then, as now, progress on road building was slow—too slow to satisfy the populace and particularly those living near Biscayne Bay, which could be reached only via ocean travel along the famed and hazardous reefs offshore from the south Florida coastline, or by walking the beach with the "Barefoot Mailman." Early editorials in the *Tropical Sun* called for opening a road to Biscayne Bay, and in 1892 Guy Metcalf secured a contract from the commissioners to build the road with a low bid of $24.50 a mile. The construction went slowly, and Metcalf's response to complaints about the delays was reported as follows:

> The Sloop "Oliver" having on board contractor Metcalf and a force of workmen, bound for Lantana passed here Friday last, to com-

mence the work of opening the county road to Biscayne Bay. Mr. Metcalf intends pushing the work right through, so that by the time the season opens a stage line will be fully established between Lantana and Biscayne Bay. Some one ought to open a half-way house to be convenient for stopping over night, as the ride would be rather tiresome to go through in one day, particularly if there are many palmetto roots left in the road.[21]

While the reference to palmetto roots causes one to question the contract specifications for completing the road, it was actually not uncommon for early road builders to leave stumps up to fifteen inches—ostensibly short enough for wagons to clear. This is also the first indication that Metcalf might be contemplating operating a hack line along the route.

Completion of the road was "pushed" as Metcalf had promised, and on November 14, 1892, the Dade County Commission accepted it as a county public road.[22] Although the road was open and in use, much work remained to be done. On February 13, 1893, commissioner N. W. Pitts reported on the condition of the completed bridges, found they met the required specifications, and recommended that they be accepted by the county commission. This report was adopted, and at a special session of the commission on March 20, notice was given that "the County Commissioners of Dade County will receive sealed bids for the construction of 2230 feet of corduroy work, twelve ft. wide across sloughs, bogs and bay heads between New River and Hillsborough River, crossed by the County Road."[23]

Immediately a controversy arose over the route of the county road, most of it generated by Mary Brickell of Miami, who was not happy with the road's approach to the New River. The route she preferred would not bisect her property, the "Frankee Lewis Donation," but run along its western boundary and the east line of Section 10. On April 13, 1893, she notified the commission, "I have had a road cut and grubbed on the Section Line at New River. Please have the Ferry moved, and use the new road within thirty days."[24] In July the county commission considered the Brickell protest. The clerk was instructed to write William and Mary Brickell that if they would do the corduroying and bridging that was necessary on the section line at New River, the county commissioners would declare the same a public road.[25] Mary Brickell ultimately won her point, and the river crossing for the county road was moved to the area where the U.S. Highway 1 tunnel under New River is now located.

The disagreement between the Brickells and Dade County over the location of the New River crossing is understandable. County officials originally selected the "old government road" constructed by Capt. Abner Doubleday in 1857 as a route between New River and Lemon City (now part of Miami). That choice required no bridging between New River and Arch Creek since it bypassed the Tarpon River.[26] It would have been the most economically advantageous route since the county estimated the cost of an additional bridge at $500 and Tarpon River was less than a mile south of New River at the point where the Brickells wanted to place a ferry crossing. The commissioners wrote to the Brickells indicating that Dade County was agreeable to moving the road provided the Brickells would do "bridging and corduroying at New River." However, it seems unlikely that the commissioners actually meant for the Brickells to build a bridge over New River itself since they had, considerably earlier, authorized the construction of a ferry for use at New River. It is more plausible that the county meant for the Brickells to bridge the much smaller Tarpon River and prepare the approach to it.

During construction of the county road, the Metcalfs remained actively involved in a variety of enterprises for their names appeared frequently in both the *Tropical Sun* and *Indian River Advocate*. Many of their activities responded to fast-breaking events in Florida, such as a meeting of railroad titans reported by the *Indian River Advocate:* "Messrs H. M. Flagler and H. B. Plant were hob-nobbing in Jacksonville and St. Augustine this week, and the knowing ones say that it means railroad building in South Florida, and that Indian River 'is in it.' Intelligence also comes from New York that the building, at an early date, of the Canaveral and South Florida railroad from Kissimmee to Canaveral is an assured fact. Ah, well! We will see what we will see. All things come to those who wait. We wait with patience."[27]

In the last quarter of the nineteenth century, the names Flagler and Plant were synonymous with economic expansion and railroad development in Florida. During the 1880s, capitalizing on the discovery of phosphate deposits near Tampa and cultivation of citrus in the region, Henry B. Plant of Connecticut developed a network of railways and hotels along the state's west coast. In like manner Henry Morrison Flagler became the preeminent railway and resort developer along the Atlantic coast. The multimillionaire Flagler made his fortune in association with John D. Rockefeller, as a founding partner of the Standard Oil Company. In 1883 he and his second wife honeymooned in Florida, and he became enthralled with the state's potential as a place both to retire and to indulge a second career. By 1885 the fifty-five-year-old Flagler had taken control of the Jacksonville, Saint Augustine, and Halifax River Railway and had begun construction on the opulent Ponce de Leon and Alcazar hotels. Soon the nation's oldest city became the Florida destination of choice for affluent northern tourists.

Flagler continued to acquire land and determined to push his railroad southward. Prior to 1890 he received state permission to build as far south as Miami, although that was not his initial intent. Nevertheless, as one of his biographers observed, "The Standard Oil magnate received a big thrill from watching the two ribbons of steel roll southward; he had employed more than 1,500 men to complete the task. But the task was only half completed, and Flagler's nature would never allow him to stop until a thorough job was done."[28] The line reached New Smyrna by November 2, 1892, and was headed for towns in the undeveloped Indian River region. At that time his company was more appropriately named the Jacksonville, Saint Augustine, and Indian River Railroad. Anticipation of the explosive growth that always accompanied the arrival of a railroad was enough to excite astute businessmen such as the Metcalfs.

As if the completion of a road all the way to Biscayne Bay and the possible extension of rail service even farther south was not enough, still another transportation project was generating great excitement. Although the earliest surveys had been made in 1844, actual construction was now to begin for a series of canals connecting the chain of creeks, rivers, lakes, and sounds along Florida's east coast to create one continuous waterway. Richard Fitzpatrick's vision of the 1830s was coming to fruition. The *Tropical Sun* carried the following item on November 24, 1892:

> Capt. Wright, who has had charge of the dredge boat Chester, now cutting the canal from Jupiter to Lake Worth, for the past few months, arrived here on the belated through steamer on Monday on his way to his home in Mobile, Alabama, for a two or three weeks vacation. Captain Wright is of the opinion that an opening cut into

Lake Worth will be reached by next February or March. He also informs us that another Dredge will shortly reach Lake Worth and commence cutting from the lower end of the lake towards Boca Raton and New River Inlet, and that another dredge will start work at New River and cut south toward the north end of Biscayne Bay.

Ultimately the Florida Coast Line Canal and Transportation Company would receive over a million acres of land along Florida's east coast in return for the construction of this toll canal.

During the time Guy Metcalf oversaw completion of the county road from Lantana southward, he was also busy with plans to establish a hack line between Lantana and Lemon City that would provide commercial overland transportation to Biscayne Bay. While this venture ultimately lasted just three brief years, it brought Frank Stranahan to New River. Stranahan was a young man in the right spot at the right time, and certainly he had the right family connections. The opening of south Florida was an exciting prospect, and young Stranahan's relatives seemed to be well positioned to profit from that—or were they? Rapid developments in Florida rail transportation must have given Guy Metcalf some worried moments as he contemplated the competition that his fledgling hack line would face. Ironically, Metcalf himself foresaw the ultimate replacement of the hack line, predicting that the East Coast Line would be at the head of Lake Worth by the winter of 1893–94, and he wrote in the *Tropical Sun* of November 24, 1892, "This year a hack line will serve the purpose, next year or the one after, Mr. Flagler may see fit to go Metcalf 'one better' and put an Iron horse on the route."[29]

While the Metcalfs were busy expanding their enterprises, Frank Stranahan remained employed at a store in Melbourne, gaining valuable business experience. It was also in Melbourne that he first undertook some of the public-spirited community involvement that marked his later life. On November 22, 1888, Stranahan signed the notice of incorporation for the city of Melbourne, along with his cousin Guy Metcalf and others. However, when balloting took place the following month, his name was not listed among those eligible to vote on the incorporation issue. This may well have been because Stranahan did not own property in the area proposed for incorporation, although he was a registered voter in Melbourne for the years 1889–92. Guy Metcalf voted, but his father did not. Immediately following the positive incorporation vote, city officials were elected, and Guy I. Metcalf, a notary public, swore the first mayor into office. When the municipal election was held two years later, in December 1890, Frank Stranahan was chosen as Melbourne's marshal and collector. On December 19 he was sworn into office along with other city officials. Evidently Stranahan served for only one year because the report of the election the following December does not list him as a city official. But his political career was by no means at an end, although it would be another twenty-five years before he was again elected to public office.

The local newspaper mentioned Stranahan on several occasions. On September 4, 1891, the "Melbourne News" section of the *Advocate* reported that Frank Stranahan and others had "returned Thursday from a trip to the lower river. They encountered no mosquitoes." A front-page item in the November 27 issue announced that "Frank Stranahan has gone on a mission to Titusville; his place in the store of E. I. [sic] Thomas & Co. being filled during his vacation by Robert Carson of Eau Gallie." Stranahan appears to have been well thought of in the community, as attested by this item in the June 30, 1892, *Tropical Sun:* "Mr. Frank Stranahan, head clerk and valued assistant to E. C. Thomas & Co.s merchandise establishment is off for a two weeks trip to Jacksonville and other points in the State. Frank has been a faithful employee, and constant attention to his many duties for so long a time will make his vacation all the more enjoyable."

By late fall of 1892, Metcalf's plans were sufficiently well along that he began promoting the hack line. The November 15, 1892, edition of the *Times-Union* in Jacksonville reported that "Metcalf, while in St. Augustine, stated his Lantana–Lemon City hack would be running by December 1st." But something—perhaps a delay in completion of the two tallyho coaches being built in Jacksonville—evidently caused the service to begin later than first planned. The *Times-Union* announced on January 1, 1893, that the coaches had been shipped and the first run of the hack line would occur on January 15. Other necessities for the venture began to fall into place slowly, and the January 27, 1893, issue of the *Indian River Advocate*, reporting Lake Worth news, stated, "Guy Metcalf's mules for the Hypoluxo–Lemon City stage route, arrived Saturday [January 21]. There are eight of them. One of them is an immense fellow. From their appearance one would judge they would do good work. They are from St. Augustine."

On January 13, 1893, the "Lake Worth News" column in the *Indian River Advocate* reported, "The Hack line from Lemon City to Hypoluxo is being used almost constantly now-days. Four passengers came up Friday and three went down on Saturday." The next issue of the *Advocate* contained this item: "Mr. Guy Metcalf, editor of *The Tropical Sun* was in town Tuesday, on his way home after an absence of some weeks from Juno. He gave us a pleasant call on Tuesday, and said his hack line to Biscayne Bay would commence running on Monday next. Metcalf said a wrong impression had gone abroad that his hack line was connected with the J., St.A. & I. R. Ry. It is run entirely by himself; has nothing to do with the above railway, and that he would connect with any railway or steamboat company that felt like connecting with his line."[30]

Another Metcalf venture was announced earlier in the month by the *Indian River Advocate:* "The Dade County Real Estate and Abstract of Title Company is the name of a new firm which has just hung out its banner in Juno. It is composed of the following members: W. I. Metcalf, Attorney at Law, A. E. Heyser, County Judge, Guy I. Metcalf, Editor of *The Tropical Sun*, and Notary Public. The size of Dade County ought to be large enough to support two good real estate firms, especially when we take into consideration the great interest now being manifested by prospective settlers in regard to the Lake Worth and Biscayne Bay regions."[31]

In January 1893 Frank Stranahan was wrapping up his personal affairs preparatory to leaving Melbourne and venturing into an even more remote frontier area. He had been hired by his cousin Guy Metcalf to manage the hack line's camp at New River. On Saturday, January 21, Dr. A. E. Lyman of Melbourne wrote a receipt to Stranahan for "$25.00 for payment in full of dental work up to date."[32] On the same day he secured a letter of recommendation from a former employer in Melbourne, E. P. Branch, who wrote, "Mr. Frank Stranahan, the bearer of this note, has been for several years in my store at Melbourne. I can confidently recommend him as a man of strict honesty, industrious, and closely attentive to business. He can be trusted in any business position he may undertake to fill."[33] Another letter written on the stationery of "E. C. Thomas and Co., Successors to E. P. Branch," attested that, "Mr. Frank Stranahan the bearer of this note has been associated with us since we succeeded Mr. E. P. Branch one and one half years ago. We speak of him as a man of the strictest integrity, ——— [illegible] and ——— [illegible] at his business, and capable to successfully further any undertaking, and we cheerfully tender this ———— [illegible] to him at his parting with us. /s/ E. C. Thomas & Co."[34] This appears to have severed his connections in that Indian River community.

At age twenty-eight, Frank Stranahan headed for New River to manage the tent camp where hack line passengers spent the night and took their meals before journeying onward. The *Tropical Sun* announced on February 2, 1893, "Mr. Frank Stranahan, of Melbourne, Indian River, arrived at Juno last Wednesday [January 25] and on Thursday proceeded down to Hillsborough at which place he will have charge of the half-way house of the new hack line." During his five years in Melbourne, Frank Stranahan earned recognition as an able, industrious young man. From these modest beginnings as the first merchant–Indian trader in the raw frontier community that sprang up on New River, Frank Stranahan eventually achieved economic success. He also earned recognition as a civic leader with the reputation of being a "rich man," a degree of success that was probably beyond his wildest youthful dreams.

3

The New River Camp

Frank Stranahan arrived at New River on January 26, 1893, and reported finding Seminole Indians living nearby. Only three whites resided in the immediate vicinity. One, Dennis O'Neill, served as the keeper at Life Saving Station No. 4 on the beach.[1] Another, W. C. Valentine, a civil engineer who had come to New River from Biscayne Bay, also lived at the life-saving station. Valentine became the local postmaster in 1891.[2] The third was W. C. Collier, who farmed on seventy-one acres three miles north of Middle River, land that he was negotiating to purchase.[3]

Using letterhead from Metcalf's Tropical Real Estate Exchange, Stranahan wasted no time in writing to brother Will describing his new situation in detail. He enclosed a sketch of the camp showing its relationship to the road between Lantana and Lemon City. This letter is generally considered to be the first communication from contemporary Fort Lauderdale.

New River Jan 31 1893

My Dear Bro:

One week ago to night I left Melbourne. Here I am in camp, two of us, myself and darkey cook. Will you join us. My nearest neighbor is Capt. Oneil. Guy and Uncle Will were here last week with a party of four gents. Met them on the road as I was coming. Came through with one mule wagon, and saddle mule driver two passengers and myself. Fare one way 10 dollars round trip 15 dollars. Two dollars a day at camp. At present, I have most of the say, or sort of act Supt. Guy is off on a two weeks trip in the northern part of the state. The Hack is carrying the mail. Pays 15 dollars a trip once a week at present. Hope to have it three time in the near future. This is the only P. Office on the line. It is settled up at each end. The county road clearing and grubbing cost the county two thousand dollars, bridges and ferry three thousand six hundred and think there is about five thousand in the Hack Line, 8 head of mules, 2 hacks, one baggage wagon and one mule wagon, 1 buckboard, 1 saddle, last three belong to camp. Have the tents, all have floors in and furnished equal to any hotel, oil gas stove and granite cooking ware, all decorated chinaware, silverware, six bedroom sets complete, twelve spring cots, brass lamp, have one bill of table linen and bedding and towels which I will copy.

1 doz comforts	16.00
16 pr. blankets	48.00
8 pr. blankets	16.00
18 counterpanes	16.00
3 doz lin towels	6.00
1 doz cot "	1.25
4 " "	4.00
1 doz combs	1.25
1 piece T linen	15.93
1 " " "	3.00
3 doz napkins	4.50
Dish rags	.75
18 pr sheets	21.00
3 doz pil slip	9.00
40 yd crash	4.00
½ gross soap	2.40
½ doz brushes	1.50
1 T cover	2.00
10 pieces plaid for petitions in tents	27.18

The furniture is as good as any one need. 1 doz card tables, rocking chairs, camp stools & chain folding chairs, both wood and iron, hammocks, carpenter tools, everything you can think of. I want you to come down and spend the winter. If you want to work all right, if not you can sport. Wont cost you a cent. Will give you a pass over the Hack line, buy a ticket to Jupiter unless you have passes. You ought to get there round trip 30 or 40 dollars for sport here. After day work today cook set under his tent with gun and killed 4 gray squirrels, all we wanted for couple of meals, coots, ducks, all kind of fish, Tarpon or silver King. Will send you some of the scales. Manatee or sea cow weigh from 500 lb. to 800 lb. Porpoises, Sharks, Wild cats, Otters, Deer, Alligators all the game any one wants. Boats and fishing tackle. Two mules in camp all the time. You will probably see quite an article in the *Tropical Sun* this week don't let it scare you out on account of a family being murdered on this camp ground in 1825. The Indians here are Seminoles and talk very good English. I think I will get along with them all right. When I get fixed up I will be living like King. Hope not like the Kings of old get their heads taken off any day. You can get a chance to take up a homestead or buy canal or state land. Land that I am camped on is taken up and held at one to two hundred dols per acre. When can I expect you down address Lantana Dade Co. Fla.

/s/ Your Bro Frank S[4]

Shortly after Stranahan arrived at New River he was named postmaster, taking over from W. C. Valentine. This was a logical transfer since the mail was now being carried by the hack line, replacing the picturesque "Barefoot Mailman" who walked a route along the beaches. The old beach mail route was adjacent to the area where Valentine lived, but with the initiation of hack line service, the mail was being transported to a point that would have required Valentine to make a two-mile boat trip. Congressional registers listing postmasters were published in odd years, and Stranahan's name appeared for the first time in 1895. He continued to serve as postmaster until the settlement on New River came to be known as Fort Lauderdale and was incorporated in 1911.

The New River Camp under Stranahan's management seems to have won immediate public acceptance. On February 17, 1893, the Jacksonville newspaper, the *Florida Times-Union*, carried this item taken from the *Indian River Advocate:* "Go to Biscayne Bay via the new stage line.

Tri-weekly trips between Lake Worth and Bay Biscayne in well-equipped roomy, easy-riding, covered stages, leaving Lantana at the foot of Lake Worth and Lemon City at the head of Biscayne Bay every Monday, Wed., and Friday at 7 A.M. and passing at New River, where comfortable accommodations are provided for ladies and gentlemen. Good board and comfortable lodging at New River, the finest tarpon fishing grounds in Florida. $3. per day. Round trip fare $16.; one way $10. M. B. Lyman, Lantana, Fla." A few days later the same paper reported that Guy Metcalf had been in Jacksonville for two weeks "drumming up business."[5] This was Guy's trip to the northern part of the state alluded to in Frank Stranahan's letter to Will.

The *Tropical Sun* also publicized the camp regularly; typical was an item appearing February 23, 1893: "The New River Camp—the half-way house on the new stage line, is becoming a favorite resort for sportsmen; the fishing on New River 'can't be beat.'" Another item in the *Sun* of March 30, 1893, stated, "The New River Camp, under Manager Frank Stranahan, meets with many encomiums, for its conveniences and cuisine. 'A better bed I never slept on in Florida,' says one delighted passenger." A week later the *Sun* reported, "The passengers coming and going over the Bay Biscayne Stage Line continue to sing praises of the ——— [illegible] and novelty of the trip and of the splendid accommodations they find at New River Camp. Sportsmen will find this Camp one of the most delightful places in Florida at which to enjoy fishing, hunt for game, large and small, and at the same time, enjoy the comforts and convenience of first class accommodations."[6] Initially the hack line seems to have had no difficulty attracting customers, for another item proclaimed, "The New River Country, thanks to the Hack Line, is coming into prominence now. For several weeks the vehicles, large and roomy as they are, have been filled to the last seat every trip by both ladies and gentlemen. On arriving at the New River station and finding the novel camp accommodations offered, many remain to more closely inspect the country, and also to enjoy the fishing and hunting which is simply unexcelled."[7]

Ed Moffat of Lemon City became one of the drivers for the hack line. According to local historian Thelma Peters, "He drove a pair of mules hitched to a springless wagon with benches for seats and a canvas top for shelter. This was his schedule: one day from Lemon City to Fort Lauderdale, spend the night at Stranahan's tent hotel, next day return to Lemon

City, spend night at home. He made three round trips each week and had Sunday off. This was actually a short driving day and he was back in Lemon City by early afternoon on Tuesdays, Thursdays, and Saturdays."[8] In his spare time the enterprising Moffat built several small frame cabins known as "Moffat's Camp," which he operated in competition with Stranahan. Apparently the competition did not last long for nothing further is known of Moffat's venture at New River. Moffat did, however, take over as mail contractor. Peters wrote, "When torrential rains closed the county road the *Tropical Sun* of October 18, 1894 reported: 'The Hack Line has yielded up the ghost as the county road is *non comatibus* in swamp. Mr. Moffat, the mail contractor, has taken to the high seas and is bringing it in on the [schooner] *Pearl*.'"[9] But the rains subsided, and by November the *Sun* announced that the hack line would soon be put back in first-class shape with Moffat as manager.[10]

Two additional drivers for the stage line have been identified. One was J. N. Brantley and the other a J. Farrow. They drove for at least two months in May and June of 1894. Brantley was paid $50 for his services and Farrow received $60. Farrow was known to be a friend of Stranahan and lived in the vicinity of Fort Lauderdale when the 1900 U.S. Census was taken. Farrow was identified as having been born in Georgia and as a "hunter" by trade. Each was paid the money due him on September 3, 1894.

According to Peters, Garry Niles of Lemon City "anticipated the opening of the county road from Lantana to Lemon City and bought a ferry to operate across the New River that he later sold to Frank Stranahan."[11] Occasional complaints were lodged about the tolls being charged for the ferry at New River, and these became sufficiently serious that the Dade County commissioners considered the matter, as reflected in their May 1, 1893, minutes: "A petition from Lemon City signed by W. T. Pent and ten other tax payers for an endless wire cable be put on the lighter at New River and that parties be prohibited from charging toll."[12] Nevertheless, after examining the issue, the commission voted to grant a license to operate a toll ferry across New River to anyone making legal application. On August 9, 1893, the commission granted a license to Guy Metcalf to maintain a ferry across New River at the county road for a period of one year. Metcalf was to pay $5.00 dollars for the license and furnish a good bond in the sum of $200; he was also to have use of the lighter at New

River and keep it in good condition in lieu of rent. Commissioners also set rules governing operation of the ferry. Metcalf was to attend his ferry every day of the year including Sundays from 6 A.M. to 9 P.M., and persons desiring to cross were not to be delayed more than one hour. For this service he was allowed to charge:

Passengers in any vehicle (Except driver)	25 cts each
Persons on horse back	40 cts each
Two horse wagon & driver	60 cts each
One horse wagon & driver	40 cts each
Cattle, Lead Horses or mules	25 cts each.[13]

Metcalf was late in providing the stipulated bond, and on January 22, 1894, the commissioners ordered the clerk to advise Guy Metcalf to have his bond for operating the New River Ferry before them at their next meeting. By April 3 the commission minutes contained the following entry: "Guy Metcalf furnished a bond in the sum of $200. for to operate a ferry at New River, with Geo. R. Edwick and W. Whidden as surety."[14] The fact that Metcalf was slow in making his bond may have been a sign of impending financial difficulties.

Apparently the Dade County Commission's decision to allow operation of a toll ferry across New River did not mitigate the reluctance of local residents to pay tolls. Peters reports an incident in which two Lemon City men "took a train to West Palm Beach, then walked the county road. Between them they had six dollars. When they came to the ferry at New River and believed the ferryman was trying to overcharge them, they decided to swim, holding their guns and their few clothes tied to a stick up in the air as they swam. As they touched the opposite shore some large alligators were disturbed and slithered into the water. Only then did they realize what a risk they had taken, and in anger and fright they shook their fists at the ferryman and cursed him."[15]

Although Frank Stranahan had come to New River to be superintendent of the hack line camp, he also planned to make money by trading with the Seminole Indians in the region. This plan surfaced after Dr. F. M. Welles of Boston, who had been in Melbourne before Stranahan's departure, made a trip to New River in May 1893. Whether Welles and Stranahan had discussed a joint venture at New River before the latter left

Melbourne is unclear. Nevertheless, preparations began for building and stocking a trading post at New River.

Little is known of Welles's background other than that the 1893 Boston city directory lists the real estate firm of F. M. Welles Co., located at 61 Ames Building in Boston. It also shows that the Welles home was at Winthrop. It would appear from the frequent mention of Welles's name in the newspaper that he had business interests requiring numerous trips back north during his stays in Florida. Dr. Welles and his family arrived in the Indian River community during the holiday season of December 1892. The January 6, 1893, edition of the *Indian River Advocate* reported, "Dr. and Mrs. F. M. Welles and their five children, and the Misses Lucette and Eugenia Daly, who arrived here from Boston last Tuesday week, leave here for Eau Gallie on Tuesday morning. . . . Dr. Welles is about to have a winter residence erected on his fine property, situated about 5 miles above the Eau Gallie post office, and the younger members of his family are all anxiously looking forward to its completion, so that they may have a 'house warming.'"

The first item of the Stranahan-Welles correspondence implies that plans for their enterprise on New River had been made prior to Stranahan's departure from Melbourne. Since none of his letters to Welles are known to exist, it is necessary to rely on the Bostonian's letters for a story of their ill-fated venture. The first Welles letter, written on stationery of the Carleton Hotel in Jacksonville, was begun on May 4, 1893. It provides considerable information about the planned endeavor:

My dear Frank:

I arrived here yesterday noon but the "Reynolds" has not got here yet. I sent you from Banyan[16] case containing scale, scoop, box starch, 200 Empty Shells #12, H keg FFFG powder (which had been opened), pkge primers, some cans of salmon, etc., all being things I had there & could spare. I have also left word for a part of bbl. syrup & part bbl. vinegar to be shipped to you from there.

I am buying here just as closely as possible for spot cash a small but quite varied stock of goods to go down on the Reynolds as soon as she is ready for them. I cannot find here all we want & we cannot afford to pay the prices asked for some goods, i.e. Butter is .34 to

.35c!! Could we afford to pay $4.mo Butterine license & pay .18 to .20c for good Butterine? Hope you will *do all you can to rush through the surveying & completing of purchase of land at New River* & as soon as done let me know & I will apply for the lisence.

There are many things I would like to explain to you about the stock purchased but the bills & goods will, with your experience I hope make things clear to you & I hope you will find everything satisfactory. My family are all with me & I expect to go North from here Saturday. When you get selling I would advise at first letting me know what goods you need frequently & my policy is to buy now as small lots as I get bottom prices on, but all the variety there is a call for. I hope you will write me your ideas & needs freely as I want to do all I can to make the business a booming success.

Later—Noon, May 6th '93

I can sell here in Jax any hides or skins you are likely to buy but hope to get better prices offered for them in N.Y. 'Gator skins are low—can only get here from 10 to 80 c for "green salted" according to size of from 3 ft. up. Indian *dressed* Deer skins I am offered abt. $1.-per lb. for cow hides 3 to 4H c. lb. I can sell any kinds of skins or furs, beeswax, Tallow, 'Gator teeth, Live gators etc. I think. I enclose you some bills & some others will be mailed direct to you. Anything that is not plain or satisfactory to you please write me abt. at once. Also want you in sending for goods to give me full details of just what you can use best. The Schr. has not arrived here yet but I have left word with Capt. Cunningham's son at Merchants Bank where I have left goods for him to get.

Yours truly,

/s/ F. M. Welles[17]

Welles wrote to Stranahan from Boston on June 2 assuring him that an account in the amount of $300 had been established in his name at the Indian River State Bank of Titusville. He also noted that Captain Cunningham's schooner had sailed on May 20 with 8,500 feet of lumber and shingles for the store, plus most of the goods previously mentioned. Welles, anxious to confirm title to the New River property where he hoped to build the store, asked, "Would it not be best, if you can, to get the deed of the land all solid before Mr. Bricketts [William Brickell] has a chance to get up to New River and '2' hear about the store. And as soon as the deed is secured you must write me, so that I can get out a lisence. Also if you run across any bargains in the way of good land around New River you might let me know. . . . Well, whoop her up all you can and I wish you good luck in doing so but it seems to me very important to clinch the land purchase before there is any chance of our getting tripped up on it. I shall not rest easy till I hear from you that the deed to Metcalf from Bricketts and from Metcalf to me of the store lot has gone on record."[18] Guy Metcalf's part in this doomed undertaking remains obscure, but since he was active in real estate sales, he could have been involved solely in that capacity. However, a conspiracy obviously existed to conceal from the Brickells the entry on the New River scene of at least one new source of development capital.

Welles wrote again later that day with bad news, initiating a sequence of communications that spell out the demise of his joint venture with Stranahan. "I have just received the following telegram," he wrote: "'Jacksonville, Fla. June 2nd Schooner D. N. Reynolds wrecked and cargo and vessel lost. P. A. Cunningham.' I therefore hold back the enclosure mentioned in within letter & shall act promptly to see what can be done. If you can do anything to lessen our loss I hope you will of course do so & let me know what ever you can about other ways of getting lumber and goods to New River, either by way of Key West or otherwise."[19]

News of the *Reynolds* wreck dazed Welles, but by the following day he had composed himself enough to write again to Stranahan, stating that he had telegraphed Captain Cunningham to send by first mail full details on the disaster and a list of the goods on board. He asked Frank Stranahan to make a duplicate copy of the list that Cunningham had provided earlier and return the original to his Boston address. He also wanted any information that Stranahan could get about the wreck. This reversal of fortune did not dampen Welles's enthusiasm for the store, however, and he wrote: "Of course for so short a run along the coast I took out no insurance and am afraid that I am at a heavy loss as the stock was a particularly good one for such a store and I hoped great things from it. I am also soory to miss the trade of the Indians June festivities; but of course the only way to do is to learn first all the details of the wreck, whether anything was saved or not. And then, as soon as I can, get another stock and send you, though I think that will have to be considerably smaller until we see what luck we have with it. Please let me know anything that you can learn about the best way to get more lumber and goods to you."[20]

Welles's letter of June 29 came in response to Stranahan's intelligence that Captain Cunningham had sent their goods to sea on a schooner manned by an inexperienced crew, and that led to the wreck. Wrote Welles, "I am very glad to get the information in your second letter and have already arranged to make use of it. I certainly don't think that after making the agreement he did, Capt. Cunningham had any right to put our goods on another persons schr. and send them out to sea in charge of such incompetent parties and I think by so doing he must have made himself liable to us for the value for our goods. I am trying now to see what can be done about it."[21] Naturally, Welles would not trust any more business to Captain Cunningham, but he was at a loss over how else to get lumber and goods down to New River. There remained in Jacksonville about $100 worth of groceries and some grain that had not gone with the lost shipment. He suggested that Stranahan use the original lumber bill to order new materials if he could find a safe, inexpensive way to transport them to the New River. Welles ended with the cheerful admonition "And never say die!" To this typed letter Welles appended a handwritten note inquiring if Stranahan had received his checkbook, and he enclosed a message from the cashier of the Indian River State Bank in Titusville advising that Frank Stranahan was credited with $300 on April 28 and that a checkbook had been mailed.

The following day Welles confided, "I think there is no doubt from all the evidence that the fault of the wreck and loss of our goods was Cunningham's and I have already communicated with Judge J. W. Archibald of Jax. to see what can be done to recover from him. But so far have not heard from him though it is time that I did and I fear that he is out of town. Cunningham wrote that he intended buying a larger vessel and that he remained in Jax. to build his house so he must have something at least. I am hoping daily to hear from Archibald and if I do not soon shall get some one else to act in the matter."[22] Welles mentioned that he had written to Guy Metcalf asking about his own contract with Captain Cunningham but had received no response. He was still anxious to secure the land and move ahead with plans for a store. "[I]n the meantime," he wrote, "we must see what can be done about getting transportation regularly, as we want it, for goods, either from Jax. or Key West to New River. Have you received the parts of bbl. of Syrup and Vinegar sent from Banyan and how do the beads go?"²³ This last was an obvious reference to the anticipated trade with Seminoles.

In an undated letter written from Boston, Welles informed Stranahan that he was attempting to send goods on the schooner *Tortugas* to Lemon City. From there they could be transported by road or small boat to the New River for their joint venture. Welles still hoped to build a store and believed lumber could be brought in the same way. He remained interested in pursuing a legal remedy to their earlier loss, noting, "I have not had a word from Metcalf yet. I hope the wedding did not 'wreck' him. I would like very much to have him see J. W. Archibald, lawyer, in Jax. on his way south."²⁴ This reference to the marriage of Guy Metcalf, which took place in June 1893, indicates the letter was probably written in June or July of that year.

By summer 1893 the prospects of the New River camp were in doubt. Welles's letter of July 18 commented, "I am verry sorry to learn of Metcalf's business troubles and hope they will prove only temporary. I also hope that the change of the stage line will make no difference with your position unless it improves it. But I think you are right about our not beginning until we know how things are going to be. Though I hope there will be no trouble about our going ahead with the business as I believe there is a good chance for us both to make some money."²⁵ One can only speculate about the extent of his difficulties, but this clearly implied that Metcalf was about to lose control of the hack line. The controversy between the Brickells and Dade County over the route of the county road at New River was still unresolved, and movement of the camp to a new location was looming. There was also difficulty keeping the mules and wagons for the hack line in good condition during the hot summer months. According to Stranahan's letter of January 1893, it appears that Metcalf had invested about $5,000 in setting up the hack line. Possibly the investment was too great for the returns that could reasonably be expected. If the rumors of the railroad coming farther south proved true, it could spell doom to the hack line. Then, in the fall of 1894, Metcalf lost the mail contract to Ed Moffat. As Sidney Martin, Henry M. Flagler's biographer, explained, Metcalf reportedly incurred the enmity of Flagler when he "defaulted in the payment of a debt amounting to $3,750 which Flagler felt he was fully able to pay. The railroad builder hated debt. In the first place he hated to lend money to his friends because he realized the strained feelings which might result. After the break with Metcalf over the debt, Flagler made it a rule never to lend money to a friend, though often he made money gifts to people close to him."[26]

With Stranahan's position at New River uncertain, he and Welles decided to postpone the store venture indefinitely. Welles requested that Stranahan return the $300 held in account at the Titusville bank, explaining, "as you will not have to use the money I left with you for some time I wish you would send me a check for the amount by return mail so I can have the use of it and then when we are ready to go ahead I can return you what is needed."[27] Nevertheless, at this point Welles still had high hopes of doing business at New River, again inquiring, "How have the beads and other things gone? I also think well of your suggestions to have the goods in Jax. put back in stock if possible and let the amounts stand there to my credit. Please write me as often as you can, keeping me posted and let me know as soon as there is a chance for us to go ahead."[28]

Meanwhile, Welles encountered difficulties in pursuing a legal case against Captain Cunningham. Attorney J. W. Archibald refused to take the case, and another lawyer requested a fee of $100, payment of all court costs, and 25 percent of any compensation recovered through the suit. This distressed Welles, who had dealt with lawyers elsewhere, and he inquired if Stranahan or Metcalf knew any able attorneys in Jacksonville who would take the case on more reasonable terms, which they did not. Moreover, Welles may have encountered business difficulties of his own for he seemed relieved to receive Stranahan's reimbursement for the Titusville account: "I was very glad to hear from you again," he wrote, "as well as to get the check enclosed in your favor of the 7th inst. for money has been very scarce here lately and hard to make collections from anyone."[29] He concluded with a reaffirmation of his confidence in Frank Stranahan's judgment about the store and expressed hope that the land deal would be concluded quickly; only then could they decide the best course to pursue concerning the store.

Three communications are known from Welles in 1894, all written on the stationery of F. M. Welles and Company at 177 Broadway, New York City. These letters bring the Stranahan-Welles joint venture to what appears to be an amicable end. On January 8 Welles wrote Stranahan:

> I feel about as you do regarding our enterprise there & for that reason thought best for us to come to a settlement about the goods sent, & of which you send me a list, I don't see just how I can put a figure on them (though I suppose I should do so) as I have not my bills, showing cost, here. I should be satisfied to get back what they cost me & if you can afford to do that, suppose you send me by return mail what you think enough to cover their cost. I expected to get down the Indian River at least before this but have not been able to get started yet, though we hope to before long. I wish you would kindly deduct from amount you are to send me for the goods 1 year's subscription for "*Tropical Sun*" & have it sent to me here."[30]

When he had not received a remittance by March, Welles wrote again urging settlement by check or money order, and confiding, "Just now I am a little short" so anything Stranahan sent would be acceptable.[31] The following month Welles acknowledged receipt of Stranahan's checks in the amount of $31.45 as settlement for the goods. His letter concluded rather apologetically: "I am sorry our proposed venture ended so but I fully expect now to make a short trip to the Indian River, to look after some matters at our places near Eau Gallie, this spring & to certainly spend next winter there, when I shall hope to see you again, even if I cannot do so before."[32]

In retrospect, the Stranahan-Welles enterprise appears to have been ill timed. On May 3, 1893, the day before Welles's first letter, a major financial panic began in New York. Numerous U.S. banks and brokerage houses subsequently failed, and a prolonged business depression ensued. The national economic malaise evidently impacted F. M. Welles's business fortunes before he could get the New River venture underway. Recall that in August 1893 he wrote, "Money has been very scarce here lately and hard to make collections" and in March 1894, "Just now I am a little short." It seems that Welles was no longer in a position to bankroll another venture on New River.

Concern over the fate of the trading post may have caused Frank Stranahan to neglect writing his parents in Ohio. A letter from Robert Stranahan, dated August 21, 1893, hints that the family had not heard from him for some time. Reading between the lines of his father's letter, it appears that Frank Stranahan's health had been good during his six months at New River. There was much information about family members, including the news that Frank's sister Lucy and her husband, Charles Dunlap, whom he visited in Iowa, had returned to Ohio. But with a hint of family discord Robert mentioned, "Lucy and Charles are going to leave the farm this fall. They have got enough of Metcalfs. I am sorry to know that they have had such a time as they relate. But it is no more than I expected. I wish they had never gone there." It is not clear just which members of the Metcalf family were involved in this dispute. On a more pleasant note Robert reported, "I heard from Will an Al a few days ago. They were both in Minnesota. I will write them tonight or tomorrow and give them your address. I gave them your address in my last letters to them. I hope they may drift toward your place as winter approaches. I would like very much to be there myself. I doubt whether your mother would like it. What do you think about us going to spend the winter with you. I do not mean to go there and loaf. I do not believe in loafing no matter where I am."[33] He concluded by inviting Frank to come stay at home if he wanted to visit the 1893 World's Fair in Chicago and by expressing doubt that there would be a great economic panic. After such a prolonged absence from Ohio, it is likely that Stranahan welcomed a visit from some of his family during the coming winter.

While Stranahan pondered a possible family visit, problems arose concerning the location of the overnight camp. Guy Metcalf had built his hack line camp at the site selected by Dade County for a river crossing. Unfortunately, the property belonged to the Brickell family of Miami. There is no evidence of a title dispute between the Brickells and Metcalf, although the subsequent relocation of the camp and Stranahan's comments indicate that some conflict existed. Ultimately the matter was resolved amicably between the parties, and decidedly to Frank Stranahan's advantage. One indication of a problem was noted in the *Florida Times-Union* of October 18, 1893, which reprinted an article carried earlier in the *Indian River Advocate:* "The camp at New River has changed its location about 1 mile upstream. This was done to satisfy Mr. and Mrs. Brickell, who claim the land first occupied. It seems that the Brickells agreed that if Mr. Metcalf would move his camp, they could cut a road through to the new location.

For some reason, this promise remains unfulfilled and passengers are put to the inconvenience of leaving the county road and driving north nearly a mile to the new camp, then in the morning have to drive back to be ferried over."

Exactly when the overnight camp was moved from its original location to the property that Stranahan later acquired from the Brickells is unknown. An article appearing in about 1923 in the *Fort Lauderdale Herald* recounts that Stranahan's camp remained in its original location for only five months before being relocated along the New River. The move came after the Brickells "proposed to him to move his camp and ferry up to where he now lives, offering as an inducement a gift of 300 feet river frontage. He didn't hesitate a minute in accepting that and entered at once on a two months job to clear the ground sufficiently to get in, and to tear down and move and put up his tents again." In addition, the article reported that Stranahan placed a bridge across Tarpon River: "The commissioners of the sparsely settled country had rebelled at building a bridge across Tarpon River, declaring that it would cost $500.00. Stranahan said he could build it for $80. and they told him to go ahead. With the help of a negro he put it across for $45., for with the advance of the railroad project down this way many settlers began to drift in, some negroes among them." This newspaper item indicates that at about the same time F. M. Welles was seeking to acquire land on New River, Stranahan was making a deal with the Brickells to move the camp and ferry. No mention is made of Metcalf's involvement in reestablishing the camp.

Despite the dismal business climate throughout the country, Frank Stranahan weathered the storm from his remote New River location. In fact, it appears that he had begun to achieve a degree of success. Only two months after the letter from Welles spelled the end of their business relationship, Frank Stranahan acquired 10.7 acres of property on New River. By deed dated June 4, 1894, Mary A. and William B. Brickell transferred the property to him, although the deed was not recorded until over a year later, on August 4, 1895. The land adjoined the county road on the west. It was the site to which the "Metcalf" tent camp had been relocated and exactly where the Brickells wanted the New River ferry crossing.

A *Miami Herald* story about Frank Stranahan published on May 9, 1926, sheds some light on that acquisition. The reporter recounted that

The Brickells, as an inducement to him to move off their land, gave him 10 acres, including and surrounding his existing homesite. . . . On his newly-acquired property, at a point where his house now stands, Mr. Stranahan built a shelter of saplings and palmetto thatch. . . . This was later replaced by a wooden structure which, in turn, in July 1895, was torn down to make way for Fort Lauderdale's first store. This was a two-room building, measuring 20 X 24 feet operated by Stranahan & Co., the company being M. B. Lyman of Lantana who joined Mr. Stranahan in his venture.

Other published materials about Stranahan reiterate that the Brickells gave him property as an inducement to move the New River Camp.

One can only speculate why Frank Stranahan, who was then Guy Metcalf's employee, received the gift. He obviously bore no legal or financial responsibility in connection with establishing the hack line's overnight camp on Brickell property. It is possible that the Brickells elected to deed the property to Stranahan rather than Metcalf because the former was willing to cooperate in moving the camp. Another possibility is that the Brickells and Stranahan reached an understanding whereby he would represent the Brickell interests on New River. He did, in fact, serve as their land agent in later years. In any case, the ten acres of property on New River deeded to him by the Brickells was the first Frank Stranahan acquired in what is today Broward County. It was not only the first of his many real estate holdings but also the property on which the original Stranahan and Company trading post was built. Today part of that property is the site where historic Stranahan House still stands.

The summer of 1894 was significant for Frank Stranahan because he became a landowner on New River. It was also important for another reason: he severed economic ties with his relatives, the Metcalfs, and took over the total operation of the New River camp. Although the families remained close over the years, some dispute apparently arose between Stranahan and Guy Metcalf during the transfer of the camp operation. In November 1894, Stranahan received a letter from the well-known Juno law firm of Robbins, Graham, and Chillingworth, stating, "We beg to hand you herewith bill for services and expenditures in settlement of your claim against the hack line."[34] The nature of this claim has been camouflaged by the passage of time, but it marked the end of Stranahan's financial association with the Metcalfs. He continued providing overnight camp accommodations for several years and achieved prominence in doing so. But without adequate personal resources to finance the trading post after severing connections with F. M. Welles, Stranahan needed another partner. For this he turned to his contacts among the settler community farther north on Lake Worth.

1. The modern city of Fort Lauderdale grew up around Frank Stranahan's trading post on the New River, seen here in 1896. Stranahan served as postmaster for the small community and managed the overnight camp for passengers of the hack line that ran from Lake Worth to Lemon City on Biscayne Bay. (Negative #5–42, Fort Lauderdale Historical Society)

2. In 1893 Frank Stranahan, shown here, arrived from Melbourne to manage the overnight camp at New River. Within a few years he acquired property from William and Mary Brickell, established a profitable trade with the Seminoles, and became a leader in the small frontier community. (Negative #5–8162, Fort Lauderdale Historical Society)

3. This 1890s view shows the overnight camp at New River managed by Frank Stranahan. He soon began trading with Seminoles who brought otter pelts, bird plumes, and alligator hides to sell and used the money to purchase manufactured goods. (Negative #5–24, Fort Lauderdale Historical Society)

4. This photograph from the late 1890s shows four Seminole children admiring a two-wheeler in front of Frank Stranahan's trading post. The boys are wearing long shirts typical of the period, while the girls already wear many strands of beads although their skirts are relatively unadorned. (Negative #5–21, Fort Lauderdale Historical Society)

5. Frank Stranahan's brother Will and unnamed Seminoles display an otter pelt stretched on a board known as a "shingle" (ca. 1896). Otter pelts were among the most valuable items that the Indians traded at Stranahan's store on New River, often bringing seven or eight dollars apiece. (Negative #5–1, Fort Lauderdale Historical Society)

6. Seminoles often camped on the trading-post grounds for several days at a time after concluding their business. These women (seen in the 1890s) were (*left*) the wife of Jimmy Gopher and (*middle*) the wife of Billy Stewart, with Lake Wilson standing. The women wear many strands of beads, but their skirts are relatively plain in a pre-patchwork era. (Negative #5–30, Fort Lauderdale Historical Society)

7. In 1899 the community on New River had enough children to warrant a school. The residents built one, and Dade County supplied the teacher. Eighteen-year-old Ivy Julia Cromartie arrived to become Fort Lauderdale's first schoolteacher. The following year she married Frank Stranahan. (Negative #5–11721, Fort Lauderdale Historical Society)

8. Ivy and Frank Stranahan enjoyed taking the train for a day's entertainment on Palm Beach. Here they are, ca. 1900, being transported in two of Palm Beach's famous wheelchairs. (Negative #5-8093, Fort Lauderdale Historical Society)

9. Frank Stranahan's new store on Northwest River Drive, ca. 1906–8. The store burned in the devastating Fort Lauderdale fire of 1912. (Negative #5–8175, Fort Lauderdale Historical Society)

10. Ivy Cromartie Stranahan and her mother-in-law, Mrs. Robert Stranahan (Sarah McFadden Stranahan), were photographed by the New River with the Stranahan home in the background, ca. 1908. By this time Frank Stranahan had relocated his store a half mile west, in the heart of Fort Lauderdale, so the riverfront home was rather isolated. (Negative #5–37166, Fort Lauderdale Historical Society)

11. In 1913 Frank and Ivy Stranahan's home was perhaps the easternmost residence in Fort Lauderdale. The narrow path leading to the river on the right is now the location of the New River Tunnel on Federal Highway. (Negative #5–2860, Fort Lauderdale Historical Society)

12. This close-up view of the Stranahan home shows renovations after it was no longer used as a trading post. Bay windows had been added on the first floor and a cement seawall fronted on the New River. (Negative #5–2852, Fort Lauderdale Historical Society)

13. A City of Fort Lauderdale program on January 18, 1937, featured Seminole children from the Dania (now Hollywood) reservation. The singers are (*left to right*) Mary Parker, Mary Tommie, Betty Mae Tiger, Howard Tiger, and Agnes Billie. The girls are wearing elaborate Seminole patchwork skirts. Ivy Stranahan befriended these children and encouraged them to attend school. (Negative #5–3508, Fort Lauderdale Historical Society)

14. This photograph of Frank Stranahan was taken shortly before he committed suicide in 1929. His exploits and family name remain an integral part of Fort Lauderdale history. (Negative #5-8570, Fort Lauderdale Historical Society)

15. Ivy Cromartie Stranahan is pictured in 1961, on the second-floor porch of her home overlooking the New River. The structure was built in 1901 and originally used as a trading post, but the Stranahans made it their home a few years later. Ivy Stranahan, who died in 1971, is acknowledged as the "mother of Fort Lauderdale." (Negative #H47794.23, Gene Hyde Collection, Fort Lauderdale Historical Society)

4

Stranahan & Co., 1894–1911

Frank Stranahan encountered a formidable and challenging array of obstacles and opportunities during his first eighteen months on New River. The long-standing controversy over the county road crossing at New River was resolved, and Stranahan acquired sole control of the New River Camp in the summer of 1894. Following the collapse of F. M. Welles's financial support for a trading post, Stranahan turned for financial backing to Morris Benson Lyman, a member of one of the earliest families to settle on Lake Worth. The two men became acquainted because Lyman served as the hack line's agent in Lantana. Little is known of the exact business role that Lyman played in Stranahan and Company. Business cards printed after their association began show that M. B. Lyman served as treasurer. Members of the Lyman family recalled that M.B. and his brother George owned at least 50 percent of the business in its early years. Certainly it was a fitting association for the Lymans, since their Lantana store operation was similar to the one that Stranahan developed. The Lymans supplied goods to settlers living around lower Lake Worth while also doing a brisk trade with the Seminole Indians. The Lyman family was well regarded by the Indian people, and always made a point of providing a market for their pelts and hides. The Seminoles would come to have an equally high regard for Frank Stranahan.

Stranahan's acquisition of New River property created a financial asset that provided collateral for his future business arrangements. After

Guy Metcalf relinquished his interest in the New River Camp, the Dade County Commission on August 6, 1894, licensed Stranahan to operate the ferry at New River for a $1.00 fee. The ferry was to operate by the same conditions contained in the license issued to Metcalf. At the same meeting, the commission ordered that a warrant in the amount of $65.86 be drawn to Stranahan for work done on the county road. In September 1894 Stranahan presented the commission with the $200.00 bond required for operating the ferry. His sureties were Dennis O'Neill and James L. Nugent. That these two well-known residents of Dade County would stand his bond indicates the high regard Stranahan had earned during his relatively short stay in the area. O'Neill was keeper of the federal Life Saving Station when Stranahan arrived at New River. Nugent was a Dade County commissioner at the time the county road was built, and his wife, Florence, had purchased property on the New River in May 1894. The French-born Nugent had been in the United States since 1885, and his wife was English. The Nugent family initially lived in the Bay Biscayne area (now commonly known as Biscayne Bay), although by 1898 they were residing at New River.

Stranahan's original tent camp and the trading post made of saplings and palmetto thatch were soon replaced by permanent buildings. Later Mrs. Stranahan recalled that in the late fall of 1895, a severe hurricane blew away the "paper houses," which necessitated the building of more permanent structures. Perhaps it was the same storm reported in the September 19 *Gazetteer*, a West Palm Beach newspaper, which noted, "The long expected storm arrives and does considerable damage." Certainly 1895 was a year for hurricanes; three hit south Florida in October alone.

After the permanent store building was completed, it underwent an almost yearly series of alterations, reflecting steady growth in the trading operation. Porches were added on the south, west, and east sides. Later a room was added north of the east porch. A photograph of the Stranahan camp taken in 1898 shows a new boat landing constructed at the mouth of the slough running just west of the store building, with a wharf extending to the west for approximately 100 feet. The inscription states that the river is twenty feet deep at the point of the wharf, and that the river is thirty-five feet deep in the middle. No written records remain of the trading post operations during its early years. Unquestionably it was a hub of Indian trading activity, and numerous photographs attest to its popularity. They show that large groups of Indians frequented the store, with many canoes tied up at Stranahan's waterfront location. The slough or creek to the west of the store provided an especially convenient location for canoes to be pulled ashore. To the east, Stranahan constructed a large canvas-roofed structure somewhat similar to a Seminole *chickee*. This was intended as a temporary shelter for his Indian visitors, and pictures show them making use of it. Seminoles were welcome to camp anywhere on Stranahan's property; some even slept on the store's porches. The fact that Frank Stranahan continued to expand his operation, build permanent facilities, and make subsequent additions attests to the growing success of his business.

Other events in south Florida combined to create a healthy climate for business expansion in different directions. Several photographs show luxury yachts tied up at Stranahan's dock—yachts whose owners were men of national reputation. According to the *Dade County Directory*, "During April, 1893, it began to be whispered that there was a probability of Mr. H. M. Flagler extending the East Coast Line to Dade county."[1] By 1893 Flagler had completed the railroad as far south as Rockledge. Despite the rumors, many concluded he would stop there for a few years, or possibly go only as far as Melbourne. Julia D. Tuttle, owner of a 640-acre parcel on the north side of the Miami River, was anxious to have Flagler's railroad extended to Miami as a stimulus to development. One staple of Florida folklore is the famous story of Tuttle sending Flagler a bouquet of orange blossoms following the 1894–95 freeze to show that the Bay Biscayne area had remained frost-free.

Further, Tuttle had stated publicly that she would share half of her holdings with any railroad company bringing a track into Miami. Tuttle had first approached Flagler in 1893, but he rejected her offer; he believed that the Palm Beach and Lake Worth area was a semitropical paradise with great potential as a winter resort, and additional expansion in Miami would be a duplication of effort.[2] The freeze apparently reshaped Flagler's thinking. In a five-page letter written to Julia Tuttle on April 22, 1895, Flagler outlined some of his plans for the Miami area and the conditions he proposed to the largest landholders in the area if he were to bring the railroad that far south. (This letter also shows that he had given some thought to the New River region, although he had no extensive plans for developing it.) After detailing the difficulties of putting the line through to the Miami River, Flagler stated, "In view of all that I have said, which I believe to be true, I do not now feel any hesitancy in accepting all that you have offered me in the way of land, and even asking for more. Included in Mr. Brickeel's propostion, was one hundred acres at New River. You mustn't think it strange that I have 'cheek' enough to ask at least, as much from you in that vicinity, not that I expect to build up a town at New River, but I think it is good farming land, and I should hope to recoup myself to some extent, by the sale of property given me in that neighborhood."[3]

Eventually, Julia Tuttle gave Flagler a 100-acre tract for a railroad depot and hotel site, keeping 13 acres for herself. Another 527-acre lot was laid out in alternate plots, half of which she gave to Flagler. In addition, Flagler received half of the Brickell's 640 acres south of the Miami River. Both families realized that the arrival of a railroad assured the profitability of their remaining real estate holdings. Likewise, the largest landowners in south Florida contributed acreage to insure the value of their properties. The Florida East Coast Canal and Transportation Company pledged 1,500 acres for each mile of the seventy-mile line from West Palm Beach to Miami, while the Boston and Florida Atlantic Coast Land Company promised 10,000 acres. In 1895 the Flagler railroad interests were formally organized as the Florida East Coast Railway Company (FEC) with Joseph R. Parrott serving as vice president in charge of operations and James E. Ingraham heading its land operations.

While a decision was pending on the ultimate destination of the FEC, another means of bringing people to the area was well underway. Dredging of the Florida East Coast Canal was already progressing southward. About November 1893, the cutting of the canal between Lake Worth and Bay Biscayne began. James L. Colee of Jacksonville, one of the engineers on the project, had purchased property on New River in 1891. Thus he joined other Jacksonville and Fernandina financial interests that had much earlier bought considerable properties in the New River region. As the crews on the dredges reached the New River area, Stranahan, as the only merchant between Lake Worth and Bay Biscayne, could expect some business from the workers.

The 1896 *Dade County Directory* contained an unflattering description of a trip via the hack line between Lemon City and Lake Worth during this time: "We commence at Lemon City on the Bay, and riding up, taking notes as we ride up on the old trap then called a hack, the motive power being mules that had not been curried since their arrival in Dade County, and had seemingly lost the devilish spirit supposed to be forever lurking beneath mule hide, ready to break forth at the most inconvenient time and tear things all to smash. These did nothing of the kind, but seemed to be at the point of lying down and going to sleep at any moment."[4] Clearly a new mode of transportation by water or rail would be welcome. That section of the Florida East Coast Canal between New River and Lake Worth was completed in April 1895, one dredge working south from Lake Worth and meeting the one cutting north. On May 18, 1895, the *Gazetteer* reported, "the canal dredges meet, completing the canal between New River and Lake Worth." By August 10 the paper could report, "Steamer Hittie begins regular service between here and New River."

From time to time the *Gazetteer* reported significant events in the development of the New River region, and in its 1895 editions one can trace the progress of Flagler's railroad. On June 15 grading for the Florida East Coast Railway extension began. By July 27 the newspaper reported that A. L. Knowlton had gone to New River to survey the site for a town. In mid-September work began on the Lake Worth bridge. On September 21 track-laying on the East Coast Railway extension commenced. In November the construction gang went south to put up railroad bridges. On January 18, 1896, a survey for the town of Fort Lauderdale, at New River, was completed.

During the 1920s it became known that although the Brickells owned the property platted into the Town of Fort Lauderdale, Henry Flagler initiated the survey with their consent. The ten acres of land that the Brickells had deeded to Frank Stranahan, although excluded from the platting process, was actually within and on the eastern boundary of the new town. How fortunate for him that his property was not included in the original plat! The exclusion of his holding enabled Stranahan to retain title to the river frontage when the city of Fort Lauderdale successfully sued other property owners in 1914 to gain riparian rights along New River.[5]

As owner of the camp and trading post, Stranahan stood to profit from an influx of people into the area. His store provided supplies and his camp offered the only accommodations for visitors. The camp had acquired an enviable reputation. The *Florida Times-Union* of May 8, 1897, carried botanist A. H. Curtis's romanticized account of a visit to Fort Lauderdale and New River:

Stranahan's Camp for several years has been the only object of interest at Fort Lauderdale, and I was sorry to learn from Mr. Stranahan that he plans to strike the dozen or so floored and furnished tents. It is a most romantic spot. At night a bonfire was lighted, causing the tents to stand out white against the surrounding blackness. There was a wild wind spawning in from the ocean. There was a flapping of canvas, a crackling and flaring of the fire and a roaring in the tree tops, and ever and anon the yells of an Indian, far away or near, would rise above all. And when, occasionally, the dusky forms suddenly appeared in the firelight, the situation became one of delight to a lover of border romance.

Extension of the railroad into lower Dade County produced benefits probably not anticipated by Flagler. The severe winter freezes of 1894–95 brought financial ruin to many engaged in agriculture in the central and northern part of the state, so employment on the railroad gangs provided badly needed jobs. Since the completed railroad also provided transportation to northern markets, farmers came to the New River to start over again. A number of those who built the rail line remained on New River, engaging in various business activities along with farming. Certainly rail service provided a more comfortable and expeditious means of transportation for those who came seeking choice lands. Periodically the newspaper reported the arrival of people seeking property, such as the following: "Jas Struthers went to Boca Ratone Saturday to meet Mr. Rickards, when they will look over some land there and at New River. Mr. Struthers is looking for a 60-acre tract that will combine muck and pine suitable for vegetables and pineapples."[6]

As agriculture in the region gained prominence, the *Tropical Sun* predicted, "New River will be heard from when the time comes to ship garden truck from Dade. Even the orange men from northern counties are delighted with the certain prospects of golden fruit in that favored region, and are setting out groves of oranges, lemons and grapefruit. The New River section will soon be found to be far from the tail end of the procession."[7] The same issue reported that Frank Stranahan, "postmaster at Fort Lauderdale and proprietor of the famous New River Camp resort," had visited Melbourne on Saturday and then spent Sunday in West Palm Beach with Guy Metcalf and his wife. The article added, "This is Mr.

Stranahan's first recreational trip away from the classic shades of New River in eight months past."[8]

Dade County records show that Stranahan and Company was licensed as a merchant for the period October 1, 1896, to October 1, 1897, with stock valued at less than $1,000. The licensing fee was $3.00 for the state and $1.50 for the county. Licenses issued to Stranahan in 1899 and 1901 show a like value in merchandise. The Seminoles provided Stranahan with some produce for shipment. The *Tropical Sun* of May 27, 1897, reported, "Huckleberries from Stranahan's New River Camp have been much in evidence in town this week, in fact about all the town's supply came from there."

By February 1898, the renovation of the camp at New River referred to earlier was apparently underway. On February 24 the *Tropical Sun* advised, "Our friend Stranahan, down at New River, wants tourists to know that his camp there is not yet open for guests. If he opens it this season, he will give all due notice through the columns of the *Sun* and *Palm Beach Breeze*." There is nothing to indicate that the camp was open in the spring of 1898, but Stranahan's ability to refurbish the camp bespoke a degree of prosperity. In the summer of 1898, Stranahan made his first trip to Ohio since arriving in Melbourne ten years earlier. On July 7 the *Tropical Sun* mentioned his journey and identified Stranahan as being "of the New River Camp fame, and postmaster and merchant of Fort Lauderdale." Stranahan had returned from Ohio by September, and the *Tropical Sun* carried this note on September 9: "A couple of weeks ago *The Sun* man had the pleasure of seeing what the industry of truck-growing really was in Dade. A ride by rail to Fort Lauderdale and a day's visit at that most hospitable and interesting resort, Stranahan's Camp, put one in splendid trim for a ride a la buckboard down through the settlements of Four Mile Hammock, Modello, Ojus and on to Snake Creek, where the travelers were most kindly received and entertained."

Military activity associated with the Spanish-American War in 1898 had a salutary impact on Dade County. The newly incorporated city of Miami became the site of a military camp, and many individuals brought into the region by military service chose to return following the war because of its choice climate and economic opportunities. By 1899 the New River community was poised on a new threshold of growth and Stranahan was prospering, although he no longer had a monopoly on business; there was at least one other merchant in town. In February it was reported that J. N. Brantley had a new packing house and storeroom built in Fort Lauderdale. J. W. Marshall, formerly of Valdosta, Georgia, and his wife came to live on the riverfront. Late in the year Marshall purchased the merchandise stock and business from Brantley.

The closing year of the nineteenth century also marked an auspicious personal milestone for Stranahan as a romantic interest entered his life. The increasing population of Fort Lauderdale included several large families, which in turn created the need for a school. The Dade County School Board agreed to provide a teacher if the community would construct a school building. The community project began, and the school board fulfilled its part of the agreement by appointing as teacher Ivy Julia Cromartie, a resident of Lemon City, who received a salary of $48 per month.

Cromartie was born on February 24, 1881, at White Springs on the Suwannee River in north Florida. Her father, Augustus Whitfield Cromartie, a native of Garland, North Carolina, whose father had immigrated there from Scotland, wanted to teach school and came to Quincy, Florida, where an uncle lived. He then moved into the White Springs area, where he taught school and farmed; he also met and married Sara Elizabeth Driver. Driver's father was a farmer who had come directly to the Jasper–White Springs area from England. Ivy was the first child of Augustus and Sara Elizabeth Cromartie. As his family increased in size, Augustus Cromartie homesteaded near Arcadia for a while. He planned to plant orange trees on the homestead, but the freeze of 1894–95 prompted him to move farther south. The family crossed the state in a wagon and lived in Juno a short time before continuing south to Lemon City, where the Cromarties settled and began farming.

Ivy Cromartie completed her education at Lemon City but never graduated from high school. (In 1900 the nearest high school was at Key West.)[9] It is known that Ada Merritt, a pioneer Lemon City educator, tutored her so she could pass the examination required for a Florida elementary teacher's certificate. The certificate was issued by her mentor's brother, Zachary T. Merritt, the superintendent of schools for Dade County, who assigned her to the New River district.[10] In the fall of 1899 she made the trip from Lemon City by train, leaving there at 6:00 A.M. and arriving two hours later. The selection of eighteen-year-old Ivy was a good one. Growing up in a hard-working pioneer family enabled her to adjust to the austere life of a nascent New River settlement. Ivy Cromartie Stranahan later described the place as "a perfectly wild community. . . . There were only about five families and nine pupils."[11] Upon arriving, she found the frame building uncompleted, which delayed the start of the school term. It had been arranged for the teacher to live in the home of E. T. King, who had several school-age children and was influential in pushing for a local school. King had come to the area to work on the railroad and remained after the rail line was finished. His family joined him later, coming on the first train to arrive in Fort Lauderdale.

In so small a community, the young teacher soon became acquainted with all the residents, including the bachelor Frank Stranahan, who was sixteen years her senior. As postmaster and storekeeper, he had occasion to see Ivy Cromartie whenever she came for her mail or to make purchases. Before long postmaster Stranahan began calling at the King residence, ostensibly to deliver the mail when Ivy failed to call at the post office. The charming young schoolteacher's arrival must have created quite a stir in the settlement. Her popularity was virtually assured. The 1900 census shows no families in the immediate area with single daughters in her age bracket whereas a number of single men resided in the community, including several who were nearer her age than Frank Stranahan. By the end of the school year their friendship had blossomed into romance. Although she was reappointed for the following school year, Ivy Cromartie's teaching career ended after one year. After agreeing to marry the postmaster-merchant, she returned to Lemon City for the summer months before their wedding.

Portions of the letters Frank wrote to Ivy that summer offer glimpses of life in the Fort Lauderdale community at the turn of the century. Among the pleasures people enjoyed were beach parties and other activities associated with the ocean. In one note Frank commented, "As you know we will expect you here Sunday the 13th as that is near the full moon, when we use to have our camping trip and Turtle hunt."[12] Evidently Ivy was quite popular and received invitations to many social gatherings. In mid-May 1900, Frank wrote her to say, "There is going to be an ice cream party at Mr. King's Thursday night. From rumors you will have several invitations from men. Kindly accept this as one."[13] The letters also provide a picture of Frank Stranahan's devotion to his future bride. At one point the usually laconic Stranahan implored, "Remember be brave and true to me and I think I can say you will not forget or regret the many pleasant days we have passed together lately especially on last Sunday on the beach."[14] Another time he penned, "dull as it is, I can keep busy, and live through the coming month, with the hopes of 'more pleasant' days to come. Hope time is not dragging slowly along with you. Will try and write occasionally, but you will find me a poor letter writer. With regard and love I remain . . . "[15] Closer to their wedding date the pragmatic Frank wrote, "Time is short, wish to ask you question that I should have done several days ago. In getting the License how do you wish your name to appear on it and age."[16] The couple's plans appear to have been a well-kept secret, and according to the *Miami Metropolis* the marriage came as a surprise to their friends.[17]

Frank and Ivy were married in the Cromartie's Lemon City home at an extremely early hour on the morning of August 16, 1900. The hour of their wedding was dictated by a 6:00 A.M. scheduled departure on the FEC train. Taking no time for a reception, the couple immediately departed for an extended wedding trip, traveling first to Asheville, North Carolina, which Ivy Stranahan recalled as a very popular place in that day. While in North Carolina, Ivy met her paternal grandparents for the first time. Then they went on to Ohio to visit Frank's parents and family. Leaving Ohio, they proceeded to Niagara Falls and into Canada before returning to Fort Lauderdale. In her elder years, Mrs. Stranahan recalled that it was exactly the trip Frank had promised her before they were married. Upon their return to Fort Lauderdale, the Stranahans did not live at the New River Camp but rather boarded in the E. T. King home for a year. During this period Stranahan built a small cottage near his camp and store building. When the cottage was completed, the couple moved in and lived there for some five years.

Stranahan's business ventures flourished in the early years of the twentieth century. Ivy's family moved from Lemon City to Fort Lauderdale and her brother, Bloxham Cromartie, came to work in Stranahan's store. Although Frank had invited his brother Will to New River as soon as he arrived in 1893, there is no evidence that Will came before 1900. We know that Will did work for Frank, keeping books and helping in other facets of the store operations, but the only evidence of his arrival is a letter written in 1900. Although signed "Frank Stranahan," it appears to be in Will's penmanship. The letter was not drafted in Frank's less legible style, and neither is it in Ivy's distinctive handwriting. This letter indicates Stranahan's concerns about his Indian neighbors apart from his trade with them. Possibly he had an economic interest in the proposed trip, but most likely Ivy influenced his role in the matter. The letter was addressed to J. E. Ingraham of the Florida East Coast Railway, whom Stranahan knew from previous business dealings.

Nov. 1900

Dear Sir:

I am very much interested in the "Gala Week" fairs at Jacksonville and intend to go and a number of the indian boys have all expressed a desire to go with me. The indians are all out on a big hunt and will be in the last of this week. They brought in over 2000 gator skins in October and we expect at least 1200 to 1500 on this hunt. I have written a letter to the executive committee at Jacksonville about rates etc. but got but little satisfaction, and if it is possible I would like to hear from you whether the Indians can get transportation to Jacksonville and return. There will not be over six or eight and Tom Tiger or Frank Jumper or Robert Osceola will be the head man of the party. I would be pleased to hear from you by next Friday's mail or sooner if convenient.

Yours Respectfully,

/s/ Frank Stranahan[18]

Despite their close association, Ingraham was powerless to grant Stranahan's request. Evidently other individuals were less sympathetic to the Seminoles. On November 22, 1900, Ingraham received a letter from George L. Bahl, a member of the Jacksonville affair's organizing committee, stating, "I think Mr. Stranahan took this matter up direct with the committee and they wrote him that they would be unable to use them. To speak frankly I would state that the committee are all quiet peaceable men and that none of them would under take the responsibility of looking after the indians knowing their failing and the fact that a few years ago when they were here they simply tore things up and at such a time as this we would simply be unable to look after them and know if they did come that it would be our place to keep an eye on them. Under the circumstances we therefore were very loath to tackle this question and decided that we had better leave the red men alone this year at least."[19] The FEC vice president, J. R. Parrott, also nixed the plan, commenting, "I have had several applications in regard to movement of Indians. The one which you call my attention to this morning is not the first one. I know of no reason, under the circumstances why we should move Indians any cheaper than white men."[20]

One evidence of Frank Stranahan's increasing affluence was his ability to replace the old store, to which additions had been made over the years, with an imposing two-story building fronting on the New River. Construction began in 1901, and this notice appeared in the *Miami Metropolis* of January 4: "Stranahan's Camp, at Ft. Lauderdale will not be open to the public this season." E. T. King began building the structure, which was used as a store for five years before being renovated and converted to residential use. There was other evidence of change in Fort Lauderdale the same year; a "fishhouse" was constructed on New River, close to the railroad tracks, to process fish for shipment north.

There is nothing to indicate how many employees the trading post required during this time. Frank Stranahan had taken on his brother Will in 1900, and added another full-time employee in 1901, one with whom he was associated for ten years. At age twenty-one, W. O. Berryhill left North Carolina on a doctor's advice to recover his health in Florida. He stopped at Winter Beach on the Indian River for a time, then in 1900 came to Fort Lauderdale, where he grew beans and tomatoes. A year later he began to work as a clerk for Stranahan, serving as both storekeeper and postmaster. Later Grace Dunlap—the niece who was a small child in 1885 when Stranahan visited her family in Kansas—came to Fort Lauderdale and worked in her uncle's store until 1909.[21]

Berryhill related that most of the trading post's business was with the Seminole Indians, who came from distances as far as forty or fifty miles in the Everglades, bringing a variety of items to sell. It is known that

> After abolition of the egret plume trade in 1901, otter pelts became the most valuable trade item with a single skin priced from $7 to $8 during the winter season. . . . In summer, alligator hides brought

$1.80 to $2.00 for specimens 6 to 8 feet long, but only 50 to 75 cents each for smaller hides. Newly hatched alligator eggs were also important. The Indians would place moist leaves around eggs and hatch them at the store for Stranahan who sold them to tourists for 25 cents to $1.00 each, depending upon size. Garden produce in the form of corn, pumpkins (the special Seminole variety), and beans were often offered to the store as were huckleberries and wild grapes. But the old custom of bartering preserved quail, doves, parakeets, or live turkeys seems to have died out, although deerskins remained a common trade item. *Kunti* (*koonti, compte*) the famous Seminole starch and famine food, constituted a significant item of commerce at Stranahan's store.[22]

The Seminoles did not trade with Stranahan as such—that is, they did not barter their commodities for his merchandise. Instead, the Indians received cash from Stranahan for goods sold; they then made individual purchases and paid cash for them, keeping any surplus.[23] Stranahan's store provided the Indians with practically every item necessary to survive during their long stays in the wilderness. They bought good-quality traps, as well as the shotguns, rifles, and ammunition used for hunting. They also needed pots, pans, axes, hatchets, saws, hammers, and nails. The Seminoles showed a marked preference for canned goods, coffee, sugar, and grits for making the semi-liquid food known as *sofkee*, plus lots of salt—much of it used for preserving alligator hides. For making both men's and women's garments, they purchased "books of Calico" (a ten-yard bolt of cloth folded to resemble pages of a book) and hand-cranked Singer sewing machines that could easily be transported among the camps. The men were particularly fond of Panama hats, train conductors' caps, and watch fobs and chains, while women wanted a great quantity and variety of beads for making necklaces. Silver coins were often punctured and strung together to be worn as adornment. Chewing tobacco, pipes, and snuff never became popular among the Seminoles, but they purchased large quantities of cut tobacco and cigarettes, which were used by both men and women. W. O. Berryhill indicated that the trade in hides and skins in one day could amount to $1,500 and that such days were not uncommon. Despite this thriving business, the state and county licenses issued to Stranahan and Company for the years 1900 and 1902 show that the stock was valued at less than $1,000. However, it was not uncommon to undervalue stock in the mercantile world.

Letters written by brother Will to the family in Ohio between May and October 1902 tell of the activity at Stranahan and Company. More important, they reveal the drive that animated Frank Stranahan. In one, Will also described his own business interests, noting that he had acquired forty acres of land and an option on twenty more, which he expected to lease for a net of at least $1,000 in the next two years.[24] Another time he wrote of plans to plant 400 orange trees and grow vegetables. This correspondence implies that Will Stranahan was considering a more stable lifestyle, like his brother's. If so, the notion did not last long. On September 4, 1902, Will wrote to his parents:

> Today is my birthday and I have celebrated my 40th year by buying 500 orange and grape fruits and doing a hard days work in the store. I have as fine a prospect as I could wish for and in fact I would not exchange places and conditions with Frank under any consideration whatever. Frank talks of taking a trip this month or next but I think he will be kept busy fixing up the place as he has only put in about 9 years at it now and he will have to hurry up or he will be a hundred years getting it finished to suit him. He is just as he used to be at building up and tearing down all the time and only a few days ago he said the store was to small by at least 12 feet. I will stay in the store until Frank takes his vacation and then join the Farmers Alliance and try and grow some vegetables for the northern winter market.[25]

A third letter from Will to his parents, written in October 1902, comments on the business activity at Stranahan and Company:

> I have been very busy since I came back the first of July. My farm is 2H miles from the store and I walk out on Tuesday and Friday in the afternoon so that I have to keep moving and keep up with my book work. . . . I will stay in the store next month and perhaps longer. . . . I think that Al could get a job here keeping books for Frank at any time if he wants to come down. Frank has a first class man working in the store with us who is going to stay until next June or July and it keeps them busy behind the counters while I keep the books and work in the post office and help out in the rush.[26]

Will's letters to his parents during this time contained many references to his chronic poor health, and mentioned that he wanted to go to Hot Springs, Arkansas, which he hoped would prove beneficial. He told his father about his insurance and that he had paid the premiums in advance. Will was a totally different personality from Frank—a fun loving, gregarious individual, with little, if any, of Frank's steadiness and persistence to see a job done. A newspaper article appearing in the Miami paper in 1901 reported Will missing after a trip to Miami, but he reappeared shortly. The *Free Press* of Fort Lauderdale carried articles on "Pioneer Days in Fort Lauderdale" written by Eva Bryan Oliver, who, in 1902, was the first woman married in the town. In a 1936 column she wrote, "He [Frank] had a brother, Will Stranahan, who kept books for him for a while and would come and go as he was of a rambling nature. He used to play the piano nights on the old Joe Jefferson boat then tied up at the Stranahan place. The beautiful music carried up and down the river and people would gather to listen. He built a dance pavilion on the beach about where Port Everglades harbor is. He left here in a small boat and none of his family have ever seen him since."[27]

Will wrote to Frank from Arizona in November 1904, after leaving Hot Springs, promising to pay money that he owed and saying he could be reached through General Delivery in El Paso. However, by February 1905, Will was in Jacksonville, and Frank admonished his brother severely for failing to let the family know his whereabouts, particularly those who were his insurance beneficiaries. Frank also angrily reminded Will of the money he owed on the forty-acre farm. Evidently Will made one more trip to Fort Lauderdale for on May 29, 1905, he sold the forty acres to Frank and the deed was executed in Dade County. It seems nothing more was heard from Will. In 1927 action was taken in Ohio to have him declared legally dead so that Robert Stranahan's estate could be settled.

True to Will's assessment of his brother's business acumen, Frank Stranahan's holdings continued to expand. W. O. Berryhill remained to work with Stranahan, and he recounts that by 1903 trade at the store had so increased the business was incorporated. At that time Berryhill acquired an interest in Stranahan and Company, along with Bloxham Cromartie and Frank R. Oliver. In January 1904, Stranahan and Company bought two lots from the Brickells, representing Frank Stranahan's second purchase of Broward County property. The following July he bought an adjoining lot. This property was located within a block of the railroad, close to the FEC docks and rail yard. It was here that Stranahan and Company built a large two-story building, moving the business there in 1906. It fronted on the west side of Brickell Avenue, now Southwest First Avenue in Fort Lauderdale, just north of the river. As the business expanded, even this building would be enlarged in 1908. According to the *Florida Times-Union* of August 15, 1908, "Stranahan & Co. is preparing to build a store addition on the rear of the already large store."

Despite the growth of Stranahan's mercantile operations and the many expansions the store underwent, one of the original functions that brought Frank Stranahan to New River in 1893 continued relatively unchanged. New River had never been bridged, and the ferry continued to operate. For eight years between the railroad's arrival and opening of the Andrews Avenue bridge, Stranahan conducted "business as usual" at the point where traffic crossed the river by ferry. In 1903 the Dade County Commission paid Frank Stranahan $450 to operate the ferry for a year. It was not until 1904 that a bridge was built over New River, and its location at Andrews Avenue was just one block east of the new Stranahan store. No doubt the impending construction of the bridge was an influential factor in Stranahan moving his mercantile operations from its original location when he did.

With the relocation of his store into an area that became the center of Fort Lauderdale's business life, Stranahan began renovation of the large structure built in 1901. It was converted to a comfortable and, by local standards of the day, imposing residence. Family records of furnishings for the home reflect the Stranahans' tastes and lifestyle. A piano was shipped to Mrs. Stranahan on October 31, 1908, and the contract with the Cable Company called for the payment of $400, with $25 down and $10 per month. Frank also acquired a Buick automobile, and a county license was issued for it April 20, 1912. Several sources reported that Frank never drove a car, and that Ivy always did the driving. The Stranahans also owned a motor boat named *Heloise*, but it is unclear whether it was used for pleasure, business, or both. The *Florida Times-Union* of June 26, 1905, carried an item noting that, "Frank Stranahan has just completed a sea wall in front of his residence." The seawall signaled the end of an era; no longer could Indians land their canoes and unload cargoes of pelts and hides easily. Thus the Seminole trade at Stranahan's home on New River came to an end.

Following his election in 1904, Florida governor N. B. Broward initiated the long-discussed Everglades drainage project. This monumental undertaking began in 1905. The first step was the construction of two dredges, which began in Fort Lauderdale that year. The project called for digging canals from Lake Okeechobee to connect with the New River and Miami River. Fort Lauderdale was to grow greatly as a result. With no rail lines extending into the Lake Okeechobee region, produce grown there was brought by barges to New River for rail shipment to northern markets. Completion of the canal in 1912 allowed Fort Lauderdale to claim the title "Gateway to the Everglades." The drainage project and associated land development schemes drew nationwide attention to the community. There was agitation for a new vegetable packing house at Fort Lauderdale long before the canal project was finished. In March 1905, J. R. Parrott of the FEC wrote to Stranahan and Company inquiring about a packing house-site. There had been friction between the FEC and the Vegetable Growers Association over the location of a packing house on railroad property. The FEC did not want the facility built on its grounds because it would hamper plans for future development of the property. Furthermore, Parrott wrote, "We are willing to put in another side track which will cost us a great deal more than to have the side track accommodate the location first suggested, and it seems to me this would answer all purposes, and furnish better facilities. If the packing house is located far enough north of the river it would obviate the difficulties you complained of as to obstructing the river front. I do not know whom the property belongs to but have suggested to Mr. Barrett that he and you get together and solve the problem."[28] This letter indicates the reliance that FEC officials placed in Frank Stranahan's ability to arbitrate difficult situations. The packing house was not built on FEC land.

Stranahan's business continued to flourish at the new location. The extent of growth is reflected by the State and County License no. 111 issued to Stranahan and Company for the period October 1, 1909, to October 1, 1910. It showed a mercantile stock valued at $15,000. A *Fort Lauderdale Herald* advertisement from the period describes the scope of the merchandise carried: "Dry Goods, Lingerie, Ladies' and Children's

Shoes, Gent's Furnishings, Hardware and Builders' Material of all kinds, Sash, Doors, Blinds, Locks, etc. Poultry and Garden Fence."[29] Although strong demand for these items existed among Fort Lauderdale residents, trade with the Indians continued to be a large factor in the success of Stranahan and Company. The original ledgers for Stranahan's business for 1906–11 are still available and reveal the extent of the Indian trade.

In 1910 W. O. Berryhill and Bloxham Cromartie, Frank's brother-in-law, left Stranahan and Company to form their own general merchandising business. The new firm erected a store building at the corner of Andrews Avenue and North New River Drive, where the bridge spanned New River. From the time Frank Stranahan was first named postmaster for Fort Lauderdale, the post office was located in his business establishment. On April 21, 1911, he relinquished that responsibility to Susie M. Bryan, and she signed a receipt for transfer of the post office property.

The year 1910 also saw the organization of a bank in Fort Lauderdale. A Board of Trade was formed the same year, and Frank Stranahan was soon elected its treasurer. The town's population grew, and Fort Lauderdale was incorporated in 1911. The Stranahans assumed an active role, and Frank Stranahan became involved in so many facets of community life that he apparently had little time for merchandising. His business interests had expanded into many other areas, so in 1911 Stranahan and Company was sold to the Oliver Brothers. However, Frank Stranahan did not totally forsake dealing with his Seminole friends. For several years he continued to provide an outlet for Indian products, especially handicrafts and baby alligators; Stranahan always purchased what his Seminole friends brought. Although he was not a particularly sentimental man, it was probably done less for profit than as a nostalgic connection with the bygone days of the Indian trade.

5

Stranahan

Land Agent, Banker, and Promoter

The sale of Stranahan and Company to the Oliver brothers in 1911 freed Frank Stranahan from the daily demands of running a business, allowing him to devote his time to whatever activity he chose. For several years he had been acquiring properties that required his attention, and there would be other opportunities as well. Early in 1912 Fort Lauderdale experienced a population explosion and business was booming, due primarily to land speculation and the anticipated completion of the North New River Canal connecting the area with Lake Okeechobee. This civic enthusiasm was dampened somewhat in June when a fire leveled the downtown business district, including the former Stranahan store. It is unclear whether Frank Stranahan witnessed the conflagration.

In the summer of 1912, Stranahan took an extended trip to his native Ohio. Correspondence addressed to him in Warren, Ohio, shows he remained there until at least December. He kept in touch with events in Fort Lauderdale, however, especially efforts to rebuild the business district following the fire. It is likely that property he owned, or in which he held an interest, would be impacted by these improvement efforts. He received a letter dated August 24 from prominent civic leader and businessman E. C. Parker, describing work in progress along Andrews Avenue. Parker commented, "There has been a general inclination on the part of the lot owners to do their part of the work, the only refusal we have had so far to the contribution has come from Mr. Oliver, and I presume when he gets back that we will have no trouble in convincing him to do his part of the work."[1] Further, Parker advised they had been able to make new arrangements for dirt fill, which reduced the cost of hauling about 50 percent. He continued, "If the Council and County get together on the proposition of furnishing the rock, I think that we will be able to start rocking by next Wednesday. We are making the fill 24 feet wide, and the deepest runs a little under two feet, that will give us about a 28 inch raise through the lowest part after it is rocked."[2]

Parker also confided his strategy for overcoming opposition to placing a power plant and water tower on a lot at the corner of Las Olas Boulevard and Andrews Avenue, which a committee had recommended that the city purchase. His letter concluded, "I am pushing the matter with the Council, and getting all the concessions possible, for you know there is some very hard opposition to the opening of Andrews Avenue, and there are some persone who would like to give it a black eye if it were possible, and they sure will have to do some rank work, because I have started the proposition and am going to see it finished."[3] The mayor, W. H. Marshall, favored acquiring riverfront land for a city hall and water plant and opposed the Andrews Avenue site, which he considered too expensive. A compromise was reached whereby less expensive lots on another part of Andrews Avenue were secured for a city complex.

Three weeks later E. E. Rogers wrote with information that the city had passed an ordinance authorizing construction of a sidewalk from Andrews to Stranahan Avenue. Rogers also mentioned having a contract to finish the walk from Andrews to East Avenue on South River Street, near the Stranahan home. Another ordinance approved widening North Second Street ten feet and providing a five-foot walk on both sides from Andrews to Valentine Avenue. Rogers reported that a number of new buildings were being put up, and people were beginning to come in at a good rate. He concluded by predicting a "prosperous winter for Fort Lauderdale."[4]

Following the lengthy Ohio stay, Frank Stranahan's father, his brother Allen, and sister-in-law Alice visited Fort Lauderdale in 1913. So far as is known, this was the first visit to the New River home for Allen and Alice, although Frank's nieces, the daughters of his sister Lucy, had come earlier. Letters written from Ohio indicate the family there kept well informed about events in Fort Lauderdale via correspondence and newspapers. Earlier in the year Allen Stranahan commented in a letter to Frank, "Glad to hear you have got some good streets to get in-and-out on and hope you may get the cross State R. R. and deep water [port]."[5]

Although no longer operating a mercantile establishment, Frank Stranahan continued to receive orders for baby alligators for sale to tourists. He maintained business contacts in such places as Jacksonville, Clearwater, and Saint Augustine as late as 1915. In 1914 Osky's, a Jacksonville firm specializing in alligator products, offered to purchase live alligators on a scale from fifteen cents for "baby size" to thirty cents for those three feet in length.[6] Tony Tommie, a young Indian who had attended the Fort Lauderdale elementary school, was one of several Seminoles supplying them. He was entrepreneurial and wrote Frank Stranahan in 1916 asking for a loan of $10 with which to purchase "little alligator[s]," which he would raise and sell to tourists for a few cents each.[7] It is not known whether the loan was made. Stranahan provided a pen for the young gators on his property until they were shipped. A small creek or drainage ditch ran west of the Stranahan homesite, and a portion of this area was fenced to provide a suitable containment for the alligators.[8]

When Stranahan became a licensed land agent is unknown; however, his papers contain a license issued by Dade County for the year 1911. Yet it appears that he performed some land-agent functions from the time he first came to New River. It will be recalled that Stranahan's cousin, Guy Metcalf, owned two real estate firms in northern Dade County, and Frank surely was alert to opportunities along New River for Metcalf interests. In addition, his erstwhile partner, F. M. Welles, had asked Stranahan to report any possible investments in real estate. Stranahan was also in contact with the Brickells of Miami, who owned over 3,000 acres in Dade County, including many tracts in the area around New River. His files contain a volume of correspondence from the Brickells concerning property matters in Fort Lauderdale. Stranahan left an early plat of the town of Fort Lauderdale on which he had marked real estate that had been sold and to whom. He also indicated the names of prospective buyers for other lands.

Stranahan disagreed with the Brickells from time to time over the prices for certain lots and other matters pertaining to the growth of Fort Lauderdale. On October 9, 1908, Mary Brickell wrote, "I have heard that you were the first to give the commissioners permission to open the Rock quarry on the Frankie [sic] Lewis grant to make roads with. They tell me that you were my agent at Lauderdale, as I do not believe that you did give any one such permission I thought I would write and ask you as I thought of bringing suit against them for digging such a large hole and damaging the land and refused to recompense me in any way. Kindly let me here from you in reference to this."[9]

Mary Brickell appears to have been ill-informed about events along New River, or she may have routinely opposed governmental efforts to change the status quo. For example, her letter to Stranahan of September 3, 1914, stated: "Your letter received in reference to widening Andrews Ave. I did not give any part of the lot to the City of Lauderdale for the ave. to be made wider and I had it Posted so if the city takes it by force they will have to pay the expense for so doing I have tried to do right but your board of City officials want to pick a quarrel with me on every occasion. They will have to condemn it before they get it and pay for the same. I was in Lauderdale yesterday and called at your place found no one at home. Kind regards to Mrs. Stranahan."[10]

Stranahan and the Brickells continued their amicable association for some time longer, for when the Stranahans renovated their home in about 1915, the Brickells gave them some palms and other plants that adorned the grounds at least until the 1980s restoration of the house began. However, their land sales connection was evidently terminated by April 17, 1916, the date when a large advertisement in the *Fort Lauderdale Sentinel* stated that C. C. Ausherman and Company were "Agents for Mary Brickell." Moreover, by 1916 Stranahan had become one of the city officials whom Mrs. Brickell characterized as wanting "to pick a quarrel with me on every occasion."

Another Stranahan business connection was the firm of Frederick S. Morse in Miami. The Morse letterhead indicated it was the land agent for the Model Land Company, the Florida East Coast Railway, the Florida Coast Line Canal and Transportation Company, and the Boston and Florida Atlantic Coast Land Company—all major corporate landowners in south Florida. Morse was a long-time associate, for in a letter that Frank wrote to Ivy in 1900, before their marriage, he mentioned having gone to the beach with Mr. Morse. The Morse papers include several canceled notes that Stranahan gave to him in connection with properties bought from the companies that Morse represented. When G. C. Varney and his associates subdivided a tract of land along East Broward Boulevard under the name "Edgewater Addition," correspondence with Varney indicates that Stranahan also assisted in the sale of these lots.

There were others for whom Stranahan acted as a land agent in the early days. People like Hugh Taylor Birch, who owned a large tract on the Atlantic Ocean, and Thomas E. Watson, also a beach-front property owner, were only resident in the area for a short time each winter. Correspondence from these men and others reveals that they looked to Stranahan to handle affairs for them during their long absences. In fact, Watson's properties were eventually deeded to Stranahan "as trustee," and Stranahan represented him for a number of years. The Birch relationship also existed for many years, as this letter shows:

Dear Mr. Stranahan

During our conversation the other day—reference was made to a possible exchange of our properties fronting south fork of Middle River. It occurred to me that you might not know the exact location of my lot. Therefore I am sending you inclosed a small sketch which sufficiently indicates the situation of our respective pieces. Yours in green & mine in yellow joining it on the west.

I think the acreage about the same. You will note that my piece fronts on the north street of the Progresso subdivision, and I believe that street have a crossing over the RailRoad to the Dixie highway.

The strip of land in my lot, lying within Section 35, is 200 feet north & south in width by 660 feet ——— [torn] west & bordering on the above street. The ——— [torn] of the tract lies in Section 26 & is bounded by the south fork of the Middle River the east & north. The Exchange would give you an outlet by the 50 foot street along the south side of the tract & a fine river frontage too.

Let me hear from you as to what you conclude in the matter. My interest lies in having my holding in a single body, as you can well see. I am more than pleased to remember that you are not in favor of the incorporation into the city of Lauderdale of the swamp lands surrounding and including my home properties and of your own large unimproved acreage either.

I sincerely trust that the wild scheme will never be attempted in earnest. (Over!) The whole people are suffering terribly from the heavy burden of taxation. I hope you will use your conservative influence to lower taxes and help bring back to the Citizens the consolation of peace and happiness and the assurance of prosperity.

With the kindest regards

I am sincerely

/s/ Hugh T. Birch[11]

An early land promotion on New River in which Frank Stranahan took a prominent part was known as the "Harvest Home Picnic and Barbecue at Seminole Park, New River," held on May 22, 1906. Plans for the event were elaborate. Special rail fares were arranged from Miami and West Palm Beach, so that a round-trip ticket to Fort Lauderdale could be purchased for the price of a one-way fare. The picnic area was in the same locale where Frank's brother Will had his beach pavilion. Publicity in advance of the event appeared in the local papers of April 23, and was signed by Frank Stranahan, P. N. Bryan, and J. G. Farrow. In part, it stated:

> We, the executive committee, having decided in behalf of ourselves and the people of Ft. Lauderdale to take advantage of the attractions of a bank of music and balloon ascension accompanying the sale of house lots at this place Tuesday, May 5, have decided to add free excursions up New River and a political meeting, and herewith extend a cordial invitation to all candidates for state and county offices to be present and take part and to all to come and enjoy the following program. . . .
>
> Free excursion up the river in the morning, followed by auction sale and balloon ascension, then political speeches for the remainder of the day until train time, all accompanied by a band of music. We will arrange excursion rates from West Palm Beach and Miami and all intermediate points. We are going to have an entertainment costing hundreds of dollars, all free to everybody. Come by land, come by water, come by rail, by auto, by horsepower, by manpower, come in a balloon.[12]

The entire community was involved in the event. Excursions to the Everglades and the beach were arranged by Reed A. Bryan, while the transportation on New River was furnished by "Braddock & Stranahan." A flyer promoting this event shows the location of the Everglades canal that would ultimately connect New River with Lake Okeechobee. The informative poster-size flyer located the properties and farms of many, if not all, the people then living and farming along New River.

Stranahan acquired the trading post site from the Brickells in 1895. He purchased his next property in 1904, buying the lots near the railroad where he ultimately erected a new mercantile establishment. That year New River was bridged at Andrews Avenue, eliminating the need for a ferry. Between 1906 and the creation of Broward County in 1915, Stranahan recorded a total of forty-two deeds giving him title to various properties. Seven other deeds were recorded in the name of Stranahan and Company. Some of these represented individual lots while others involved considerable acreage. It is interesting to note that all of these properties were in rather close proximity to New River. According to the deed books, Stranahan bought no land as far north as present-day Oakland Park Boulevard, which was approximately the southern boundary of Palm Beach County prior to 1915.

Broward County was created from parts of Dade and Palm Beach counties on October 1, 1915. After that time, Stranahan recorded another thirty-five deeds for properties in Broward County. Among these were two tracts owned by former keepers of the life-saving station, C. W. Coman and Dennis O'Neill. Stranahan also bought property from the Jenkins family, although land records do not indicate that Washington Jenkins, the first keeper, ever owned Broward County land.

How many different corporate entities Stranahan may have used to buy land is unknown. He may well have been a principal in companies whose identities are now lost, and he could have participated in land purchases with others through some corporate name. Most frequently, though, it appears he bought property in his own name. Only rarely was the title to property taken in his wife's name. Stranahan gave eleven deeds before the creation of Broward County, and ninety-eight deeds are recorded in Broward County. After Stranahan died, thirty-seven properties were deeded by Ivy Stranahan. Eight subdivisions within the Fort Lauderdale city limits include "Stranahan" in their name. The earliest plat was dated January 4, 1911. In some instances the property was Stranahan's alone while in several subdivisions his land was platted with adjoining properties. In October 1923, Stranahan and his wife platted a forty-acre tract in the northwest area of Fort Lauderdale under the name "Tuskegee Park." It was then a black residential area consisting of ten blocks, lying west of the railroad and north of Broward Boulevard. Records reveal that Stranahan financed his real estate investments in various ways. For example, canceled notes show that he bought properties from the Brickell family "on time," giving notes for the balances due. In the pioneering days of south Florida, Stranahan's principal banking connection seems to have been the First National Bank of Saint Augustine. Later he developed associations with the Bank of Bay Biscayne in Miami, as well as the First National Bank of Miami.

Stranahan apparently carefully calculated the timing of his store's sale. The days of leisurely settlement on New River were coming to an end, marked by the incorporation of the town of Fort Lauderdale in the spring of 1911. Although prospects for the future appeared bright, one wonders whether Frank welcomed the inevitable changes that accompanied growth, changes that he had a role in bringing about. The 1906 "Harvest Home Picnic and Barbeque" promotion was designed, in great part, to capitalize on the growth possibilities that completion of the North New River Canal would bring. The gigantic land-sales promotion of Richard J. Bolles tied farming acreage in the to-be-drained Everglades to lots for homes in the townsite of Progresso. By 1911–12 some 12,000 lots had been platted north of Fort Lauderdale. This widely publicized property development began to attract people from the middle and western sections of the United States.

Completion of the North New River Canal brought a great celebration, with Florida's governor Albert W. Gilchrist present for the official ceremonies on April 26, 1912. Also joining the festivities were Fort Lauderdale's first mayor, W. H. Marshall, and other dignitaries. The advent of the railroad in 1896 had provided the growers along Florida's lower east coast with reliable transportation to northern markets, and farming operations had increased. However, until 1912 there was no way of shipping produce grown in the Lake Okeechobee region to northern markets expeditiously because no transportation network reached into the area. The North New River Canal changed that. It enabled growers around the lake to ship fruits and vegetables by barge to Fort Lauderdale for transshipment north by train. Although the drainage canal had an extension into Miami, produce brought to Fort Lauderdale reached northern destinations sooner. Predictions about the canal's economic impact on

Fort Lauderdale soon came true. By January 1916 between 300 and 1,000 crates of vegetables were shipped daily by express during the height of the harvest season, with 400 to 700 carloads shipped annually.[13] The town of Fort Lauderdale appropriated the name "Gateway to the Everglades," and it freely used the additional sobriquet "Winter Vegetable Capital of the World."

Regardless of their occupation or social status, it was customary for practically all Fort Lauderdale area residents to engage in some type of truck gardening or grove keeping, and Frank Stranahan was no exception. He had a large orange grove and some grapefruit just north of his home, at the corner of what is now Las Olas Boulevard and Southeast Sixth Avenue. Stranahan had a shed on his home property where he kept tools and stored fertilizer; he also kept a mule. This may have been the animal that Roy Nash referred to in his 1930 report on the Florida Seminoles, when he noted, "Many of his neighbors wondered why Frank Stranahan kept a horse long after the automobile had relegated most stables to the past. Few knew of his trips in the dead of night with that old horse to bury some Indian baby or friend who had died in camps on the edge of town."[14]

There is also evidence of more extensive farming operations. Both the *Florida Times-Union* and the *Daily Herald*, published only briefly in Fort Lauderdale, carried items in March 1911 about Frank Stranahan irrigating his farm. A photograph of Ivy Stranahan, accompanied by land developer J. P. Taravella, appeared in the *Fort Lauderdale Daily News* of October 20, 1954. The caption read, "Here Was the Watermelon Patch," and these comments followed: "Coral Point subdivision, now largely built up in beautiful waterfront homes, originally was one of the first farms in Ft. Lauderdale. Two years ago this week the land was sold to Coral Ridge Properties by Mrs. Frank Stranahan, widow of the city's founder, and the event was commemorated by a caravan to the site. Here, Mrs. Stranahan points out the spot where 'the finest watermelons you ever tasted' were grown over a half century ago."

During his years as the town's first merchant and owner of its largest mercantile establishment, Stranahan reportedly served also as an unofficial banker. Lacking local banking facilities, people turned to Stranahan, and most of the town's financial transactions took place at his store. During this era the First National Bank of Saint Augustine served Stranahan's major banking needs. When he heard talk of organizing a local bank,

Stranahan immediately wrote his bankers in Saint Augustine. In May 1910 he received a lengthy reply with sound advice from G. B. Lamar, vice president and cashier of the Saint Augustine bank. While that institution would regret losing Stranahan's business, it viewed the proposed Fort Lauderdale bank as no great competition. Past experience suggested that its chances of success were doubtful. Banks had opened in other small towns along Florida's east coast, usually after successful crop years, and initially accumulated handsome deposit accounts; then they began to make loans secured by agricultural property. Lamar noted that farmlands were the only sizeable assets at New River other than Stranahan's store. Due to the vagaries of agriculture, most of a new bank's patrons would not be depositors but rather borrowers who secured their loans with land. Following a bad crop year or two, it would be difficult to collect these loans. For this reason many banks had failed or were struggling to get by. Further, in a small community if one man or a small group controlled the bank, it would be difficult to get various interests to act together to support the new institution.

The banking official advised Stranahan,

> It would seem to us that so far as you are personally concerned, you ought either control the Bank if one is organized, or else keep out of it except to the extent of very few shares as evidence of your good faith and desire to assist what you consider a worthy enterprise in your community. We say this because if you held any considerable amount of stock, but less than the controlling interest, others not in sympathy with your ideas might combine to secure control and jeopardize your large but minor holdings. It is our belief that no one in your community would be better fitted for the active direction of the bank, such as making loans, etc, than you would be.[15]

When the new bank was organized as the Fort Lauderdale State Bank and granted a charter on September 10, 1910, Frank Oliver became president. As he had been advised to do, Stranahan became a stockholder. While his involvement in the banking field began in a passive way, it continued until his death, and he took a more active role as time passed.

Even though the Oliver brothers were instrumental in organizing the new bank, they turned to the Saint Augustine institution for financing when they purchased Stranahan and Company the following year. Two letters written to Stranahan from the First National Bank of Saint Augustine tell part of the story. The first, dated February 3, 1911, advised Stranahan that F. R. and J. D. Oliver had notified the bank they were purchasing Stranahan and Company, including M. B. Lyman's interest. The Olivers wanted to continue a line of credit with the Saint Augustine bank on the same terms it had granted Stranahan. The bank solicited Stranahan's opinion about the Olivers' business acumen and specifically about their plan to discontinue certain lines of merchandise from the store. It also asked him to assess the Olivers' credit worthiness: "We should like to know what you regard as a reasonable line of credit and what you have regarded as your line of credit; that is to say, Stranahan & Company's line of credit with this Bank?"[16] In closing the bank requested a prompt reply and assured Stranahan that his answers would be held in strictest confidence.

Evidently Stranahan was able to reassure the Saint Augustine bankers, and the sale of the store went forward. On March 29, 1911, Stranahan received a second letter from G. B. Lamar notifying him that, "Yours of the 28th is received and by the same mail we have received instructions from Stranahan & Co., to pay your note of $6,000 which we have done, and we are returning to you herewith the note in question together with certificates Nos. 26 for ten shares; No. 27 for ten shares, No. 28 for ten shares, No. 29 for ten shares; and No. 30 for eight shares; total 48 shares of stock of Stranahan and Company, together with mutilated power of attorney which we have been holding."[17]

Contrary to the predictions of the Saint Augustine bankers, the Fort Lauderdale State Bank did well, and by 1918 Frank Stranahan had become its president. In 1912 the Withan banking chain of Miami met with Mayor Marshall, W. O. Berryhill, and other local residents to discuss forming a second bank. Later the same year, the Dade County Bank opened its doors with W. C. Kyle as president. In another three years it built its own building and changed its name to Broward State Bank, following the creation of Broward County in 1915. The federal Liberty Bond program used to finance World War I was popular, and both local banks suffered from the large withdrawal of savings that were converted into government bonds. The two institutions found it necessary to merge in order to survive, and W. C. Kyle of the newer bank became president of the merged institution, with Frank Stranahan serving as vice president. In March 1916, the state of Florida granted Frank Stranahan a registration certificate as a banker. Following the merger, the new bank outgrew its Brickell Avenue location and built a stately new structure at the corner of Las Olas Boulevard and Andrews Avenue. The bridge over the New River on Andrews Avenue had made this the predominant business street, replacing Brickell (now Southwest First) Avenue. At the same time the bank's name was changed to the Fort Lauderdale Bank and Trust Company.

The phenomenal growth of Fort Lauderdale during the "roaring twenties" must have caused Stranahan to ponder earlier, simpler times. In 1923 he wrote his friend G. C. Varney, "We are getting in too much of a rush here. City life too fast for me."[18] Other financial institutions were organized in Fort Lauderdale, but the destructive 1926 hurricane, following the stalled land boom, took its toll. In November 1927 the First National Bank merged with the Fort Lauderdale Bank and Trust Company. At the time of that merger, the latter institution was unaware of the extent of the problems facing First National. Two and a half months later the Fort Lauderdale Bank and Trust Company failed also.

Failure of the bank was a blow to the town and spelled financial ruin for many stockholders, who were required to pay an assessment double the value of their shares. In a way, Stranahan fared better than many of the other stockholders. His holdings were small, only 207 shares, and his assessment was $20,700. He settled this obligation with a promissory note secured by a mortgage on Fort Lauderdale real estate. The bank receivers were later forced to foreclose the mortgage. On March 1, 1929, Frank Stranahan borrowed $22,410.67 from Edith Burnham, giving as security a mortgage on his home, which she, after his death, also foreclosed.

Stockholders of the defunct bank attempted to form a new banking company, filing application for a state charter. However, a second group of investors headed by John Lochrie, a wealthy Pennsylvania financier, also petitioned for a banking charter, which the state of Florida awarded. A major difference in the proposals presented to the state banking authorities by the rival groups tipped the decision in favor of the new group. The Lochrie group presented a plan to repay depositors in the failed bank to the extent possible and thus won the state's approval. Eventually, by April 1940, depositors in the defunct Fort Lauderdale Bank and Trust Company received 31.5 percent of monies on deposit at the time of the bank failure.

Frank Stranahan engaged in widely diverse enterprises, and in several he either held or exercised the controlling interest. One of these was a pavilion built on Las Olas Beach. Other local residents were involved in this project on property that reportedly was leased from the Alexander Holding Company. The structure was a large two-story building located about 200 feet south of the present-day Alexander Park. It fronted on the ocean between the International Swimming Hall of Fame and Atlantic Boulevard (state road A1A). Evidently Stranahan was brought into the pavilion project by a neighbor, George W. Hall. Hall had come to Fort Lauderdale in 1913 from Wyoming, and his home was built on property he bought from Stranahan. In October 1916, George Hall, as secretary of the Las Olas Beach Company, which was organized to build the pavilion, advised Stranahan that he had been elected a director. Thereafter Stranahan seems to have taken the lead in the project; licenses and permits for its construction were granted to him as an individual, although Hall and others put up the money. On February 22, 1916, George Hall, by then city clerk, issued Frank Stranahan a license to operate a "Public Hall for Hire," and that may have guaranteed his place on the governing board. Construction of the building proceeded slowly because all materials had to be transported from the downtown area to the beach by water. Only a few documents remain on this project.

Robert Hall spoke extensively in 1979 about the friendship between his father and Frank Stranahan.[19] The two men conferred frequently on business matters as they visited in the yards of the two homes. Although the Hall children were never present during these talks, the entire family did participate in operating the pavilion. It had seventy-two dressing rooms, shower stalls, and rest rooms on the lower floor. A refreshment stand was also provided. The second floor was used for dancing. The conventions of that time did not allow people to go to the beach in their bathing suits, so suits were rented. Robert Hall's mother was in charge of the ladies' locker-room while his father handled the one for men. Young Bob's job was to gather the wet suits, wash them, and disinfect them in Lysol water, and hang them to dry. The other Hall son worked also, selling soda water and other refreshments. Frank Stranahan did not take an active part in running the facility, although he was part owner of the concession stand.

Robert Hall recalled that Stranahan never hesitated to put a little "risk capital" into anything that looked promising, and he followed operations closely to assure they were properly managed. Before the completion of a causeway and bridge to the beach, the bath house was open only Sundays, the Fourth of July, and Labor Day. A boat ferried passengers back and forth from town. Once the beach road was finished, use of the dancing pavilion became more practical, and the bathhouse was open more frequently. The pavilion was operated until the structure was virtually demolished by the 1926 hurricane.[20]

A group composed of Stranahan, the Bryans and Olivers, W. C. Kyle, and Fred Barrett undertook construction of the beach road. D. C. Alexander owned beach property at the proposed eastern terminus of the road; he named his property "Las Olas by the Sea" and agreed to provide land for the road's construction. In January 1915, the Las Olas Bridge Company was chartered and capitalized at $15,000 with Stranahan serving as treasurer. There are indications that Stranahan's financial interests may have clashed with those of developer D. C. Alexander, and the families never had a cordial relationship. In 1914 Alexander borrowed $40,000 at 8 percent interest from Malinda J. Lawrence in order to purchase thirty-two acres of beach property, and Stranahan was administrator of the loan.[21] Alexander believed that a bridge would be built quickly, enabling him to sell lots in Las Olas by the Sea and repay the loan. When the bridge was still not completed after two years, Alexander may have believed Stranahan was delaying the project because he had an eye on the property for himself.

The idea of building a causeway and bridge to Fort Lauderdale's beach created a stir in the newly created Broward County. As the automotive era began, other communities also wanted access to the ocean. The west Broward town of Davie requested several short bridge spans to make the beach more accessible. Pompano and Dania also wanted bridges to the ocean. Finally, Broward County passed a bond issue worth $400,000 to build bridges to the beach areas, as well as to improve access to the Davie community. By far the most difficult problems were in the Fort Lauderdale area. Nearly a mile of dense mangrove swamp separated the mainland from the ocean. A further complication was the width of the bay between the mangroves and the beach itself. Champion Bridge Company of Mansfield, Ohio, was selected to build the single-lane, turn-style bridge at what is now Las Olas Boulevard. In January 1917 the road, causeway, and bridge were completed, and a parade of cars formally opened the new access to Las Olas Beach with much fanfare.

Another civic venture to which Stranahan devoted time was the creation of a deep-water harbor for Fort Lauderdale, a project that had been discussed as early as 1913. The winds and tides have always created an unstable south Florida coastline, and the New River inlet changed location a number of times. The shallow inlet south of the life-saving station had virtually closed and another opened near present-day Port Everglades. But except for the inlet, New River was still a clear and very deep stream, capable of accommodating ocean-going vessels. Given a deep inlet and channel through the bay, local businessmen foresaw the possibility of ocean-going ships docking at the downtown Fort Lauderdale riverside. Building materials were needed for the town's growth, and shipping them directly to Fort Lauderdale seemed preferable to having them transported to Miami, then brought up to the New River area by train, small boats, or wagons over the county road. The difficulty of maintaining the depth of artificial channels was not considered, for knowledge of hydrology and geology was still not well developed.

Frank Stranahan joined other prominent citizens in forming the Deep Water Harbor Company. The firm was incorporated and capitalized at half a million dollars. Mayor W. H. Marshall was elected president, with Frank Stranahan serving as treasurer—his accustomed role in many enterprises. The company dredged the channel south of the life-saving station, and granite boulders were put in place to create the north and south jetties of the inlet. (Some are still visible from the municipal parking and picnic area along the ocean, north of the old Yankee Clipper Hotel.) With completion of the dredging, certain ocean-going vessels could come up New River and dock near the Andrews Avenue bridge to unload lumber and other cargo.

By 1926 Joseph W. Young, a town founder and developer from Hollywood, Florida, had announced grandiose plans for a true deep-water harbor in the Lake Mabel area. The Young plan ultimately became a joint Hollywood–Fort Lauderdale venture, and today the line separating these two cities runs down the middle of slip number one of world-famed Port Everglades. It was the realization of those early New River residents' dream when, on February 22, 1928, an elaborate celebration marked the dynamiting of the final sand bar between then Lake Mabel and the Atlantic Ocean. This was one bright spot in an otherwise dismal month for Fort Lauderdale, as only six days earlier the Fort Lauderdale Bank and Trust Company had failed.

On May 2, 1925, the Mortgage Security Corporation of America, headquartered in Norfolk, Virginia, notified Frank Stranahan that he had been selected as one of their Fort Lauderdale appraisers. Stating that the company wished to broaden its local operations, it expressed confidence that Stranahan could assist materially. His recognized expertise in the real estate field and long residence on New River, coupled with his own land ventures, were deemed ample qualifications. In addition to the formal appraisal reports required from time to time, the company urged Stranahan to give them the benefit of his knowledge of special situations through informal letters.

Over the years Frank Stranahan's name was associated with numerous and varied enterprises. He helped organize the Fort Lauderdale Mutual Loan and Building Association soon after the creation of Broward County. Although a member of the association, his name did not appear either as a director or officer on its 1916 letterhead. On June 23, 1916, R. A. Horton, secretary of the association, sent Stranahan a warrant in payment for his shares in the institution, which later failed. There is little to indicate that Stranahan was a major investor in most enterprises, except in the early days of the trading post, the mercantile store, and his associations with W. C. Kyle. For many of these ventures Stranahan probably only "lent the use of his name." For example, he owned one share of stock in the Gate City Transportation Company and two shares in the Atlantic, Okeechobee, and Gulf Railway issued in 1912—an ill-fated early attempt to connect Lake Okeechobee by rail with each Florida coast. Stranahan had six shares of stock in the Everglades Lumber Company, a venture with W. C. Kyle, and he did become a director of that company. When the Everglades Telephone Company was formed in 1915, Frank Stranahan took one share of stock.

Around 1920 Fort Lauderdale residents caught oil fever. Many hoped to find oil or gas in the southwest part of the city, and the Mecca Oil

Company actually drilled a well—with disappointing results. Frank Stranahan, who held 77 shares of the stock, took an active role in the company, becoming a director, treasurer, and trustee. In 1915 Stranahan built a roller-skating rink, and in January 1927 he acquired 20 shares of stock in the Lauderdale Amusement Company. When the Fort Lauderdale Securities Company was formed in 1914, Stranahan held 135 shares. Indeed, it seems that Frank Stranahan had a "finger in every pie."

Stranahan's last major venture, an equal partnership with W. C. Kyle, was a twenty-nine-unit, three-story apartment building on the north side of New River immediately west of the Stranahan home, called the Lauderdale Arms. The Bank of Bay Biscayne in Miami provided the financing, and the Stranahan Building Company was incorporated on February 28, 1925, to build the structure. The Bank of Bay Biscayne was pressing for some payment on the financing at the time of Stranahan's death in 1929.

Over time Frank Stranahan's financial interests and business investments covered a broad spectrum. The ambitious young man who in 1893 came to manage an overnight camp and ferry passenger vehicles across New River became a merchant, real estate tycoon, and banker. What was his principal occupation? A precise answer is difficult. He was essentially an investor and entrepreneur; however, in a broader sense he became the leading promoter and booster of a fledgling settlement on New River that eventually grew into the thriving city of Fort Lauderdale.

6

Stranahan

Civic Leader and Politician

Over a century after Frank Stranahan first came to New River and some seventy years following his death, the city of Fort Lauderdale still bears his imprint. The family's name is found on a public park, high school, river, and several subdivisions. The building opened as a store in 1901 and later remodeled for the family home, now called Stranahan House, has been restored and designated a national historic landmark. Over time Frank Stranahan exerted his influence in both prominent and subtle ways. He was active in supporting community improvements and other projects aimed at enhancing the cultural amenities of the community. Yet he and his wife maintained a reclusive and aloof personal lifestyle.

In 1904, when the first bridge over New River was being planned, Stranahan pledged cash support. The proposed bridge site was some six blocks or so from the County Road. He joined thirty-seven others in signing this commitment, which was typed on the letterhead of Reed A. Bryan:

> We the undersigned residents of Fort Lauderdale, and vicinity, do hereby pledge our-selves to give the amount set opposite our names, same to be paid either in cash or labor. If labor, to be allowed the rate of $1.25 per day for man, $2.50, per day for single team, and $4.00, per day for double team and driver,—For the purpose of building a

rock road on Second St. and Andrews Ave. from the County road to the river, same to be given on condition that the County build a bridge across New River, as petitioned for at the meeting of The County Commissioners June 8th, 1904.[1]

The pledges ranged from one dollar to a single $50 contribution; two pledges were for $25, one coming from Stranahan.

The Fort Lauderdale settlement grew slowly, and by 1910 it had some 200 residents. Prospects for growth during the next decade seemed promising since the North New River Canal was then over half completed. A board of trade was organized in that year with Frank Stranahan acting as treasurer. On January 6, 1911, a committee was formed to investigate incorporating the settlement. Those on the committee included J. L. Billingsley, W. H. Marshall, H. G. Wheeler, and Frank Stranahan. The committee did its work well. Incorporated on March 27, 1911, the town encompassed one and one-half square miles. Its boundaries extended a quarter mile beyond the square-mile area originally platted and subdivided by Henry Flagler in 1895 as the "Town of Fort Lauderdale."

W. H. Marshall was elected mayor, and a long-time Stranahan business associate, W. O. Berryhill, sat on the first city council. J. L. Billingsley became city attorney. Interestingly, Frank Stranahan did not seek a seat on the first council; but even without holding elective office, he was a dominant political force in the earliest years of the city. On October 17, 1913, the council named him auditor, along with P. N. Bryan and C. M. Davis, to handle proceeds from its last bond issue. The $12,000 issue, voted in September 1913, was to pay the city's debts and build a city hall. That Stranahan was a popular choice testifies to the faith residents placed in him beginning when he served as the town's first informal banker. In November 1914, he was named to fill a vacancy on the city council created by the death of a member. The following spring he became a candidate for the position and was elected on April 4, 1915. This was the first elective office Stranahan had held since serving as Melbourne's marshal and collector in 1890. Dr. C. G. Holland became mayor, while F. T. Fisher was named president of the council. Stranahan was reelected in the spring of 1916, when an old friend, J. G. Farrow, was also selected to the council. After the members took their seats, Stranahan's neighbor, George W. Hall, was named city clerk.

Four years after the town's incorporation, a serious effort was mounted to create a new county. Following an unsuccessful attempt in 1913, Stranahan and other prominent citizens played active roles in bringing the new county into being on October 1, 1915. Broward County—carved from Dade and Palm Beach Counties—was named in honor of former Florida governor Napoleon Bonaparte Broward, whose plan for draining the Everglades had profoundly affected the New River community. Fort Lauderdale was selected as the new county's seat of government. Creation of Broward County and its potential impact on the community were mentioned by Frank's brother, Allen, in a letter written October 24, 1915: "[H]ope you come out all right on the reperian rights proposition. I am not surprised at the drop in real estate values from three years ago. It looked to me a little like Frenzies Finance your community will be in on a sliding scale for the next two years. It will take some time to find out just what value the new county will mean to your town."[2] Although Stranahan was known in Fort Lauderdale as a man of few words, the correspondence from family members in Ohio indicates that community affairs were a topic on which he kept his relatives fully informed. Before ending his letter, Allen commented on their cousin Guy Metcalf: "[H]ope Guy will come out all right but everything goes in politics love and *war*."[3] This was undoubtedly a reference to Metcalf's political problems in Palm Beach County, where he was planning to run for school superintendent.

Frank Stranahan never sought an elective county office. Rather, he seemed content to focus his attention on affairs in Fort Lauderdale. Although he was reelected councilman in 1916, politics became quite heated during that spring, and Frank and Ivy appear to have been in the thick of the fray. Ivy Stranahan's letters of this period reveal that the couple were subjected to charges they felt were unjust, to put it mildly. When Ivy went to New York for a Federation of Women's Clubs convention, Frank kept her informed about local events. The items he reported must be surmised from two fiery letters Ivy wrote to him. The first, dated May 30, 1916, was written on stationery of the Hotel Netherland:

My Dear Boy—

Your letter yesterday was so interesting. I am sorry that Bro. Frost has had his plans so upset. But you know that ridiculing people publicly from the platform is a preachers privilege[.] [A]s far as harming me is concerned that is utterly impossible, for he and a dozen Holdings cannot prove that I ever stood only for the cause that needs assistance and against the wrongs that need resistance. As for what Holding says regarding any graft just let him have all the rope needed he will hang himself—just as surely as he and Frost are doing these things they will have to reckon for them. They are both good church members as is usual you know. However if Holden [*sic*] goes too far with his graft I would make him swallow some of it but keep your head. You and I have seen many ataching [attacking] us go down in defeat and we scarcely notice it. [R]ealy I should have just as leave Frost kept my name out of his mouth. I am sure what you told him was a plenty.[4]

Ivy added that Mary Barr Munroe, wife of the well-known author of outdoors books, wanted her to spend a week in the mountains after the convention and that she might do so since she had had "no rest" to that time. She concluded the letter saying, "I am glad you are getting on so well. Don't work too hard, and don't let those political scapegoats trouble you. I wish they could hear some of the addresses being made on citizenship and legislation, they would shrunk [*sic*] into the runts they are. I am getting on fire."[5]

Ivy did go to the mountains with Mrs. Munroe, and a week later she wrote her husband from Wildemere House, in Winnewaska, New York:

June 7, 1916

My dear Boy—

I received your most interesting letter this A.M. Judging from it things will be going fine soon. I thot of you on yesterday. I am sure it was a most interesting day and that all will come out well. [D]on't let Frose [Frost] and Mahany trouble you[.] [T]hey are not worth one thot of a progressive citizen who has the good of the community alwas at heart. I don't believe I would ever say I told you so after election. Mahany I was told before I left was not even a registered citizen. I feel it would lower our standard and ideals to attact them on a plain upon which we wish to meet out problems.

I am just praying that Mr. Rickards will not attack them and that it has been possible for him to refrain from any form of mud slinging.

It will only cheapen him and make it hard for him to lift himself from their sphere again which he must so quickly do and treat every one as tho this had never taken place—the same with ourselves. I am somewhat surprised at the Olivers changing their stubborn determined way.

I trust the searchers of the Dade Co. records will take good care of them. I should like very much to know just what they do discover. I was amused at Holden's credit given E. T. King, T. M. Bryan in his record of Lauderdale school work. Great isn't it. I am anxiously awaiting your next letter and papers too.[6]

Brother Allen was also well aware of the turmoil in Fort Lauderdale during that spring, for his letter to Frank dated April 3, 1916, contained these comments: "I know you have been very busy for I see by the papers there is a great stir on there in your town hope your Fair will be a success and that the beach drive will go through."[7] Ten days after the June 6 election, Allen wrote again to his brother: "I must say you have had some political strife in your county as well as in the state."[8]

A review of the *Fort Lauderdale Sentinel* for March through June 1916 identifies some of the controversies on which Ivy Stranahan commented so vehemently. While some of the names she mentioned appeared in the paper, newspapers in those years were more reticent than now about publishing personal charges and countercharges. Hence, the *Sentinel* omitted the name-calling. Nevertheless, elements of the parochial dispute can be pieced together from its columns. A long article concerning the Broward county fair appeared in the *Sentinel* on April 17, 1916. Credit for its success was attributed primarily to J. M. Holding, H. T. Brown, and S. L. Drake, while the efforts of Frank and Ivy Stranahan were noted almost as an afterthought. The same edition mentioned that J. M. Holding was announcing his candidacy for reelection as superintendent of public instruction. Four days later the *Sentinel* stated that the Women's Club was busy on proposals to be presented to the council for park sites on the north and south sides of town. City action appears to have been somewhat slow on the issue, for the May 15 *Sentinel* carried the headline, "Parks Again—The Council Laid It on the Table." On May 5, 1916, it reported that W. J. Frost had declared his candidacy for superintendent of public instruction in the June election. Obviously, the school system was one of the most sensitive issues for in the *Sentinel* of May 19, James S. Rickards announced, "Fort Lauderdale High School is accredited." Rickards was then principal of the school. On June 9, following the election, the *Sentinel* reported that J. M. Holding had received a number of votes over his two opponents in the superintendent's race.

After Ivy Stranahan's sojourn in New York State, she stopped in Washington and visited relatives in North Carolina en route to Florida. On June 20 she wrote to Frank from Garland, North Carolina, again emphasizing events at home: "I also rec'd papers yesterday and today note the news. Glad indeed to see that Guy has received the nomination of Supt. I feel sure he will know how to look after his own affairs by this. He should be able to make a success of this. I will not know Lauderdale I believe when daylight comes upon my arrival so many new buildings. [L]et the good work go on. Sounds good about the park also. [T]hings will come right yet even tho it seems a long way around."[9] Ivy's letters reveal the couple's iron-willed determination to prevail in Fort Lauderdale affairs. Her sarcastic reference to Guy Metcalf also reflects something of the family's feelings about their cousin, and implies some disapproval of his actions. Metcalf was elected superintendent of schools of Palm Beach County but proved a disappointment. After two years in office, he was indicted for embezzlement. The following day, February 7, 1918, Guy Metcalf killed himself.[10]

In the spring of 1917 Stranahan did not seek a seat on the city council. He did, however, rejoin the council on November 24, 1917, replacing F. W. Harper as councilor from District 1, and he was reelected each year from 1918 through 1923. Stranahan served as president of the council in 1918, and again for the years 1920, 1921, and 1922.

In August 1925 the citizens of Fort Lauderdale voted approval for a commissioner–city manager form of government. Frank Stranahan was not elected to the first commission. But in May 1927, following the resignation of Tom M. Bryan, Stranahan filled that vacancy and thus served for a few months on the first city commission. He successfully sought reelection in the fall of 1927 and served as a commissioner until his death two years later. Stranahan's tenure on the commission was fraught with problems resulting from the collapse of the 1920s land boom and the devastation wrought by the great 1926 hurricane. The two events combined to bring an economic depression to south Florida well in advance of the rest of the nation. In September 1927 the municipality's citizenry defeated a proposed bond issue, and an angered Stranahan apparently considered it a personal defeat. The amount of the proposed issue was $140,000, and the proceeds were intended for community improvements. The new casino swimming pool at the beach was under construction and would open in January 1928, just months away. Some $75,000 of the bond-issue funds were allocated to purchase additional beach property from J. Frank Needham to be used for a park near the new structure. A lesser amount was for the purchase of some property that Stranahan owned, although he would not benefit personally from the proposed sale. His stated intention was to distribute the entire purchase price of $57,500 in the following manner: Central High School would receive $20,000; the Women's Club, $15,000; the American Legion, $10,000; and the Salvation Army, $5,000. The remaining $7,500 would be used for improvement and maintenance of parks. Thus all of the bond proceeds would have effectively been returned to the community.

More was at stake for the beach area than the purchase of the Needham property. An effort was also underway to acquire from the U.S. Coast Guard a parcel of land measuring 100 feet by 300 feet and stretching from the beach to New River Sound. Florida's Senator Duncan U. Fletcher had arranged a meeting in Washington, D.C., between the commandant of the U.S. Coast Guard, Admiral F. C. Billard, and local community leaders C. E. Rickard and E. P. Hubbell. Their proposal received a positive hearing, and on September 17, 1927, Rickard and Hubbell wrote City Manager B. J. Horne outlining the steps that should be taken to gain a favorable decision from the Coast Guard. The letter arrived on September 22, only a couple of days before the bond-issue vote. Horne discussed the letter with another commissioner, W. C. Kyle, who advised him to have it published immediately. Horne later stated that a local newspaper executive refused publication, and the letter lay pigeonholed on this man's desk. Stranahan said he was not advised of the letter until several weeks later, when Rickard returned from Washington. Stranahan was enraged, and the "man of few words" let go a barrage in the *Miami Daily News and Metropolis* of October 28, 1927. In an article headlined "Plot Charged by Stranahan," he asserted that if the letter from Washington had been published, the news would have changed the outcome of the bond measure, which lost by a mere thirty-eight votes; and he characterized the episode as meant to discredit him and prevent his winning the upcoming election for city commissioner.

Of course, circumstances other than the supposed "plot" contributed to the bond issue's defeat. The proposal came at a time when overburdened taxpayers in Fort Lauderdale and other south Florida communities were experiencing dire financial problems. Numerous residents had fled the area, and many of those remaining were unable to pay their taxes. C. G. Rodes, an early Fort Lauderdale resident and prominent "boom time" land developer, was among those who had left. A good-natured, humorous, and outgoing individual, Rodes later returned to Fort Lauderdale and once again achieved financial success. He wrote Stranahan from Colorado Springs: "My dear Friend—Let me congratulate you on the good sensible stand you take pertaining to the welfare of our (use to be) city. It is really laughable, as well as pitiful, to *'stand on the outside & look in!'* It is one hell of a job you have on your hands but try & *hold them* in line. I know you wish you was back with the Indians & old Chas. Jenkins."[11]

Nevertheless, taxpayers were in revolt, and some became extremely vocal. The following letter, signed simply "A Resident," was written from Fort Lauderdale on September 26, 1927: "Dear Sir: Things look pretty dull here now. The Voters are getting aroused and Saturday voted down a bond issue of One Hundred Forty Thousand dollars. There are about Seven Million dollars in bonds of the City out now on which the interest amounts to One thousand seven hundred and seventy dollars a day, and Salaries are fearful. The Engineering firm of Solomon Norcross Van Kies have been paid Four Hundred and eighty thousand. These extravagances, couple with the Fiasco as to the Golf Course, looks as though some one was Criminally liable. Yours truly, A Resident."[12] Three days after its appearance in a local paper, a copy of this letter was forwarded to Stranahan by W. E. Rasey from New Haven, Connecticut, who wrote saying, "Such letters are going to hurt Fort Lauderdale whether they are true or not; ... I saw an article in a New York paper some time ago, written by some person in Miami, which said that Ft. Lauderdale with a bona fide population of 4700, paid their city officials higher salaries than other cities three times the population of Ft. Lauderdale.... If you could run the city, I am sure you would do it at a great saving from what it now costs."[13]

Another indication of taxpayer dissatisfaction is found in an undated, two-page mimeographed circular distributed by someone signing himself "A Tax Payer":

> Mr. Commissioner:
>
> A commentary upon conditions as affecting the City of Fort Lauderdale, a Corporation, and the Tax Payers as Stock Holders in this corporation, may be in order at this time. Each and every stock holder is familiar with conditions during the last two years, when the height of our prosperity had reached the peak, needs were that we prepare for a greater City. Our WISE MEN mapped out a high program of development—Calling upon the Stock Holders for their approval, which was freely given.... As a last resort appeals have been made to our BOARD OF DIRECTORS, *urging a plan of retrenchment.* ... What the influences are which animate our Directors in continueing this vast expenditure of public money is one of the unsolvable mysteries. Civic Bodies, Business Men all over the City are discussing these public matters, it means spending their money....
>
> It therefore behooves our administration to look further into the future, with but a small fraction of our 1926 taxes paid to date, and our Representative in Tallahassee working for a *further extension of time on our tax payments for last year, what are the possibilities of the payment of taxes for 1927, especially on the inflated value of today.*
>
> If great care is not exercised in the framing of our Budget and values for 1927, we are facing a still greater critical period....
>
> THE BIG QUESTION THEN—DOES our City Commissioners REALIZE THE FACTS, which are so vital to the People.[14]

Such angry sentiments contributed in great measure, no doubt, to defeating the bond issue. However, despite his charge that attempts were made to discredit him, Stranahan did win his race for the city commission in November.

Also in November 1927, C. E. Fritz replaced B. J. Horne as city manager at an annual salary of $5,000, half the amount paid Horne. As the economic situation deteriorated, the city manager's salary was further reduced the next year, to $4,200. When Glenn E. Turner replaced Fritz in

July 1928, the salary was lowered to $325 a month. Turner experienced a further salary reduction to $250 a month in November 1929.

Stranahan served as a commissioner during an extremely critical period in the city's history, and apparently he was fully aware of its financial affairs. On August 16, 1928, city manager Glenn Turner wrote Stranahan: "I wish to call your attention to the following condition of the finances of the City so that you will be fully advised. At the present time the General Fund is overdrawn $222,500 and there is no chance of reducing this overdraft before taxes start coming in next fall. The Cash Balance in all funds on August 15th was $66,691.13; from this amount it will be necessary to meet interest on bonds in the amount of $43,796.30, which will be due September 1st. Other interest items will be due between now and December 1st, in the amount of $41,987.77."[15] Turner continued by itemizing proposed projects totaling $44,399, which included an expenditure of $18,500 for the South Andrews Avenue Bridge, $350 due and payable for asphalt, and a note on the fire truck for $2,000, among other items. He concluded by stating, "From the above you will note that the interest on bonds and projects proposed amounts to $130,183.07 to be taken care of in the next three months. I have made arrangements to borrow up to $45,000. from the Broward Bank & Trust Company at 8% interest to take care of operating expenses, as I do not believe that the revenue will be sufficient to meet same."[16]

Two months later, A. W. (Bert) Erkins wrote to the city commissioners from Cincinnati, Ohio. Erkins had invested heavily in Fort Lauderdale, and he signed his letter as president of the Sunset Investment Company and owner of the Sunset Theater Building. Erkins had a strong interest in the city, which continued even after Fort Lauderdale was no longer his home.

October 26, 1928

Dear Sirs:

In these trying days of economic stress and strain, it behooves all true citizens of Florida and those interested therein, to share a just part of municipal and community burdens.

The very fact—as I understand—that all but one of your commissioners refused to agree to a cut in your salaries as paid to you by the city out of the pockets of the hard pressed and excessively taxed taxpayers seems to "smack" of selfishness. Certainly this is very far from the spirit of the "City Fathers" should show to the people,—many—*many*—of whom (surely very capable people, too) would be most happy to serve in your capacity for less than one-half of the salaries you now receive.

Rich and poor alike have suffered in diverse ways from the various set-backs that the fair State of Florida has experienced within the past two years.

I, as a taxpayer, and one who has done a great deal for the up-building and development and progress of Ft. Lauderdale, *do*—respectfully request—The City Commissioners of the City of Ft. Lauderdale, Florida, to agree to, at least a reasonable and substantial cut in salaries paid them. . . .

The following rumors have been "floating" around Lauderdale for quite some time! I assure you they carry venom!

That several of Ft. Lauderdale and Broward Counties' Commissioners do not own five cents worth of property within the above confines—and several (not all) who do own property, have not paid their taxes! Also, that several have never put a nickel into a building or structure in Broward County!

The people voted you into office as their servants and representatives—you are answerable to them. As to all your actions and motives I do not question the honesty of purpose and intent: you, of course, have stood for some abuse and aggravating trials—all public servants do.

What may we taxpayers expect?[17]

Although commissioners did not take the pay cut suggested by Erkins, Stranahan, fully cognizant of the community's dire finances, evidently was not cashing checks drawn against the city. On the day following his death, the city manager notified Ivy Stranahan that she would be receiving a check for $550 to cover his pay for a final month of service on the commission, plus other checks that he had failed to cash.[18]

Neither Frank nor Ivy Stranahan enjoyed reputations as particularly outgoing, sociable people, yet they never overlooked the social needs of the community. The Stranahans offered the second floor of the trading post on the New River for dances and social gatherings until they remodeled it for residential use. When Frank Stranahan opened the large store near the railroad in 1906, the second story provided space for community gatherings. Mrs. W. H. Marshall remembered that a New Year's dance was in progress at Stranahan's store on the night in 1909 when she arrived in Fort Lauderdale as a bride. Bob Hall recalled that a stairway leading to the second-floor hall was located near the Western Union office on Southwest First Avenue.

Providing such facilities for social events demonstrated Stranahan's accommodating attitude toward the community. Several years after selling the store to the Oliver brothers, he took another step to provide the community with a gathering place. Frank and Ivy Stranahan deeded property to the Fort Lauderdale Women's Club on which the club erected a building. The deed recorded on March 18, 1916, stated that the property was intended for a building to house a library, but the structure served also as a clubhouse and community center. The low and marshy site, located at the western end of a long slough that began as a narrow inlet to the west of the Stranahan home, went northward and turned west just south of today's Broward Boulevard. The cypress trees that stand today around the Women's Club building attest to the marshy terrain. Landfill was needed, and in the May 19, 1916, edition of the *Sentinel*, the Women's Club thanked citizens for their help in filling the lot "which Stranahan had given for a Library building." The building still stands, although the original structure is obscured by an addition that almost totally engulfs it.

Frank Stranahan took an active part in fostering the Fort Lauderdale Baseball Club, which began play in 1913. Two Fort Lauderdale historians have reported that community enthusiasm for such an enterprise was fired in a meeting at which Stranahan offered to donate ground for a ball field, stating that he would have it cleared himself.[19] Evidently this should have read "offered the use of ground," since title to the property was retained by Stranahan for many years, as shown by the Broward County land records. Funds were needed to get the club operating, so he endorsed a note at the Fort Lauderdale State Bank for $100. On September 24, 1913, the note was unpaid and overdue. The bank called on Stranahan as endorser for payment.

Although they had no children of their own, education was another matter of concern to Frank Stranahan and his wife. By 1914 the area's population had increased to a point where the school located on South Andrews Avenue, the second Fort Lauderdale school building, was inadequate. On November 27 of that year Frank and Ivy Stranahan sold to the trustees of the Fort Lauderdale Special Tax District No. 1 a plot of ground measuring 250 by 300 feet. A deed shows the Stranahans were paid $3,000 for this land, which was located within a larger tract that they owned. It was a good business decision as the presence of a school made the remaining Stranahan holding more valuable. The Fort Lauderdale Central School was built on this property, which later became the site of the Landmark Bank building.

School board acquisition of additional Stranahan property took place in incremental fashion. In 1917 an additional 200 feet was deeded to the school board, although they waited four years to record the deed. Only Frank and Ivy signed the deed, although in April 1921 an agreement was entered into between the school board, Stranahans, and nine other prominent couples. The agreement called for the school board to pay the ten couples the sum of $10,000 over a period of several years. The deed and agreement were both recorded April 9, 1921. These instruments covered the 200 feet adjacent to Central School and the north 180 feet of Lot 1, Block 60, Fort Lauderdale, the site where the Southside School was later built on Andrews Avenue.

On August 8, 1923, the Stranahans entered into another agreement with the school board for the acquisition of more property adjacent to Central School. The agreement contained the following covenants: "said parties of the second part hereby further covenant and agree to commence and complete the building of a school building on said land within six months from the date of this agreement. Also that the land East of and adjoining said above described land and extending to the ball part [sic] shall be placed in good and proper condition as a play ground at the expense of the District, and should a road or street be constructed through the above described land from Third Street to Valentine Avenue, it will be sufficiently posted to be used, and used only for school or athletic purposes."[20] If the school board failed to make full payment or to adhere to the specific covenants, the contract would become void, any monies already paid would be forfeited, and the property with all improvements thereon would revert to the Stranahan family. Forty years later, when the school was moved to another location, the school board negotiated a release with Ivy Stranahan before it disposed of the property. The original agreement and the deed specified that the purchase price was $4,500. Five years after the agreement was executed, the Stranahans gave a deed to the school board for the west 169 feet of Block E in Stranahan's subdivision.

The Stranahans were not only interested in schools for the community's white children; it is believed that around 1920 they gave the school board property for a school in the black community. However, it was not until 1924 that Frank and Ivy Stranahan officially deeded to the school board a plot of ground in their Tuskegee Park subdivision measuring 200 by 250 feet. It was the location of the original Dillard school. On February 17, 1938, many years after Frank died, Ivy deeded the remainder of the block to the school system.

Stranahan made another interesting contribution to the city's development by artfully skirting the letter of the law. In 1918 the developer of Fort Lauderdale's first tourist hotel was short of capital with which to finish the project, and he sought local help. Stranahan was a member of the city council and had considered giving the municipality property surrounding the Women's Club building, which would become known as Stranahan Park. The sum of $6,000 was needed to complete the hotel fund drive. The city council could not use city funds for such a purpose, and, as a council member, Stranahan was prohibited from selling property to the city. Thus a deal was struck whereby Stranahan "sold" the property to John Sherwin for one dollar. Sherwin then sold it to the city for $6,000, and he turned the funds over to the hotel developer.

Stranahan is often credited with providing the site for a hospital. In reality he owned a considerable amount of property in the northeast section of the city, and sold a 480-foot piece of land bounded by A and Fifth Streets, and Avenues F and G, to Dr. Scott Edwards. Edwards recorded the deed on June 13, 1923, and a hospital was subsequently built. Stranahan was evidently involved to some extent in the construction; the previous year he received a letter inquiring about the need for elevators "in the hospital."[21] In 1924 Stranahan sold the property surrounding the hospital to Alfred G. Kuhn, who developed the Victoria Park subdivision. The hospital had a short and hectic history and finally closed, and the building has since been destroyed. The Salvation Army was another organization that benefited from the Stranahans' largesse. For a consideration of one dollar, Frank and Ivy Stranahan deeded the organization Lot 19, Block 12, of the town of Fort Lauderdale on April 6, 1927.

This account of Frank Stranahan's contributions of real estate for civic purposes is presented with some trepidation. Those mentioned here were compiled following a review of his land transactions as entered in the Broward County public records and listed in the files of the Fort Lauderdale Historical Society. Stranahan may have made other donations that only his contemporaries could have known about, but they too have passed from the scene. Even though Frank Stranahan unquestionably realized economic gain from many of these transactions, his public-spirited nature and interest in Fort Lauderdale and its citizens of all races is undeniable.

7

Ivy Stranahan, Civic Activist

One can only imagine the thoughts of eighteen-year-old Ivy Julia Cromartie on October 1, 1899, when she arrived to teach school at New River. It is unlikely that the inexperienced young woman could have anticipated that within the year she would marry Frank Stranahan, a prosperous man nearly twice her age. Stranahan's business was established and doing well, he was highly respected, and the marriage would afford Ivy the status of "first lady" in the community. Could her wildest youthful dreams ever have envisioned the influential role she would play throughout a long and productive life? Whatever her thoughts, Ivy plunged into the new role with characteristic enthusiasm. Until completion of their small house near the trading post, the newlyweds boarded with the King family, as Ivy had done while teaching. The couple lived on the north side of New River while most other area residents had homes on the south side. Although the river created a barrier to frequent socializing with other area families, this did not prevent Ivy Stranahan from actively pursuing causes in which she was interested.

Ivy Cromartie was raised a teetotaler Methodist, and she took an active part in the local Women's Christian Temperance Union (WCTU) meetings. She remained steadfastly opposed to alcohol all her life, and it gave her great satisfaction when the Eighteenth Amendment was adopted in 1919. Its repeal after little more than a decade must have been a bitter disappointment. Her views on alcohol set up an immediate conflict concerning one of her husband's most profitable revenue sources. At the turn of the century, it was an accepted practice at Florida frontier trading posts to sell liquor to the Seminole Indians, and Stranahan's was no exception. But so firm a temperance advocate was Ivy that she reportedly prevented Frank from selling anything containing alcohol to the Indians, even such seemingly innocuous items as patent medicines or vanilla extract.[1] Thus the strong-willed young bride quickly came to influence her husband's business affairs.

When the Seminoles finished their transactions at her husband's store, some of the men would take the train to West Palm Beach, where they could buy liquor at Zapp's or other saloons and celebrate before returning to the Everglades.[2] However, one might question whether it was necessary for the Indians to make such a journey, since there were probably moonshiners around New River who trafficked in that commodity. Frank Stranahan encouraged the Indians to leave their guns at his store when they went carousing, which indicates that most of their drinking sprees took place in the vicinity of the trading post. Of course, an intelligent and observant young woman had to be aware of the illicit liquor trade that flourished in the vicinity of New River even while the "noble experiment" of Prohibition remained on the statute books. Nevertheless, Ivy Stranahan was firm in her convictions—so much so that in the 1930s, when the lower floor of her home was turned into a restaurant known as Pioneer House, the lease contained a provision that neither alcohol nor narcotics could be sold or used on the premises. This clause was added in her bold, distinctive handwriting. Despite Ivy's opinions regarding the use of alcoholic beverages and her influence on her husband's affairs, Frank was known to imbibe on occasion. Material evidence of this—a small stash of used liquor bottles—was found when the attic of their house was cleaned out prior to the beginning of restoration in January 1980.

Another cause Ivy fervently espoused was the conservation of south Florida bird life, much of which was being slaughtered early in the twentieth century. Well-equipped and organized bands of commercial "plumers" could shoot out a rookery in a few days, destroying mature nesting birds and hatchlings alike. The plumage of birds such as the snowy egret and roseate spoonbill became a mainstay of the international millinery industry; at one time an ounce of feathers was said to be as valuable as an ounce of gold. Against the allure of such wealth, even the National Audubon Society, organized in the early 1900s, found it difficult to protect the birds. The assassination in 1905 of Guy Bradley, the Audubon game warden for Monroe County, polarized the community and energized an effort to put a stop to the ruthless destruction. It is likely Ivy knew the Bradley family from her days in Lemon City. His father had been a keeper at the Fort Lauderdale life-saving station for a brief time, some ten years before Frank Stranahan's arrival on New River, and Guy Bradley's boat, the *Pearl*, was well known throughout the Biscayne Bay region.[3]

In 1885, as a lad of fourteen, Guy Bradley went on a hunting expedition with Jean Chevelier, who lived on the Miami River and was considered "one of the most devastatingly effective of all the early plume hunters."[4] Guy shot his share of birds, selling the plumes for twenty-five cents each. However, as an adult he turned against the plume trade and accepted the Audubon job protecting bird rookeries. It has been conjectured that the conservation-minded author Kirk Munroe and his wife were responsible for converting Bradley to the Audubon movement, since they were its leading exponents in the Miami area. Ivy Stranahan came to find that she and Mary Barr Munroe shared many mutual interests. Guy Bradley's death evidently fired Ivy's resolve to become involved with the Audubon cause, and before long Frank Stranahan ceased buying bird plumes from his Seminole clientele. Since plumes were among the most valuable commodities that Indians brought to sell at the store, along with alligator skins and otter pelts, this was another way in which Ivy's principles directly influenced Frank's business.

At a Fort Lauderdale Board of Trade meeting in January 1911, a committee was named to investigate and prepare for incorporation of the community. At the same session a motion passed that "all energetic ladies of the town be asked to meet with the board to form a civic organization."[5] At the board's next meeting, it was announced that the Women's Civic Improvement Association stood ready to help. The newly formed organization gave Ivy Stranahan a vehicle for direct involvement in public life, although it appears to have had a very brief life, almost immediately metamorphosing into the Fort Lauderdale Women's Club. Information in the collection of Women's Club yearbooks at the Fort Lauderdale Historical Society is contradictory. In one place it is stated that the Women's Club was organized in 1910, but another book gives 1911 as the date. In any case, the organization became "state federated" in 1912, incorporated in 1913, and affiliated with the General Federation of Women's Clubs by 1914. In 1923 a county federation of women's clubs was organized.

Lists of officers appearing in early yearbooks show that Mrs. Frank Oliver served as president of the Women's Civic Improvement Association in 1911, Mrs. D. C. TenBrook was Women's Club president for 1911–12, and Mrs. H. G. Wheeler became president for 1912–13, with Mrs. Stranahan serving as second vice president. Ivy Stranahan was elected president for 1913–14 and held the post for three years.

In her capacity as president, she formulated a plan to hold a Suburban Day on December 11, 1914. All residents of surrounding communities were invited, the merchants prepared special displays to entice shoppers, and prizes were awarded for various contests. James Whitcomb Riley, the famed Hoosier poet wintering in Miami, was invited as special guest for the day. Schoolchildren participated in the event, bringing bouquets of flowers with which to honor the writer of children's verse. In the afternoon attendees gathered at the Rex Theater for a program that included an address by club president Ivy Stranahan, probably her first public speech. Following the event, 300 women attended a tea at the Gilbert Hotel. Although the day was damp and disagreeable, the merchants found the event a great success and urged the club to stage more such activities.

Affiliation of the Fort Lauderdale group with the Florida Federation of Women's Clubs (FFWC) provided an avenue for Ivy Stranahan's emergence on the state level as an activist for various causes. The Stranahans had no children to claim her time and attention, and employment of household help was then a routine practice for most white southerners. Frank Stranahan's financial status afforded Ivy the freedom to pursue an active and fulfilling role outside the home. Despite her youth, from the time of their marriage she was possibly the most financially secure matron in the community. The expenses involved in travel to state and national meetings appeared to be no problem; she could hold her own with women of high social standing, and this circumstance no doubt contributed to Ivy's rise to prominence on the state scene.

Ivy Stranahan's involvement with the FFWC also focused her efforts on behalf of women's suffrage. It is likely that she first developed an interest in the issue through membership in the Women's Christian Temperance Union, and this would be reinforced through her club work. The state federation had adopted suffrage as part of its program and formally endorsed the Florida Equal Suffrage Association (FESA), founded in 1913. Although FESA held six state conventions between 1914 and 1918, the women's clubs proved the most effective agency to promote the cause. Moreover, the same cadre of women provided leadership for both the FFWC and the suffrage association. Upon the formation of the Fort Lauderdale Suffrage League in 1915, Mrs. Stranahan promptly assumed a leading role and used this as a springboard to an office in the state group. One historian of the women's suffrage movement in the state wrote, "Ivy Stranahan became one of Florida's most prominent suffragists, while a number of other Fort Lauderdale pioneers, such as Annie Beck and Frances TenBrook were active in the suffrage movement on a local level."[6]

The Florida Equal Suffrage Association held its third annual meeting at Miami in March 1917. The program included discussions led by Mrs. William Jennings Bryan on "Some Necessary Legislation for Florida" and by Mrs. Stranahan on "Sectional Objections to Suffrage." The FESA adopted a political agenda to be supported in the upcoming legislative session; it also voted to push for suffrage bills in as many municipalities as possible. When the time came to elect officers for the organization, Ivy Stranahan was named president while Annie Broward became first vice president. A legislative program was adopted, and Mary Elizabeth Bryan was named chair of the legislative committee. Initially the FFWC and FESA both supported a bill to allow women to vote in state primary elections but not in general (presidential) elections. The two groups' position was based on the assumption that the South was solidly Democratic and winning the primary was tantamount to election. Furthermore, the primaries were segregated by race, and this would not embroil women's suffrage with the controversial issue of black suffrage, as in the recently defeated effort to insert a "grandfather clause" in Florida's constitution.[7] Also introduced was a constitutional amendment allowing women's suffrage that ex-governor William S. Jennings drafted for his wife, the FFWC president May Mann Jennings. Clearly, over the next months the state capitol would occupy the attention of FFWC and FESA leaders.

The political struggle for women's suffrage in Florida placed Ivy Stranahan in close association with May Mann Jennings and Annie Broward, both wives of former governors, and Mary Elizabeth Bryan, wife of the noted orator and three-time Democratic presidential candidate William Jennings Bryan. These were articulate, talented, and sophisticated women who knew how to exercise political influence, even without the vote, through a network of personal contacts at the state and national level. Surely there must have been times when the relatively youthful Ivy Stranahan pondered the contrast between her humble beginnings and her close association with distinguished women who spent much of their time in Tallahassee lobbying for various suffrage bills.

In 1917 a young *Miami Herald* reporter, Marjorie Stoneman Douglas, accompanied these suffragists on one of their lobbying forays and left the following assessment of her companions' bravery in confronting a male-dominated legislature:

> We went to Tallahassee by Pullman train. I remember the red dust of those red hills beyond the Suwannee seeping in around the joints of the Pullman car. In Tallahassee we stayed in the old Leon Hotel, which was full of lobbyists where you'd expect to see them, down in the lobby discussing politics all night long. Mrs. Broward was sick and had to stay in bed, but she'd go over and speak to the legislators and return to bed as soon as she got back. We'd sit on her bed and she'd tell about the days when her husband was governor and when he was running guns to Cuba in the Spanish-American War. Mr. Broward was a canny old pirate, and he'd smuggled guns down the Florida coast. I liked Mrs. Broward and her stories even though my father was her husband's greatest enemy in the dredging of the Everglades.
>
> Mrs. Jennings was younger than Mrs. Broward, and Mrs. Stranahan and I were younger still. All four of us spoke to a joint committee, wearing our best hats. It was a large room with men sitting around on two sides with their backs propped up against the walls and large brass spittoons between every other one of them. Talking to them was like talking to graven images. They never paid attention to us at all. They weren't even listening. This was my first taste of the politics of north Florida."[8]

During the height of the legislative session in Tallahassee, Mary Elizabeth Bryan addressed a committee, delivering a well-received statement on suffrage that lasted fully an hour and a half. However, her efforts were criticized by some as an "outside intrusion in Florida affairs," and Bryan ceased to be active on the FESA legislative committee, although she remained its chair. Thereafter, as one historian has observed, "Mrs. Jennings and Mrs. Stranahan did the real suffrage work in the legislative vineyard."[9]

Initially, the prospects for passage of both suffrage measures—the constitutional amendment and the bill to allow women to vote in primaries—looked favorable, so most of the women returned to their homes. But suddenly the temper of the legislature grew increasingly negative, portending defeat for FESA's primary bill. Evidently, many members of the legislature supported a suffrage amendment that male voters of the state would have to ratify but balked at passing a women's primary suffrage bill that needed no approval by the electorate. When Jennings and Stranahan rushed back to Tallahassee, their legislative supporters convinced them that the bill had no chance of passing, and they allowed it to be withdrawn. This decision drew strong criticism, and suffragists over the state began to struggle among themselves.

Many women in south Florida, particularly in Miami, wanted a suffrage bill introduced that would permit women to vote in the general election, and they blamed Ivy Stranahan and May Jennings for that failure. According to Kenneth Johnson, "The legislative programs of the FESA and FFWC did not call for the introduction of a presidential suffrage bill although Mrs. Stranahan and Mrs. Jennings had a copy of such a bill ready to introduce if conditions were ever favorable. On the advice of friendly legislators, the bill was not introduced because it would have met sure defeat. . . . As the accusations circulated and feelings grew bitter, there were threats that some of the woman's clubs would withdraw from the Federation and some of the suffrage leagues from the Suffrage Association."[10] May Jennings replied to the accusations in detail, and her explanation indicated she was acting to avoid a sure defeat in the state legislature that would make passage of a later bill more difficult. After all, she had the expert advice of her husband, a former governor wise in the ways of the Tallahassee legislative process. Whereas May Jennings was measured in responding to her critics, Johnson found that "Mrs. Stranahan with less diplomacy announced that the women were out of their heads and suggested that some of their energy might be used more effectively working for municipal suffrage."[11]

The women's suffrage amendment to the state constitution (not to be confused with the previously withdrawn primary bill) passed the Florida senate in 1917 but failed to receive the required three-fifths majority in the house.[12] Thus thwarted at the state level, the quest for political equality continued at the local level—and was equally unsuccessful. The women of Fort Lauderdale sought the municipal ballot in the summer of 1917. In a referendum abolishing the town of Fort Lauderdale and establishing the city of Fort Lauderdale, provision was made for women's suffrage if a majority of qualified electors approved. The women had to fight even to secure a place on the ballot. They canvassed the town and found 154 favorable to the proposition and 117 opposed. The driving force behind this effort was Frances TenBrook, president of the local WCTU and a suffrage leader. Ivy Stranahan informed May Jennings that most of the "best people" in the city supported the proposition, but the politicians were the uncertain group.[13]

It should be recalled that Frank Stranahan did not seek reelection to the city council at that time, thereby avoiding taking a stand on the issue. The new city charter with its suffrage provision failed by a vote of ninety-three against and seventy-eight in favor.[14] That same year the Miami suffragists also decided to make another try for municipal suffrage, but, Johnson reported, "they became embroiled in a disagreement with Mrs. Stranahan and Mrs. Jennings. . . . Apparently Mrs. Stranahan and Mrs. Jennings would not support the measure, and the Miami women would make no special effort in their own behalf, so the measure failed to pass."[15] Perhaps this lack of support from state leaders in the suffrage movement stemmed from the Miami women's rebuff of Stranahan and Jennings during the legislative session.

Ivy Stranahan's tenure as president of the FESA was not an unqualified success. Shortly after she assumed office, the United States entered World War I, and the suffrage movement became a secondary national priority. Ivy soon overextended herself by accepting increased local responsibilities, heading up the food conservation effort in Broward County and the Liberty Loan drive as well. She urged all suffragists across the state to take an active part in the sale of Liberty Bonds. Despite setbacks suffered in the 1917 legislative session, the influential May Mann Jennings, in her third year as president of the FFWC and a driving force in the suffrage movement, still hoped to move forward with the organization of local suffrage leagues. She wrote to Ivy on August 9, 1917, "I want to see as many suffrage associations in the state as possible and I want the people of Florida to feel that you have done some splendid foundation work."[16] The fourth annual FESA convention was held at Tampa in November 1917, only eight months after the March meeting in Miami and planned to coincide with the FFWC state meeting. Stranahan could only report that, "Organization work has been very much retarded owing to the great war in which our country is engaged thus demanding the time, energy and finances of the women who could do this work. With the hope of overcoming this handicap, your president has written a personal letter to many women over the state with gratifying results."[17] Nevertheless, it appears that the FESA president believed that the real strength of the suffrage movement lay with the state federation of women's clubs, which numbered over 9,000 members. In August she had written, "I really feel that the majority of suffrage work will be done through the women's clubs anyway.... You know when we get equal rights, it seems to me there will be no further use for a separate organization, our aims will have been accomplished."[18] Obviously, May Jennings was less than totally satisfied with Ivy Stranahan's organizational work as president of FESA, and persuaded her not to seek the office of vice president in the Florida Federation of Women's Clubs. Perhaps because of this Ivy Stranahan never held a major leadership position in that organization. Regardless, May Jennings never wavered in her support of Stranahan's efforts as chair of Indian affairs for the federation.

In 1918 the FESA convened in Daytona, and Ivy Stranahan became first vice president and chair of the legislative committee. May Jennings, her pique evidently abated, also served on the legislative committee and worked closely with Stranahan until suffrage was achieved. Those close to the movement believed that Ivy Stranahan was totally dominated by May Jennings. Certainly the older woman from Jacksonville was one of the best known and most influential individuals in the state, and she could be overpowering. Perhaps this was also an expression, in part, of the sectional differences that continued to divide north and south Florida on occasion. That year the FESA planned a two-pronged attack on the suffrage issue. It would petition senators to support a national suffrage amendment while again pushing for a primary suffrage bill at the state level. Neither strategy met with success. During the 1919 legislative session, a resolution adding a suffrage amendment to the state constitution received the required three-fifths vote in the senate, but again failed in the house by four votes. It was the last vote that Florida would cast on the enfranchisement of women.

Despite the infighting that sometimes characterized the Florida suffrage campaign, the movement was successful on the national level. The Nineteenth Amendment was passed by Congress on June 4, 1919, and sent to the states for ratification. The Florida legislature was still in session and had the opportunity to become the first state to approve the measure. Ivy Stranahan and four other women traveled to Tallahassee to lobby for ratification; however, the legislature adjourned two days later without voting on the Nineteenth Amendment. The crafty May Mann Jennings did not make the trip to Tallahassee; she correctly judged that the Florida legislators had never seriously considered the FFWC/FESA bills, and she did not want to give them the satisfaction of rebuking the Nineteenth Amendment. The only minor victory that Fort Lauderdale suffragists gained from the 1919 legislature was a bill allowing women to vote in local municipal elections, as was already mandated in sixteen other Florida towns. In June 1919 the states of Wisconsin, Michigan, and Illinois became the first to vote for ratification of the Nineteenth Amendment, which was certified as approved on August 26, 1920, ten days after Ivy Stranahan's twentieth wedding anniversary.

While the suffrage movement was moving toward a successful conclusion, patriotic fervor swept the New River community during World War I. Although Ivy Stranahan remained involved in promoting women's rights, she did not neglect local service. The coastal community felt a direct impact from military activities that was unknown inland. Florida residents worried about a U-boat menace along the coast, although it was not realized until the next war, and activities at Fort Lauderdale's beach generated an awareness of the conflict. In 1915 jurisdiction over the life-saving station on the beach was transferred to the U.S. Coast Guard. With the 1917 declaration of war, the base was designated a defense installation, and patrols were begun along the beach. The free and easy use of the former "House of Refuge," once extended to local residents by its hospitable occupants, came to an end. No longer could it be used as a bath house for changing into swimming attire. This no doubt helped provide the impetus for construction of the pavilion on adjoining property.

Ivy took the lead in the Liberty Bond campaign for Broward County. She promoted this patriotic obligation locally as well as at the state suffrage convention. The *Fort Lauderdale Sentinel* of February 15, 1918, stated, "A thrift campaign for the purpose of assisting in educating the people of the state and nation in the habits of thrift to encourage saving and out of the savings to purchase war saving stamps, has been inaugurated among the women of the state. Mrs. W. S. Jennings of Jacksonville is in charge of the state campaign and Mrs. Frank Stranahan of this city has been appointed county chairman for Broward County." Ironically, the Liberty Bond sales may have negatively affected Frank Stranahan's business affairs. It has been asserted that the success of the bond program resulted in a great loss of savings from both local banks, leading the two institutions to merge. But this was probably not the determining factor undermining Frank Stranahan's banking interests since the community, which had only 1,870 residents by 1920, was quite small to support two successful banks.

Ivy Stranahan's patriotism was demonstrated in yet another way—formation of a local American Red Cross chapter.[19] In May 1958, she was honored by that group for "her foresight and interest in organizing Red Cross during the early days of the community."[20] With the conclusion of the "war to end all wars," Ivy's attention turned to advocacy for the League of Nations as the best chance for world peace; she also supported Near East Relief.[21] The catastrophic Second World War renewed Ivy's Red Cross activities, and she became involved in British War Relief as well.[22] Another topic that drew her attention was the social hygiene issues related to the war.[23]

Ivy Stranahan was a woman of multifaceted interests who devoted much time to issues of national scope: the Audubon movement, women's suffrage, Indian affairs (discussed at length in chapter 8), and patriotic issues. Yet she always had time for humanitarian concerns, such as Broward County welfare.[24] During the Great Depression, Ivy was distressed to learn that impoverished families were losing their homes—seeing them auctioned off on the courthouse steps because they were unable to pay their taxes. She and her supporters called an "indignation meeting" at the courthouse, and a movement was launched for what eventually became the homestead exemption law. She enlisted Dwight L. Rogers, then a member of the Florida legislature, to push the bill that allowed everyone a $5,000 exemption on property taxes, thereby saving many family homes.[25]

In the mid-1930s Fort Lauderdale and Broward County also faced a medical crisis when the county medical association refused to support existing private hospital facilities. The establishment of Broward General Hospital was not a total solution since, in an era of racial segregation, it lacked facilities for black residents. On April 27, 1937, a mass meeting was sponsored by Fort Lauderdale's black citizens, and the Broward Hospital League was formed to raise funds for a hospital to serve them. A year later Provident Hospital opened at 1400 Northwest Sixth Street. In 1938 Dr. Von D. Mizell, a young black man reared in Dania and a graduate of a Chicago medical school, returned to Broward County to set up a practice. He became medical director and chief of surgical services at the hospital. Mizell stated that he had refused an opportunity to practice in the Chicago area, preferring to return to his home area to provide better health care for members of his race. Ivy Stranahan became treasurer for Provident Hospital in 1938 and continued to be actively involved for many years. When Mizell left for military service in 1941, he was replaced by Dr. James Sistrunk.[26]

Another of Ivy Stranahan's interests was family planning. This seems to have derived from a very personal experience with her mother, Sarah Cromartie, who died at a relatively early age. Ivy was the oldest of her children, and Mrs. Cromartie's health had been impaired by many pregnancies, although she did not rear a large family by standards of that day. Thus Ivy had an intensely personal reason for promoting a family planning program.

As if the many causes Ivy Stranahan espoused were not sufficient to fill her hours, she took on an added civic responsibility. After local voters chose a city manager form of government, the first planning and zoning board was established on December 8, 1925. Among its five appointees was Ivy Stranahan, the lone female member. She served ten years and has been credited with farsighted service that fostered the orderly growth of the city. However, there was one civic duty Ivy refused. Following Frank's death, a movement was immediately set in motion to draft her to fill his seat on the city commission.[27] Petitions were circulated, but the grief-stricken widow declined to enter the political arena, although she might have achieved the distinction of becoming Fort Lauderdale's first female commissioner. Instead, the city had its first female commissioner eight years later, when Genevieve Pynchon was elected.

In her later years, Ivy Stranahan lost a major battle when she opposed construction of the New River tunnel that adjoined her home and property. The issue was a divisive one. Husbands voted for the tunnel, wives against it. The influential Gore family and its newspaper opposed the tunnel, but in balloting held on November 20, 1956, the vote was 7,040 in favor of the tunnel and 6,443 against. No wonder Ivy opposed it! Who would not have done so, given the daily disruption it created over a long period of time. Pile drivers pounded away day after day as the foundation for the tunnel was constructed. The ear-splitting noise was audible at great distances, to say nothing of what it must have been like just a few feet away in Ivy's living quarters.

On October 13, 1958, the federal highway bridge over New River was closed and tunnel construction began. Over two years later, on December 9, 1960, the $7.5 million tunnel was officially dedicated. The construction process damaged the Stranahan home, opening cracks in the aging structure. Pictures of the damage were made in August and September 1960 and damages were assessed.[28] When restoration of the home began in 1980, it was determined that damage to the foundation was even greater than that discovered during the 1960 inspection.

Religion was important to Ivy Cromartie. She grew up in a Methodist home, and the first church established in Fort Lauderdale was Methodist. Her religious beliefs influenced her long, service-filled life. Later she heard speakers describe the beliefs and practices of the Seventh Day Adventist Church, and she made a decision to cast her lot in that direction—practicing its tenets with loyalty and devotion the remainder of her days. The church offered a natural extension of Ivy's humanitarian involvement with her community. Her records contain an article from the *Miami Herald* dated June 6, 1954, and headlined, "70 Adventists in Broward Donated $17,000 to Church." The article stated, "The church maintains its own welfare center from which it dispenses food and clothing to the needy regardless of religious affiliation. Last year, working with state and county welfare workers and the Salvation Army, it helped 664 persons, taking food and clothing to some people who had no other place to live except shacks southwest of Fort Lauderdale and in the vicinity of St. Rd. 7." In 1958 a group of pioneers instituted an annual luncheon for women who had lived in Fort Lauderdale in 1935 and earlier, as well as their daughters and granddaughters. The event was, and still is, scheduled on a Saturday since so many can attend only on that day. However, the most senior "pioneer lady" never attended; Saturday was her day of worship.

Ivy Stranahan was a loyal member of a small, exclusive group of pioneer women called the 1919 Study Club, which met for many years until its membership was decimated by death. Her old associate in the suffrage movement, Annie Beck, lamented that the records of the group were never given to the local historical society. Ivy Stranahan was associated in some way with virtually every civic activity in the city. She organized the first group of Camp Fire Girls in Fort Lauderdale, and that fact was noted when the organization celebrated its fifty-fourth anniversary. Active in the Fort Lauderdale Garden Club, she served as treasurer in 1939. After formation of the Fort Lauderdale Historical Society, she provided a replica of the first "trading post" for its collection.

As the years advanced, Ivy Stranahan received recognition from numerous groups. She was awarded an honorary Doctor of Humanities degree by Drake University, which in 1968 was Fort Lauderdale's only four-year college.[29] Florida governor Claude Kirk proclaimed February 18, 1968, as Mrs. Stranahan Day.[30] The Fort Lauderdale pioneer received national acclaim for her work with the Seminole Indians, and the local Exchange Club and Amosis Society honored her. She was recognized as a Broward County "Golden Ager," and an orchid was named for her. In 1967 the National Society Daughters of the American Revolution honored Ivy Stranahan in a ceremony held at Pioneer House, as her home was often called at that time.

Over the years the *Miami Herald* contained several highly laudatory accounts of Ivy Stranahan's various endeavors. In 1956, speaking of those who had served the south Florida community, it recognized

> Lauderdale's "first lady," Mrs. Frank Stranahan, whose patience, diplomacy and understanding through a long career of civic work are a model for the young women who'll shape the city's future.
>
> Her long service on the city planning board, her efforts to retain the park-like beauty of New River, her championship of the Seminoles—even her early efforts to obtain suffrage for Florida women—all are paying off for us today.

For years she worked as a volunteer in the Broward County Public Welfare department and in the welfare center of the Seventh Day Adventist Church. She helped establish a county home for the aged. All her life she's chosen to do the work that no one else would do.

Now she's willing to let others take over except for her work in the Friends of the Seminoles, which she helped organize and headed for many years."[31]

Ivy Julia Cromartie Stranahan launched her career as an activist as the twentieth century dawned and remained an influential figure in south Florida affairs for the next seven decades. Had there been no cause for which to crusade, she likely would have created one. She personified the meaning of "emancipated woman" in the truest sense of the term and achieved many of her goals without benefit of the Nineteenth Amendment or other legislation. In a *Miami Herald* profile written shortly before her death and appropriately headlined "Mrs. Ivy Stranahan: The Tiger Mellows," she recalled being "the real poison ivy" to those who opposed her reforming zeal. Stranahan then provided a memorable valedictory to her activism: "I've been the master of my life. Now I have ceased proposing, or disposing, anything. I've settled down to the quiet life and only better eyesight could make me happier. I don't seem to notice growing old. It seems the natural condition that appears just like youth, and is not to be worried over."[32]

8

Ivy Stranahan and the Indian Reform Movement

Ivy Cromartie had little contact with Florida's Seminole Indians prior to her arrival at New River. Although Lemon City was one of the frontier communities frequented by Seminoles, her family had no known involvement with them. Once she was married to Frank Stranahan, though, they became an integral part of her existence, and she embarked on what proved to be a lifelong commitment to support Indian causes, starting at home. Prior to 1906 the Seminoles were Frank Stranahan's most consistent customers. In later years she remembered seeing "as many as a hundred canoes coming down the river, loaded with Indian families, their trade goods, cookware, and animals headed for a rendezvous at the trading post."[1] With the passing of time her recall may have become exaggerated, given that the entire Seminole population in south Florida probably numbered fewer than 600 at the turn of the century, and not all of them traded with Stranahan. Nevertheless, she painted a vivid picture of the large numbers of Indians who arrived to camp near the trading post. These groups might come in as often as every six weeks, depending on the supply of game and where they were hunting. She recalled that the Indians were taciturn—as was her husband—and took little notice of visitors, even famous ones. Henry M. Flagler, the multimillionaire founder of the FEC and former partner of John D. Rockefeller, often moored his yacht in front of Stranahan's store for several days at a time and "would just come in and quietly stand with his back to the counter, watching the Indian trade. The Indians would pay no attention to him, of course, but anyway he was a stranger and they didn't recognize strangers. . . . he enjoyed watching the Indians, and we were always glad to have him."[2]

Naturally, the Indians were curious about Stranahan's new wife, who was an attractive young woman. Seminole children were more open than the elders in expressing their inquisitiveness, often coming around the small cottage near the trading post where the couple lived and peeping in the windows to catch a glimpse of her. At first they were shy and reticent, but she soon won them over by letting the girls dress up in her large "Merry Widow" hats, and in time they had the run of the house.

As Ivy Stranahan gained the children's confidence, she began to teach them informally, using religious materials published by the Presbyterian Church. These consisted largely of colorful posters containing the names and pictures of various scriptural figures; Indian youngsters learned their letters by reading words printed on the posters. Possibly some of these materials were provided through her Presbyterian minister father-in-law in Ohio, as well as the local Presbyterian church. Had she chosen, Ivy could certainly have used secular materials, such as the Webster blue-back speller and McGuffey readers left over from her year teaching school in Fort Lauderdale. She later claimed that there was no overt attempt to convert Indian youngsters to Christianity, but these instructional sessions seem to have expressed her missionary zeal as well as interest in Indian education.

Classes were unstructured, as teacher and pupils sat in the yard or on the broad verandas of the trading post building erected in 1901. Instruction was, of necessity, sporadic. After concluding an exchange of goods, Indian families usually returned to their camps near the Everglades until hunting netted sufficient goods to warrant another transaction at the store weeks or even months later. After the trading post closed, Mrs. Stranahan acquired a Model-T Ford, which she drove over deeply rutted sand roads to the nearby Indian camps to continue the lessons. Although Seminole elders, especially the medicine men, never condoned Ivy's instructional sessions, they did not prevent the children from participating. Most Indian parents probably saw no lasting harm in infrequent visits with the white woman. Ivy Stranahan continued her informal teaching for over twenty-five years, ceasing only with the 1927 opening of a federal day school on the Dania Seminole Reservation. Her niece, Alice Cromartie Simpson, recalled, "She was a natural teacher. We used to go to the reservation and sit on the logs with the Indians with a basket of mangoes; she put those mangoes out there then go back to the car and then eventually the children would appear and sit on the logs and eat the mangoes. And then when the logs were full [of children] she would get out of the car and bring her Sunday School materials and that's how she began to teach."[3] These early contacts with the Seminoles led Ivy Stranahan into an active role championing Indian rights and welfare issues, as she saw them. Despite their lack of approval of their children's "education" at her hands, many Seminoles came to respect the woman who befriended them and to whom they could come with their problems. Over time she was given the Indian name *Watchie Esta/Hutrie*, "Little White Mother."[4]

Until she became directly involved in the statewide activities of the Florida Federation of Women's Clubs (FFWC), Ivy Stranahan's involvement in Indian causes had been undertaken primarily as an individual. Obviously, she was most directly concerned with the Indians whom she knew personally, which meant those families who traded at her husband's store or lived nearby. She had virtually no contact with Seminoles who lived on the west side of the Everglades or near Lake Okeechobee. Neither was she closely involved with the Indians who lived along the Tamiami Trail between Miami and Naples. The Seminole camp located closest to Fort Lauderdale early in the century was that of Annie Tommie, which was situated on the north fork of New River. She was the widow of a famous medicine man, Doctor Tommie, who died around 1904 and left her to raise their six sons.[5] Ivy Stranahan became interested in their welfare, and in 1915 she was instrumental in having Tony Tommie admitted to the Fort Lauderdale public school—only the second time a member of the tribe had attempted public education in Florida.[6] Although Tony was already fifteen years of age, he got along with younger classmates and developed some ability to read and write. His only surviving letter to Frank Stranahan, written in 1916, contained the request, "I wont you lone me some money $10.00. . . . I wont buy little alligator [Tony hatched and sold baby alligators] . . . I wont get my bicycles and shoh and some school books to, if I don't buy litle alligator. I paid you back soon."[7] Tony Tommie later attended the Carlisle Indian School in Pennsylvania, then returned home and became headman at the Musa Isle Indian Village tourist attraction in Miami.[8]

Ivy Stranahan became chair of the Indian affairs committee of the Florida Federation of Women's Clubs in 1915 and held that post for many years. In this capacity she assumed a prominent role lobbying for the establishment of a permanent reservation for the Florida Seminoles. As early as the 1890s authorities began acquiring tracts of land in the Everglades that would ultimately become a federal Indian reservation; even so, Seminole advocates wanted the Florida legislature to set aside land for a state reservation as well. Ivy Stranahan embarked on the crusade with vigor and was strongly supported by the state federation's dynamic president, May Mann Jennings. However, their campaign to have land set aside for a state Indian reservation became stalled in Tallahassee. Moreover, they believed the federation efforts were being undercut by the tactics of Minnie Moore-Willson of Kissimmee, who helped organize the Friends of the Florida Seminoles society in 1899.[9] Three years earlier, based primarily on her knowledge of Seminoles living north of Lake Okeechobee, Moore-Willson had written a book titled *The Seminoles of Florida*, and she fancied herself an authority on the subject. Consequently, she was not a "team player" and formed her own alliance with a national Indian-rights group to promote legislation in Tallahassee.

Through her speeches and writings Moore-Willson became the leading figure in the struggle for a state reservation, although she often alienated other equally ardent supporters of the Indian cause with her acerbic denunciations of legislative inaction and her abrasive personality.[10] In 1915 she was reprimanded by FFWC president May Jennings for charging in the federation's publication that scandals in state government were preventing the Seminoles from receiving land.[11] All future statements regarding Indian affairs, she was informed, must come through the chair of the Seminole Indian committee, of which Moore-Willson was a member. Furthermore, Jennings made it clear that the federation would not support unsubstantiated charges that could only hurt the Indian cause in the legislature.

A fundamental difference in approach distinguished the two groups. May Jennings and the FFWC took the position that advocates should lobby the legislature as long as necessary to secure good land, rather than settle for an immediate appropriation of worthless acreage. The Kissimmee group, on the other hand, felt it was urgent to secure as large a tract as possible for immediate Indian use. When Moore-Willson continued her pointed attacks on legislative leaders, Ivy Stranahan wrote asking that she disassociate herself from the Indian committee.[12] The former did not formally relinquish her committee position and may have felt it presumptuous for Stranahan, who was much younger and a newcomer on the state political scene, to pursue her own Seminole agenda so aggressively.[13] Thereafter Moore-Willson initiated a course independent from the federation while receiving assistance from the national Indian Rights Association of Philadelphia; and when the Florida legislature did establish a 100,000-acre state reservation in 1917, Minnie Moore-Willson and her Kissimmee organization received most of the credit. Only a few newspapers noted that the tract set aside was for the most part worthless swampland at the southern tip of the peninsula where few Indians could hunt or build their homes. Undaunted and almost single-handedly, Ivy Stranahan continued her struggle to assist the Seminoles who lived along the lower east coast of Florida in the ways she deemed appropriate.

Stranahan found a great ally in Lucien A. Spencer, who served as a federal Indian agent from 1913 until his death in 1930. He was an Episcopal clergyman who left a post as dean of Saint Luke's Cathedral in Orlando to take up Indian fieldwork. In this he followed the tradition of the Right Reverend William Crane Gray, Episcopal Bishop of the Missionary Jurisdiction of Southern Florida, who began mission work among the Seminoles as the nineteenth century came to a close.[14] Spencer served as an army chaplain during World War I, then returned to Indian work for the remainder of his life. His high standard of ethics and zeal matched those of Mrs. Stranahan; together they were relentless foes of bootleggers and others who carried liquor to the Indian camps.

Florida's 1920s land boom increased the problems of the Indians. Landowners who held legal title to lands where Seminoles hunted or camped demanded their removal. The Indians, generally suspicious of the government, were reluctant to move onto the federal trust land that had been set aside for their use beginning in the 1890s. Because Ivy Stranahan was trusted by the Seminoles, Agent Spencer sought her help in convincing local Indian families to take up residence on a 500-acre tract near the town of Dania that had been acquired in 1911 by presidential executive order. If the Indian community could be induced to take up residence on the tract, Spencer had promised to move his headquarters from Fort Myers to the east coast. In 1924 Ivy Stranahan took four of the Indian leaders to the reservation land in her automobile hoping to persuade them that the move would be in their best interest. She described the trip this way:

> I was worried and anxious about it because I knew that if they did not do this there would be some trouble. So, I went out there on the first week. I really walked the floor on Sunday. And my husband said they would not move, they would not go. And I said, "Well, we will have to try."
>
> ... So I went out there on a Tuesday morning, I made up my mind it had to be done.... I told them that it was their reservation, it was their home. It was beautiful, it was a wonderful piece of land. And it really was, it was a high piece of land. And if they did not take it, somebody else would take it. And if they would not go, why, they would not have any home. I said, "I want to take you out there." And I said, "White man—he your friend. Plenty of white people be your friends now. And everything be all right. So you have a meeting. You decide what you want to do and if you want to go, I will pick you up later this morning." So I parked my car about 600 feet from the gate. And then I just prayed that they would decide to go, because I knew the Indians had no choice. And in time they came out. So it shows that they were including the young people as well as the old ones. I opened the door of my car as I saw them coming, Annie Tommie leading, and never said a word because I was afraid I might change the atmosphere. I drove just as fast as I could after they closed the door, out nine miles to the reservation. It was a beautiful morning in June, and when we got there I drove out off the road. And I turned around and I said to them, "Isn't it beautiful?" ... They all stepped out. I had prepared to put them to work. I knew it wasn't just to take them out and look it over, because they had seen it many, many times. So I said, "Well, Willy Jumper, pull out your hoes and axes and go to work. This is your home. So, by and by, you will have a store." They kind of smiled and took out their hoes. Right here they wanted the largest groups ——— of the palmettos there was on the reservation. So they went to work on that. Annie Tommie and Pocahontas got out and walked over to the north to look at the rest. They had not said a word yet. And later on she came back and I said to her as she came up, "Annie, isn't it beautiful?" And she said,

"uh-huh, uh-huh." And I knew she was pleased, too, although she didn't even speak much English. I said, "Are you ready to go home?" She said, "Yes." They got in the car and I told Willy and Johnny—sometimes they call him Sam—to work there and I would be back at 5:00 to pick them up. And I said, "Tomorrow morning, you get tools and bring them out here and I will come back and get you in the afternoon." So the next morning I went and got them. That was Tuesday, Wednesday, Thursday and Friday. I wired Fort Myers to come on, that the Indians were on the reservation and it was getting too regular for me, and so the man came over.[15]

In 1926 the Dania Seminole Reservation was officially opened. The government provided a living area consisting of ten small wooden houses, a wash house, school building, and a combination office and living quarters for the Indian agent. The housing facilities were quickly occupied by the Osceolas, Jumpers, Tommies, and other Indian families from the New River region. The following year a government elementary school was opened on the reservation with Mrs. John Marshall, the daughter of agent Spencer, as its first teacher. Ivy Stranahan felt this school was the realization of her efforts to provide an education for Indian children. Unfortunately, the old Seminole reluctance to have their children educated soon resurfaced. Only a few children at Dania Reservation attended regularly; moreover, Spencer wanted a number of Indian families living in a settlement near Lake Okeechobee to move to Dania and place their children in school, but their headmen objected. This led the agent to take drastic measures to assure the Seminoles would come to his school. He reported, "The Indian Town camp which I was preparing to move here refused to come on account of the above interference, and I promptly cut off their ration supply. At the end of three weeks of starvation they moved here and placed their children in school."[16]

Among the families moving to Dania Reservation was that of Ada Tiger, whose daughter, Betty Mae, later became one of the first Seminoles to graduate from high school. In her memoir she recounts how the Stranahan home was a safe haven for Indian children when they came to town for a Saturday movie. "My mother would take us and drop us off at the show. The admission was ten cents, drinks five cents, popcorn five cents. After the show we got ready to go to Mrs. Stranahan's house. . . . We would stay at Mrs. Stranahan's house all night, sleeping in her living room. She would get us up early and feed us oatmeal. Then she would teach us Sunday school, and we would go home to the reservation."[17]

Spencer's successor, James L. Glenn, was another former clergyman who earned Ivy Stranahan's respect and support. Glenn also took a special interest in the school and later dedicated his published memoir to the Stranahans.[18] He modified the curriculum to include training in hygiene and food preparation, which he felt was needed to help assimilate the Seminole people. Among its other problems, the school was plagued by a turnover of teachers and there was only limited support from Indian parents. Adult Indians also came to the school classes upon occasion. The school was closed in 1936 as part of an economic retrenchment during the Great Depression, which curtailed reservation services. With the closing of the school, alternative means of educating Seminole youngsters had to be developed.

Glenn had difficulties on the reservations with drunkenness, and one of his goals was to stem the flow of alcohol to the Indians. He brought a special investigator into south Florida, and together they accumulated evidence and brought some of the offenders to trial. The remoteness of the Indian settlements, the poor roads, the great distances involved, as well as the mobility of the Indians combined to create formidable obstacles. Despite the valiant efforts of investigator Walter B. Lewis and Glenn, little could be done to eliminate the scourge of alcohol. Glenn had been recommended for the post by Roy Nash, who made a survey of the Seminoles for the U.S. Senate in 1931. His was the first study of Florida's Indians since Clay MacCauley's report for the Bureau of American Ethnology half a century earlier.[19] In assessing white support for the Seminole Indians, Nash reported, "It is difficult to overestimate what the friendship of people like the Stranahans of Fort Lauderdale, the Hendrys and Hansons of Fort Myers, and the Willsons of Kissimmee meant to the Seminoles during the years when they distrusted the Government and hated the missionary. They had one of the dominant race to whom they could turn for disinterested advice. . . . The Seminole can still count today as a heavy asset the interest of many stanch friends."[20]

In 1933 President Franklin Roosevelt appointed the aggressive John Collier as his new Commissioner of Indian Affairs. At that time Collier was the nation's leading voice calling for reform of Indian policy. Ivy Stranahan first met Collier in 1922, when he was named director of Indian affairs for the National Association of Women's Clubs. Mobilizing the political and economic power of the clubs nationwide, Collier mounted a campaign to reverse the previous century of government paternalism and successfully thwarted major federal legislation that would have negatively impacted western tribes. The following year he formed the American Indian Defense Association, which was in the forefront of progressive Indian reform during the 1920s. Collier was not an assimilationist; he believed that Indian tribes should be allowed to retain their religious and cultural values free of federal interference. Furthermore, he advocated a limited form of Indian self-government on the reservations. While Ivy Stranahan strongly believed that Indians would ultimately be absorbed into mainstream American society, she never overtly challenged the commissioner's anti-assimilationist position. For her it was sufficient that Commissioner Collier was acknowledged to have the best interest of Indians at heart, and she wrote frequently asking him to intercede on a variety of specific issues affecting the Florida Seminoles.

Throughout the 1920s and 1930s, Ivy Stranahan maintained an extensive correspondence concerning Seminole affairs with members of the Florida congressional delegation, especially Senator Duncan U. Fletcher. In 1930 she was invited to testify before the U.S. Senate Subcommittee of the Committee on Indian Affairs when it met at Dania Reservation.[21] Her presentation touched on most of the major social and economic ills of the Indian people and noted that few Seminole children were ready to enter school because of their poor hygiene and limited academic preparation. She was also concerned that bootlegging was still rampant and that no action was being taken by local authorities to stem the flow of liquor to the Seminoles.

Stranahan and Glenn remained frustrated by the lack of federal action in Florida, and also by the criticism of a group known as the Seminole Indian Association, headed by W. Stanley Hanson of Fort Myers. Hanson was the son of a pioneer Florida family who became a close friend of the Seminoles in the lower Everglades and Big Cypress Swamp region. Hanson's supporters on the west coast of Florida thought he should have been appointed Indian agent rather than Glenn, who had limited experience with the Seminoles. The Seminole Indian Association frequently complained to Washington that Glenn failed to serve the interests of all

Indians in Florida. Following a particularly venomous attack in the press, Ivy Stranahan rose to Glenn's defense, writing to John Collier: "Stanley Hanson has always kept the Indian at enmity with any friendly feelings toward the Government, I mean the Indians he holds contact with. I never meet or speak with him but I know how he made Mr. Spencer's life miserable by his false accusations and Mr. Spencer had not been buried when he was flying over the state politicking for the position."[22]

Shortly after Ivy Stranahan's 1930 appearance before the Senate Indian Affairs Committee, a group of Florida Christian club women took up the Seminoles' cause. After several meetings around the state, a new society was formed known as the Friends of the Florida Seminoles. Later the word "Florida" was dropped from its name to eliminate confusion with the organization founded at Kissimmee in 1899. Ivy Stranahan was chosen secretary-treasurer and would occupy an active or honorary office in the group for the remainder of her years. Education of Indian children soon became the organization's major focus. After the Dania Reservation school closed, it was the Friends of the Seminoles who provided financial support for six children to attend the Cherokee Indian School in North Carolina in the fall of 1937. Over the years Indian students attending Cherokee corresponded with their sponsors in Florida, and left a valuable record of the acculturation experience they underwent in the federal boarding school.[23]

Following World War II, the Friends of the Seminoles turned their efforts toward having Seminole youngsters admitted to local public schools in Florida. By 1946 seventeen Indian students attended the Dania elementary school. Three were enrolled in school in Immokalee, and another twenty-five attended the federal day school that had opened on the remote Brighton Reservation. A number of children also continued to attend federal Indian boarding schools; that year twenty-one were at Cherokee and two attended the Chiloco school in Oklahoma. This must have been a source of great satisfaction to Ivy Stranahan.

In 1949 the Friends of the Seminoles, Florida Foundation, Inc., was chartered as a nonprofit organization by the Circuit Court of Broward County. Mrs. Stranahan was listed as president, and her home address was given as the group's principal place of business. Mrs. O. H. Abbey was named as treasurer of the group. She worked energetically alongside Stranahan in conducting a Sunday school on the Dania Reservation and in raising funds for various Indian projects. As a moving force in the local Daughters of the American Revolution chapter, Erma Abbey was able to generate financial support from the membership of that organization, and they became the unofficial partners of the Friends of the Seminoles. It was primarily Abbey, assisted by an Indian woman from North Carolina, who prepared the youngsters from Dania Reservation for entrance into the local schools, teaching them proper nutrition and sanitation habits and assuring that they had proper clothing.

In her 1952 annual report to the Friends of the Seminoles, Ivy Stranahan noted, "The need of greatest importance to the welfare of the Seminole now, since he is friendly to the government under which he lives; has accepted Christianity, and is willingly permitting his children to attend school; is a better home for his family, he is asking for a better house."[24] This report appears to reinforce the suspicion that Ivy Stranahan's earliest efforts at Indian instruction, conducted on the lawn of her home, were aimed as much at Christianizing as at educating. Nevertheless, in the early 1950s the Friends assisted several Indian families in building new homes or remodeling the old government housing from the 1930s that they still occupied at the Dania Reservation.

Ivy Stranahan's last and perhaps most significant contribution to the welfare of the Seminoles was her participation in the struggle to prevent termination of the tribe during the 1950s. By that time she was in her seventies and in poor health, but she remained a vocal advocate for her Indian friends. Following World War II, a Republican-controlled Congress, dominated by social and fiscal conservatives, was intent on cutting government expenses to recoup the war debt. As one of the few federal bureaucracies without a natural political constituency, the Bureau of Indian Affairs and the tribal communities it served became a target for the budget cutters. Moreover, many political liberals, convinced that Indian tribes had suffered from federal paternalism as embodied in the reservation system, also called for them to handle their own affairs free of governmental control. In 1953, with both ends of the political continuum seemingly in agreement, the Eighty-third Congress passed House Concurrent Resolution 108 stating that government support services should be terminated for those tribes who were ready to manage their own affairs. The results were mixed. A number of tribes, such as the Menominee in Wisconsin and Klamath of Oregon, saw their reservation lands sold and tribal wealth distributed among individual members. In essence, they disappeared as Indian nations. Although a few have been reconstituted by acts of Congress, most tribes fortunately avoided termination and subsequently benefited from the Indian self-determination policies implemented in the 1970s.

Although among the least acculturated tribes in the nation, the Florida Seminoles were included on the list of tribes marked for termination of federal services. Such a move would place them on their own when they had neither an educated leadership nor a political structure to administer the necessary social services and carry out economic functions. The Seminoles reportedly were placed on the termination list by Congressman James A. Haley of Sarasota, who chaired the House Indian Affairs Subcommittee.[25] Haley, even though a Democrat, was a fiscal conservative who generally supported the concept of Indian termination. He apparently believed that his subcommittee should not vote to terminate other tribes unless it also took a look at the Florida Seminoles. Haley was convinced that his congressional colleagues would readily see that the Seminoles were not ready for termination and would kill the bill. Nevertheless, it was a risky strategy. When a termination plan was presented to the Seminoles in October 1953, the response was both immediate and negative.

The Seminole people held several meetings at the Dania Reservation in which they requested continuation of essential government support for at least twenty-five years, time sufficient to allow for educating and training the people to the point where they could manage their affairs. A delegation of Indian elders and an interpreter went to Washington and presented the tribal position before Congress. Florida's Seminoles were fortunate in the support they received from white friends—more fortunate than tribes in other areas of the country. Ivy Stranahan was generally supportive of assimilating Indians into mainstream American society. She had no doubt that in time the Seminole people could handle their own business affairs and spoke of them becoming "model citizens." However, that was well in the future, and now there was an immediate threat that the Seminoles might lose their land base. If the reservations were removed from federal protection and turned over to the tribe, but the tribe had no government or viable source of income, it was quite possible that the reservations might be lost for taxes.

The Friends of the Seminoles responded aggressively and marshaled other community resources to fight termination. Promptly, the Friends passed a resolution requesting "[t]hat at such time as the Government relinquishes their right and control in the Seminole Reservation, that we, the Friends of the Seminoles, Florida Foundation, Inc., ask for the right of Trusteeship of the property.... until such time as the Seminole Indians are able to take possession in their own rights."[26] Ivy Stranahan also took the precaution of notifying the Commissioner of Indian Affairs as well as the Florida congressional leaders about her concerns. Commissioner Glenn Emmons wrote to her affirming that termination was a desirable option—but conceded that there were differing estimates on how long federal supervision should continue. At the same time Senator George Smathers of Florida promised, "I am keeping in close touch with developments on this matter, and want to assure you that I shall continue to protect the welfare of the Indians on every hand."[27]

A joint hearing of the House and Senate Subcommittees on Indian Affairs was held in Washington on March 1–2, 1954, to consider the Seminole termination bills. Due to Ivy Stranahan's illness, Erma Abbey represented the Fort Lauderdale group and testified that the Friends of the Seminoles were "a coordinating and cooperating group, and all the women's clubs through the state and the Daughters of the American Revolution have helped, through our group, to give educational funds to help the different children." However, she continued, since they had been attending school regularly for only sixteen years, "these Florida Indians are not ready [to run their own affairs]."[28] Members of the Florida congressional delegation, civic leaders, a leading anthropologist, and national Indian rights groups gave additional testimony in support of the Semin-ole position. Congressman Dwight L. Rogers of Fort Lauderdale was particularly outspoken and eloquent in his opposition to termination. Rogers, like other south Florida residents, had come to know some of the Seminoles personally during twenty-plus years of residence in Broward County. Although ill health prevented Ivy Stranahan from attending the Washington hearings, Congressman Rogers made sure that her written statement was entered into the record. In part, it read:

> It is only some fifteen years now that any citizen interested in Indians can come in and work with the Seminoles. But now since this is possible, we have hundreds of well-meaning men, women and

children, organizations and clubs as well as churches of our state and community cooperating to make them feel a part of the community in which they are the real pioneers, the people the first white citizens found here when they arrived.

But gentlemen of the committee, this hard work of fifty years will lose all its meaning in moral building if we permit our government to withdraw all their protection. We as a state and community will take our responsibility as it has come to us that we have been doing to a degree but it has mislead our Government to withdraw Federal protection from the Seminole lands, cattle and property there in the short time of three years as in Bill H. R. 7321 now before your committee. Mr. Chairman you must strike the number "3" and substitute the wish and request of the Seminole Indians to 25 years. Please Mr. Chairman and members of the Committee, this is in the best interest of the most minority group in these United States. A people who are asking the least and have the least. They are asking a reasonable service for part of a race who have given up much of the beautiful country to ruling white man.[29]

No action was taken on the Seminole termination bill for the remainder of the congressional session. Florida's senior senator, Spessard Holland, who attended the Washington hearings, wrote Mrs. Stranahan: "I feel that the Interior and Insular Affairs Committee of the House and Senate were wise in not reporting out the bill which would remove the Seminoles from the guardianship of the Federal Government, and I know careful consideration will be given to the desires of the Seminoles by these committees prior to any action in the future."[30] Despite this encouragement the bill was still alive, so Ivy Stranahan, Bertram Scott of the Seminole Indian Association, and other Seminole partisans continued to lobby against federal plans to withdraw services from the tribe.

When the Eighty-fourth Congress convened in January 1955, the sentiment for termination was still strong. During the spring of that year a second round of congressional hearings was held at various Florida locations to explore the Seminole termination bill. Again, participant testimony overwhelmingly opposed immediate termination of services to the tribe and favored granting it at least twenty-five more years of government support. This position was advocated primarily by Seminoles living on the federal reservations. However, the situation became confused when attorneys for Indians living along the Tamiami Trail claimed that they owned millions of acres in south Florida. It appeared that a jurisdictional conflict between two Seminole groups might imperil the future of reservation lands. Ivy Stranahan appeared in person at one of the sessions and reiterated that the work of fifty years would come to naught if the Indians lost their land. She admitted, "I am like the Indians, I don't know who owns this land out here," but she urged that the government secure the land for a number of years as a home for elderly Indians.[31]

Following the Florida hearings, those who supported the Seminole position believed that they had won the day. In her 1954 report as legislative chair of the Friends of the Seminoles, Ivy Stranahan praised the group's efforts to influence the Washington hearings: "So well did these delegates support requests and protests of the Seminoles," she wrote, "that the Interior and Insular Affairs Committee of the House and Senate did not even report-out committee bills No. S2747 and HR7321 terminating Federal Service to the Florida Seminoles. Your personal letters and telegrams to your Congressmen gave the much needed support. . . . This leaves the status of the Florida Seminoles the same as before the 83rd Congress."[32] It was to be the old warrior's last successful lobbying effort.

As a result of the information about Seminole life brought out in these hearings, as well as pressure from committee members including Representative Haley and Senator Smathers, the Florida Seminoles were removed from the list of tribes to be terminated. Instead, they were allowed to organize themselves as a tribal government with a constitution and corporate charter authorized by the Indian Reorganization Act of 1934. The Seminole Tribe of Florida, Inc., was organized in 1957 and included all Indians living on Florida's three federal reservations as well as a few living off the reservation. Later, a group of several hundred culturally traditional Mikasuki-speaking Seminoles, who lived in camps along the Tamiami Trail, broke from the main body and in 1962 formed their own tribe, the Miccosukee Tribe of Indians of Florida. When the Miccosukee tribal council headed by Buffalo Tiger decided that their people needed education and accepted a government school, Ivy Stranahan was one of the first persons invited out to see the new facility located along the Tamiami Trail.[33]

Ivy Stranahan lived to see well-educated Seminoles assume positions of leadership in managing the tribe's affairs. Betty Mae Tiger Jumper became the first woman elected to chair the tribal council—the same Betty Mae who was in the first group of young Seminoles to attend school at Cherokee, North Carolina. Following her graduation from high school she went into nurse's training so she could return and help her people.[34] In an interview Jumper acknowledged her debt to Ivy Stranahan, recounting, "She was the first person to buy me a dress so that I could go off to the Cherokee school. She helped me much of my life."[35] The Seminoles of today have not forgotten the name Stranahan. Upon learning of her death in 1971, Howard Tommie, chairman of the Seminole Tribe and a grandson of Ivy's old friend Annie Tommie, voiced the tribe's feelings of sadness mixed with pride in having shared time on earth with a great woman. He said, "She was instrumental in a lot of ways to me and to others of the tribe in getting us to go to school. We owe her what knowledge we have of what is going on in the white man's culture. She started the Friends of the Seminoles and they are glad she gave her effort and love to make our lives better. The young ones are very sorry to see her go. She was a true friend of the Seminoles."[36] As a final tribute to their old friend, a delegation of Seminole elders attended her funeral.

9

Public Lives, Private People

A gregarious extrovert would have been unsuited to manage Metcalf's New River Camp in 1893. The job required a self-reliant, mature individual with a high tolerance for solitude. A love of nature and the outdoors were also desirable attributes. Frank Stranahan filled these requirements. Although three white families lived relatively close by, and the Seminole Indian camp of old Johnny Jumper was at Tarpon Bend, Stranahan had little time for socializing. As manager of the New River Camp, he also operated the ferry and was required to be nearby when duty called. Fortunately, Frank was reclusive by nature, for there were long intervals between scheduled arrivals of the mail stage that brought passengers and news from the outside world. Initially there was only Frank and a black cook to run the camp. But he had books for diversion, as well as hunting or fishing, interspersed with an occasional person traveling the county road between stage runs. From time to time there were visits from Dennis O'Neill, keeper of the life-saving station; W. C. Valentine, who lived near the ocean; or W. C. Collier, who had a farm at Middle River.

With the arrival of the railroad construction crews in 1895 and the first train during the following year, additional people came to work, and some remained along the New River. However, the 1900 census counted no eligible young ladies in the community. The arrival in 1899 of the new teacher, the comely and vivacious Ivy Julia Cromartie, gave Stranahan the first opportunity to enjoy female companionship since his arrival at

New River. Certainly the camp manager and Indian trader was considered the "best prospect" among the eligible bachelors. His business was prospering, and Ivy's niece, Alice Cromartie Simpson, felt that her aunt was always interested in a mature man, whose conversation was more likely to stimulate her interest.[1] Frank spared no effort in courting Ivy, who wrote, "Palm Beach and West Palm Beach were the growing areas of our world at that time. Mr. and Mrs. King, Mr. Stranahan and I visited that city occasionally. It was great fun riding around the streets of Palm Beach in wheelchairs propelled by a colored man. We would return by train that evening tired and happy after a full day of recreation."[2] The attraction between Frank and Ivy seems to have been mutual and immediate. Marriage followed the next year. Ivy recalled, "All too soon the school term was over, and I returned to my home at Lemon City. I had promised Mr. Stranahan that we would be married in August, take our honeymoon at Nashville, Niagara Falls, visit his former house in Ohio and my grandparents in North Carolina and return to make my home forever in Fort Lauderdale."[3]

There were similarities in their family backgrounds. Ivy's schoolteacher father influenced her greatly, and education was emphasized in their home. When the Cromartie family lived in remote areas, the father instructed his children. One of Ivy's nieces said that their Methodist family "was Bible oriented in the home," although the rural areas in which they lived from time to time did not always permit regular church attendance.[4] The Stranahan boys also had a church-oriented background since their father, the Reverend Robert Stranahan, was a Presbyterian minister. Prior to his coming to New River, Frank's letters mentioned attendance at church functions in the Melbourne area. The letter that Robert wrote to Frank on December 8, 1886, reveals the influence he tried to exert over the Stranahan children. Among other things he stressed the value of reading history. That early home training influenced Frank during his life and certainly in the books he selected for his library. Ivy's niece, although too young to have personal memories of her uncle, recalled the importance placed on Frank's library and recalled that it was located on the lower floor of the house.[5]

Books given to the Fort Lauderdale Historical Society by Ivy Stranahan suggest the family's broad range of interests. Among the volumes of a historical nature were Goodrich's *Pictorial History of the United States* (1873);

the four-volume set of *Ridpath's History of the United States* (1874); *The Story of Two Wars: Our War with Spain and Our War with the Filipinos* (1898); *Panorama of Nations* (1892–98); *Civil War through a Camera*, Elson's 1912 publication; and *The Building of a Nation*, by Gannett, published in 1895. The reference books included a *Standard Encyclopedia* (1896), the 1899 *American Dictionary of the English Language*, and the *Primary School Dictionary of the English Language*, published in 1871 by Webster. *Hero Tales of the American Soldier and Sailor* (1899), *Life and Travels of General Grant* (1879), and *The Illustrious Life of William McKinley* (1901) were among the biographical works found in the Stranahan library. One can speculate that Henry M. Flagler might have been responsible for Stranahan's having a copy of Ida M. Tarbell's *The Rise and Progress of the Standard Oil Company*, published in 1904. Two volumes of a different nature were *Uncle Tom's Cabin* (1852) by Harriet Beecher Stowe and Lubblock's *The Beauties of Nature* (1894). The library also included numerous volumes on the history of Florida, accumulated as they were published. While still a bachelor Frank had purchased an Edison phonograph, and the library contained the 1897 *Complete Manual of the Edison Phonograph*. The phonograph was found tucked away under the eaves in the attic when the restoration study of the house was begun in January 1980.

Following the couple's marriage, the library accumulated volumes reflecting Ivy's interests. It contained innumerable histories and proceedings concerning Indian affairs dating from the early days and continuing until the time of her death. The collection held *Common Birds*, published by the Massachusetts Audubon Society in 1901, and Faulkner's *From Ballroom to Hell* (1903). There was also a 1901 volume titled *Embroidery Lessons*. Despite the remoteness of the area, Ivy maintained an interest in the latest fashions, and she kept the December 1908 and the February and March 1909 issues of *The Delineator*, a magazine devoted to women's clothing. Her concern with diet is indicated by the publications *Let's Eat for Health, Beauty and Pleasure* and *Better Meals for Less*. The library also contained a large collection of *National Geographic* magazines and copies of the *Florida Historical Society Quarterly*.

Apart from Frank's business activities and Ivy's civic involvement, the couple seemed to live pretty much to themselves, without the social outlets essential to most people. The memories of those who knew them are consistent. Near neighbor Bob Hall recalled, "It was hard to get close to Mr. Stranahan, believe me; he wasn't—what do you call it—flamboyant; he was just the opposite. He didn't want publicity, he just didn't want it. . . . We always knew her and she was very friendly. She wasn't a person that would throw herself at you . . . I think he thought the world of her and I think she thought the world of him because when they were together they respected one another. . . . They were just quiet people all the way through."[6] Hall continued, "Mr. Stranahan wasn't a man to be out in front, he was very quiet. Consequently, he didn't get in a lot of trouble. If it was trouble, he wasn't in it. Now, Mrs. Stranahan was very forward and she was always so very benevolent. . . . Mr. Stranahan liked the Indians and they liked him. The reason they liked Mr. Stranahan was that he could tell them he was going to do something for them and he would do it and they knew it."[7] Even so, local attorney Carl Hiaasen reportedly said, "Mr. Stranahan was taciturn, unfriendly to the point of not seeming to have any friends."[8] In summary, in their personal lives, Frank and Ivy Stranahan seemed to have little need for outside friendships; for this reason they were considered aloof by some in the community.

The Stranahans did enjoy gardening around their house. Alice Cromartie Simpson described her Aunt Ivy this way: "Mrs. Stranahan was a garden freak, and her garden just to the right of the porch, there, there is a very large planting; now this was her pride and joy. She had many rare things growing in there."[9] Many of the shrubs and trees surrounding the house are said to have been gifts of the Brickells taken from their Miami property. Some plantings still remained when restoration of the house began. The couple were both nature lovers, and Frank appears to have approached the fanatical in his opposition to destroying trees.[10] Unfortunately, the grove of coconut palms that surrounded the house is now gone. Those surviving hurricanes fell victim to lethal yellowing, so only a very few remain. The magnificent live oak still standing to the east of the house is seen in a very early photograph of the house taken about 1912.

Despite reports to the contrary, Frank and Ivy entertained only infrequently at their home. In 1982 Ivy Berryhill, daughter of long-time Stranahan associate W. O. Berryhill, recalled that there was little socializing even with the members of Ivy's family who lived in Fort Lauderdale. Margaret Oliver Crews, the daughter of Eva Bryan Oliver, who wrote extensively on the history of early Fort Lauderdale and was the first white girl born there, wrote in 1982, "Mr. Stranahan was a very quiet man as far as I know. I never heard of their social life."[11] Frank Stranahan did purchase a membership in the Lauderdale Angler's Club when it was organized. The fee was $100, with membership limited to 250 people. President A. H. Brook and Secretary R. J. Blank signed the certificate. Joining the club was likely the proper thing for a town leader to do, but there is no indication that the Stranahans participated in any of its activities.

Nevertheless, newspaper accounts reveal that a few social events took place at the Stranahan home. In 1912 the *Florida Times-Union* reported that Frank's niece, Grace Dunlap, gave a party at the New River house honoring D. D. Oliver and his bride. The *Fort Lauderdale Herald* of April 8, 1921, reported a reception at the Stranahan home for a Mrs. Spring and a Mrs. Benton. On August 27, 1937, the *Fort Lauderdale News* took note of a party at the Stranahan home for Betty Mae Tiger, Agnes and Mary Parker, and Mary Tommie, Seminole students at the Cherokee Indian School. Also, Ivy once mentioned that May Jennings and Annie Broward had both stayed at her home while attending State Federation of Women's Clubs meetings.[12] Asked about his family's contacts with the Stranahans, Bob Hall replied, "Well, actually we didn't go over to his house very much. The Stranahans weren't large entertainers. They were by themselves. I mean we had no occasion to be over there unless we just happened to be going by their property, so from that standpoint, I actually wasn't in the house until later on. [After it became a restaurant] I'd see the house over there, but why should I go over there? I wasn't invited. Not because of any relations or anything, they just lived to themselves. My father was close, very close to Mr. Stranahan and my mother was very close to Mrs. Stranahan, but I mean they were people who lived by themselves, to a certain degree."[13] When asked if they had any large social gatherings in their home, Hall replied, "Not that I know of."[14] It appears the dances and get-togethers mentioned so many times as having taken place there were held during the days when the lower floor of the house was Frank's place of business, not after the structure was converted to residential use in 1906.

But Frank Stranahan had one consuming passion: baseball. Hall recalled:

He was a nut on baseball, believe me he was.... He gave the property there to the school and then the two ball diamonds. The first property he gave was way over and then he gave a lot back this way, right close to Second Street. For a while Mr. Stranahan would go out and spend as much time on that ball diamond fixing everything up as he would spend on his own work, and he had 'old Tom' who helped him and if he wasn't out there Tom was. I know of one incident where he took the pipe that he had been using for this drainage, like sprinklers that were about fifteen feet high, or ten feet. He made a bleacher out of that thing over there for people to sit on and instead of putting a roof up there he took palm fronds and made a top for the bleachers. He took these pipes and put them in, then the bleachers were sitting in here so they wouldn't get sodden. That is why he kept them over here and put a bunch of palms on top of it. He was out there fussing around with that ball diamond all the time. I don't know a man that enjoyed baseball any more than he did.... He wanted Lauderdale to have a good ball team.[15]

Frank Stranahan shared some of his family's physical afflictions. During his stay in Kansas during the 1880s, his father's letters discussed a mutual problem with catarrh. Apparently Frank found some relief in the Great Plains climate. Medical receipts among the family papers indicate Frank was being treated around 1912–15 for some type of physical disorder. Several biographical sketches of Stranahan refer to his "gas poisoning" while working in the Ohio steel mills and before going to Kansas. The gas-poisoning story has not been substantiated, although in later years it was often cited as the reason he left the steel mills. But this explanation must be treated with skepticism since one of his father's letters indicates Frank left the steel mill because of a disagreement with superiors. At least three Florida histories contain biographical sketches of Frank Stranahan. The earliest of these, published in 1923, contains no mention of gas poisoning, and Frank likely supplied the information for that book.[16] Other family information in that work, including birth and death dates, were confirmed, whereas dates in the two much later publications, issued after his death, are stated incorrectly in a number of instances.

Despite Frank's years of robust life in Florida, by 1924 he did have a severe health problem, which worried his brother Allen in a letter dated June 17, 1924:

> Dear Bro & Sister:
>
> As I have not received any ans to my last letter of some days ago I write again hoping you are on the road to health & judge by the papers you are not getting along vary fast I have done enough suffering for one family now listen Frank you write to Mayo Bros of Rochester Minn—or get on the train and go up there I have talked to several who have been there and they all feel fine They certainly have some system they have seven specialists who go over you each one in their own line and when they get through they know what ails you and sure can fix you up if it can be done anymore and a nice feature, they do not rob you[.] do not put it off[.] would be pleased to have you both come up here and we will give you the best we have[.] get away some where whatever you do. . . .
>
> [N]ow Frank pack your trunk and get away if you are able and don't forget we are here and would be pleased to have you both with us. Don't forget Mayo Bros trusting this will find you very much improved and Ivy OK.[17]

There is nothing to indicate that Frank took his brother's advice and visited the Mayo Clinic. Eva Oliver, writing on early Fort Lauderdale history, mentioned that Stranahan was hospitalized for a lengthy period of time.[18] Some years after his death, Frank's widow also referred to a long period of hospitalization. Stranahan's longtime associate, W. O. Berryhill, named his daughter Ivy after Ivy Stranahan. In 1982 Ivy Berryhill recalled that there was a time when Ivy Stranahan became deeply concerned over Frank's lethargic attitude and general disinterest in civic affairs. Ivy turned to W. O. Berryhill, and they were able to renew Frank's interest in events to the extent that he again became active in the political arena. Reasons of health may account in part for Stranahan's striking absence from the political scene over several years. He did not serve on the town council or city commission between 1922 and May 1927, although it has been reported that following the 1926 hurricane, "when city elections were held to choose leaders who might bring Fort Lauderdale out of its devastation and pandemonium, Stranahan's candidacy was soundly defeated."[19]

Stranahan was disgusted with this rejection because he felt it would hinder rebuilding the city. In an unusual display of irritation, he stated that he did not "believe that Jesus Christ and his 12 apostles could straighten out the people of Fort Lauderdale and get them on the road to prosperity."[20]

In 1925 the Fort Lauderdale city commission considered selling some city land valued at $650,000 and purchasing additional property for new police and fire department buildings, as well as golf links and additional parks. Mayor Tidball appointed commissioners Kittridge, Kyle, and Hinton to report at the next meeting. The newspaper reported that $315,000 would be devoted to park purposes, and added:

> Another motion, offered by Commissioner Kittridge and seconded by Commissioner J. S. Hinton, was adopted, and empowered Mayor John W. Tidball to appoint a committee to confer with Frank Stranahan, Fort Lauderdale capitalist, relative to the lease for 10 years, subject to purchase, for all municipal buildings except the police station and jail property on N. Third street, known as the Stranahan Ball Park, for the lease, subject to purchase, of the Stranahan home site on N. New River drive for exclusive park purposes and for lease, subject to purchase of 285 by 211 feet of vacant property on S. Andrews avenue, near the old automobile camp.... The Stranahan Ball Park property proposed as a site for the new municipal building is located north of the Central High School in the residential section, and consists of one square bounded by N. E. Third street, the Himmarshee canal, East Avenue and Stranahan avenue. It is considered one of the most desirable pieces of undeveloped property near the present business district. The Stranahan home site, located at the corner of Stranahan avenue and North New River drive, which the board desires for a public park, is located within a stone's throw of the new East avenue bridge, a contract for which was awarded at a recent meeting of the commission. The South Andrews avenue property is considered equally desirable for either public buildings or a park.[21]

This action led Frank Stranahan to have his attorney, Maxwell Baxter, prepare a proposal addressed to "The Honorable City Commissioners" and dated October 13, 1925. (The text of this document appears in Appendix A.) The first item concerned the "Home Place," which was valued at $600,000. Stranahan offered the city a lease on that property for ninety-nine years at a stipulated rental payable semi-annually. He proposed to give the Women's Club a tract of land on the northwest corner of the block in which his home was located—provided the city would purchase, for public purposes, the Women's Club property adjoining Stranahan Park. Another provision concerned the 285 feet south of the Southside School, at the corner of South Andrews Avenue and Southwest Ninth Street. The city was to purchase the school property as a public park or for public buildings. Conditional upon the acceptance of the entire proposal, the document proposed to deed to the city the parcel known as "Stranahan Field" located on the east side of Central School, with the federal highway as its eastern boundary.

The proposal listed requirements for the use and care of the properties, stipulating that they would revert to Stranahan if these conditions were not met. Finally, the entire offer was made subject to Ivy Stranahan's approval. Since Frank Stranahan was not a member of the city commission on the date the proposal was prepared, the transfer of properties to the city was possible if a mutually satisfactory agreement could be reached. Had this proposal come to fruition, Ivy Stranahan would have been assured a comfortable income by the standards of that period. Unfortunately it was not approved. Frank Stranahan's attempt to provide a secure future for his wife came at a time when the city still enjoyed unprecedented prosperity. Likewise, it was a time when Stranahan was evidently financially secure, for the biographic sketch published in 1923 stated that "from small beginnings his resources have steadily increased until they were considerably over a million dollars in 1922."[22]

The gathering storm of economic depression was felt in Florida long before it enveloped other parts of the United States. Stranahan's assets were in real estate, and, as was the case for other large land owners, his properties were heavily encumbered. There was no cash with which to pay mortgages coming due. By 1927 there was little or no market for property, even at greatly reduced prices. It seems everyone had trouble raising the money to pay taxes. When Frank Stranahan took a seat on the city commission in 1927, he assumed a share of responsibility for the city's financial woes, and that added to his personal burdens. George W. English, Jr., who came to Fort Lauderdale to practice law in 1925, became a partner of M. Lewis Hall, the city attorney. English recalled the many times he conferred with Stranahan on the porch of the latter's home, discussing means that might relieve the city of some of its pressing problems, including the heavy bonded indebtedness.

The February 1928 failure of the Fort Lauderdale Bank and Trust Company worsened an already dismal situation in the local economy. Frank Stranahan was able to sell a lot at the corner of Las Olas Boulevard and Federal Highway to the Firestone Company for $11,250, less expenses of the sale, and he sold another lot for $6,000.[23] Stranahan paid the assessment levied against him by reason of the bank's failure partly in cash and partly by a mortgage to secure the balance.

During the spring of 1929, the Bank of Bay Biscayne began to press for payment on notes against the Stranahan Building Company, which had built the Lauderdale Arms Apartments. On March 1, 1929, Frank Stranahan borrowed $22,410 from Edith Burnham, who already held one mortgage on his home dating from 1922. Then, on March 22, W. C. Kyle wrote the Bank of Bay Biscayne: "Mr. Stranahan is negotiating now to take up all notes on the Stranahan Building Company or to secure them in some way and he has agreed that within the next thirty days he will make satisfactory arrangements with you by either payment or security."[24] Kyle wrote the bank again on March 27, stating in part: "Mr. Stranhan will assume the indebtedness and properly secure or pay all that is due on this note, unless you see fit to force the matter."[25] On May 20, 1929, Kyle wrote again: "With reference to the note of the Stranahan Building Company, Mr. Stranahan has been in the hospital for about ten days due to a nervous breakdown and I have been unable to see him. I hope to be able to take this matter up with him within a few days, but if in the meantime, you prefer a renewal of the note as it stands I shall be glad to sign same if you will prepare and send to me for signature."[26]

The combination of circumstances well may have impaired Stranahan's mental and physical health. Perhaps the condition of which his brother spoke in 1924 recurred or worsened. He could have suffered from what today would be called clinical depression. On April 9 Frank wrote poignantly in his pocket notebook, "My wife gave me much encouragement but I can't seem to grasp it."[27] Two days after the Kyle letter of May 20, Frank Stranahan ended his life in the New River. What a shock for his wife! The widow was devastated. The town, and south Florida, was stunned. The newspapers carried the news in blaring headlines. The word "suicide" appeared in the bold print of front-page stories. Thereafter, the word was not used again in published accounts of Stranahan's death during his widow's lifetime. It seems that Ivy Stranahan totally rejected the term. The word was reportedly obliterated with a heavy black grease pencil in newspaper copies that she retained the remainder of her life.

Some area residents believed that Mrs. Stranahan faulted herself for her husband's death because doctors had cautioned her, upon his release from the hospital, not to leave him alone. Bob Hall described the events of the fateful afternoon:

> Of course, everybody was in the same boat, not only Mr. Stranahan, but everybody, but just his makeup couldn't stand it. It wasn't in his makeup to stand anything. He could stand certain bad times, I guess, but this, with all this bank and all of it came down on top of him at one time, it just got the best of him and it worked on him for about two years, and finally he gave up the ghost. . . . She took him to the beach that day. Dad was sitting on the front porch, we had a big, cracker porch. He had his back to their house. He couldn't see Mr. Stranahan over there and he was out there reading on the porch at the time. Mrs. Stranahan was taking Mr. Stranahan out to the beach, as he wanted to go out. It wasn't anything new. She used to drive him out to the beach in the car. Of course, he never drove, she always did all the driving. Why, I'll never know. This is just the type of fellow he was, for no reason at all, but anyway, she'd drive him to the beach and they would sit out there on the beach and watch the ocean a little bit and come back by the house and they would go into the house. This one particular day they went out—it must have been about three o'clock in the afternoon, and dad, like I say, was sitting on the front porch with his back to the Stranahans. When they came home she drove the car in the garage, but he had this all figured out. He had a wheelbarrow right along side his porch. She didn't think anything of it because he always had a bunch of clutter around there. She didn't know what he was going to do with it, but he had this old grate, cast iron grate, in the wheelbarrow and when they came back from the beach, why, she got out of the car and he got out of the car in the garage. She went on in the house through the back door as she always did. He said that he was going to work

around the garage a little bit, so she goes on and didn't think a thing about it. In fact, he got the wheelbarrow with the big grate in it and if she had seen him she wouldn't have known what he was going to do with it, because he was always puttering around. He went out there between these two palm trees and he knew where the deepest part of the river was. It was about ninety feet deep down there at one time, before it started filling in a little bit, and he got this rope tied around his foot and tied the other end around the grate and lifted it out there. Bloxham Cromartie came out and saw him from across the river; he was Mrs. Stranahan's brother. He hollered at him and he could see what he was doing and he tried to get over there. In fact, I think he dove in the water and swam over. Mr. Stranahan jumped in with the grate—he pitched it out of the wheelbarrow and jumped in. It was too bad.[28]

Frank Stranahan's funeral was held on the grounds of his home, and his body was buried at Evergreen Cemetery. It has generally been assumed that Stranahan's pressing financial problems led him to take his life, as many others did during the stock market crash some months later. Others thought Frank Stranahan suffered from cancer, and those rumors circulated at the time of his death. The Kyle letter written shortly before Stranahan's death indicated that he had suffered from a nervous breakdown, a fact that may not have been widely known. Moreover, suicide was not unknown in Stranahan's family; many years earlier his sister had taken her own life, as did his cousin Guy Metcalf.[29]

The strong-willed Ivy began to pick up the shattered pieces of her life. Incredibly, the astute businessman Frank Stranahan left no will. His widow had to wrestle with the problems of an insolvent estate in addition to the wrenching circumstances surrounding her husband's death. Administration of the estate was a difficult experience, for Ivy had no knowledge of her husband's business affairs. Her niece, Alice Cromartie Simpson, stated, "He never discussed business, his business; now she was free to do her business and she did, but he never discussed his business with her. . . . It was then that she realized [how mistaken] they had been in her doing her thing and he doing his, not doing it together cause she did not know anything about his business affairs [and] that created a hard shift at his death."[30] One of the letters that Ivy wrote to Frank while she was away on a trip implies that they may have had differing investment philosophies. Ivy suggested that they should be buying rental property that would bring in an income. Apparently Frank opposed the idea, and this could be a reason that they did not communicate on business affairs.

Settlement of the estate was a lengthy process, not completed until 1935. Maxwell Baxter served as Ivy's attorney, as he had for her husband. The estate inventory illustrates graphically the abrupt collapse in land values that had taken place. Their house, valued at $600,000 in 1925, had shrunk in value to $50,000 by 1929 when Frank died. A "friendly" foreclosure of the mortgage on the home block of property ensued. Edith Burnham was due about $49,000, exclusive of expenses incidental to the legal proceedings. But foreclosure was the only way to remove the liens resulting from other debts. Once the title was free and clear and Edith Burnham received a deed, she deeded to Ivy Stranahan the portion of the block on which the house stood, about 16,000 square feet. Thus Ivy's home was free of all indebtedness and the title was vested in her. She also retained some vacant property which in later years became quite valuable and from which she realized substantial sums. The insolvency of the estate resulted from the fact that assets were in real estate and there was a lack of cash with which to pay debts. In reality, estate records show that the assets were about equal in value to the debts.

The years following Frank's death were difficult ones for his widow, but she was not alone. The Great Depression that engulfed the United States was felt by everyone. As Bob Hall observed, "Mrs. Stranahan had a hard time in the beginning. You can be property poor. It was hard for her."[31] Ivy was a frugal person, and she weathered the storm alone. Sometimes she rented rooms in her New River home to winter visitors, and it was a delightful place to spend a sojourn in Fort Lauderdale. For a period of time Mrs. Miller Ward operated the Water's Edge Inn in the house.[32] In 1939 the lower two floors of the structure were leased to E. J. Blackwell for a restaurant, and the Blackwells lived on the second floor. Ivy Stranahan briefly attempted to live in the attic space, but she soon returned to the second floor, where she resided for the remainder of her life. Blackwell paid a meager rent of $100 a month. The lease was renewed periodically, and, although Blackwell paid for expansions to the restaurant space, the rental remained at $100 until the lease was terminated in 1979.

Many Fort Lauderdale residents remember the house only as the Pioneer House Dining Room—not as the home of Frank and Ivy Stranahan, even though the widow continued to live there. It is said that part of the reason for the low rent was that Ivy Stranahan was permitted to take her meals in the dining room. The waitresses were local young women. It soon became common knowledge that Ivy dined alone and ignored the customary practice of leaving them a tip.

Following Frank's death, Ivy Stranahan wore the mourning clothes considered proper at that time—not for a year, but for ten years or so.[33] Gradually, she resumed an active involvement with the many causes to which she was devoted. As the years rolled by and Ivy aged, she retained an iron-willed determination and made it felt even in her eighties.

By the early 1960s the Fort Lauderdale central school complex, begun in 1915, was deteriorating, and repairs would be very costly. The residential patterns of the growing city had changed and dictated new school needs, or at least the local school board thought that was the case. The board decided to relocate the school and sell the property for commercial purposes. However, the board failed to investigate the situation thoroughly before making its decision. Restrictions had been placed on the use of some of the property, and violation of the restrictions brought a reverter clause into play.

Ivy Stranahan opposed the school board's decision and did not give in quickly. Even the money offered for a release of her residual interest in the property—money which she needed badly—did not sway her. She argued that the property had "been given for public purposes" and to accept the money would have violated her sense of honor and her code of ethics. Her position was reported in the Fort Lauderdale *News*:

> Mrs. Frank Stranahan, whose husband the late Frank Stranahan sold a portion of the downtown site to the Board, said Thursday that she still objects to use of the land for commercial purposes. . . .
>
> Mrs. Stranahan stated Thursday that she will not agree to lift this restriction to make the proposed sale possible unless the land remains in the hands of the public.
>
> "We don't need any more commercial property. We've got plenty of it available all over town," she said.

Mrs. Stranahan did say that she would lift the restriction if some arrangement was made to develop the property as a civic and cultural center.

"If the school board could sell the land to the city, the people would receive double value for their money," she said. They would get the schools they need and a public park and civic center as well.[34]

Due to the title difficulty, the school board was unable to conclude the first proposed sale of the property. There appears to have been a movement to use the property to establish a Stranahan Cultural Center, but this came to naught. Finally, Ivy Stranahan's friend, attorney George W. English, Jr., presented a plan that she considered an honorable solution to the impasse. She agreed to accept the proffered $50,000 from the school board, but not one penny would go for personal gain. After all the expenses of the transaction were deducted, she would use the net proceeds to establish a foundation to benefit the Fort Lauderdale Historical Society, of which she had been an officer and director since its founding in 1962.

At the time Ivy Stranahan received payment from the school board, the necessary documents establishing the foundation had not been completed, and the tax consequences of the transaction were still to be determined. But Ivy took the steps she considered proper to assure that her wishes would be carried out should she not survive until the paperwork was complete. She prepared a holographic expression of her intent dated June 18, 1963, and witnessed by her nephew DeWitt T. Cromartie and Harriet T. True (see Appendix B). Thus, at age eighty-two she was sufficiently alert and aware of business principles to attempt to assure that her wishes would be fulfilled.

The First National Bank (later Landmark Bank) became trustee when the foundation papers were approved, and its establishment was announced in the *Fort Lauderdale News* on April 18, 1964. Income from the corpus of the foundation was to be paid annually to the Fort Lauderdale Historical Society to defray part of its operating expenses. The corpus itself could only be spent for a "worthy historical purpose." With this transaction any impediment to sale of the school board property was removed. In 1969 demolition of the old school buildings took place and construction was begun on the Landmark Bank building. After the foundation benefiting the Fort Lauderdale Historical Society was established, Ivy Stranahan lived another seven years. Unfortunately, her failing eyesight prevented completion of a project that she had long talked about: identifying her extensive collection of photographs.[35]

On August 1, 1971, Ivy Julia Cromartie Stranahan died in her home on the New River. She was buried beside her husband in Evergreen Cemetery. The good that she did is well known, and the resources she accumulated after her husband's death still benefit the residents of Fort Lauderdale. She executed a last will and testament and several codicils that made specific provisions for various family members. In addition, there was a bequest to the music program at Stranahan High School—$3,000 to the department plus two $500 scholarships for individual students. To the Fort Lauderdale Historical Society she bequeathed all of her private papers and photographs and such of her personal belongings as her nieces and nephews chose not to keep.

The value of an inheritance is not always calculated in dollars and cents. It is likely that the Fort Lauderdale Historical Society received the most valuable of her bequests—the priceless collection of photographs dating from the time that the Stranahan trading post was constructed in the 1890s, the Stranahan library, and the collection of personal and commercial documents. For example, included in the correspondence is a letter from Robert Stranahan to his wife explaining his reasons for serving in the Civil War and trying to allay his wife's fear of community criticism. The family memorabilia provide an insight into the daily activities of the Stranahans and other indomitable New River pioneers.

Many citizens expressed disappointment that the historical society did not receive Ivy Stranahan's house, as some had expected. Instead, her most precious possession—the house overlooking her beloved New River, the site of so many poignant memories—was willed to the Seventh Day Adventist Church. This bequest became a final clear expression of what the church meant to her. Ivy made suggestions as to how the property should be used, but she did not make her wishes mandatory. Perhaps she recalled the problems that attended the restrictions placed on the school property. Only a year before her death, the lease with the Blackwells was renewed for an additional ten-year period, and it still contained a prohibition against the sale of alcoholic beverages. By that time the house was showing the cumulative effects of serious neglect, and rapid deterioration of the property had begun. About three years later, Blackwell attempted to sell his lease for a restaurant and sought a waiver on the liquor prohibition. Concurrently, the church began negotiations with the Fort Lauderdale Historical Society for purchase of the property. In lieu of a restriction in the deed against the sale or use of alcoholic beverages on the property, the church accepted a statement of intent to purchase from the historical society. The trustees of the Stranahan Foundation deemed purchase of the home a "worthy historical purpose," and thus consistent with the terms of Ivy Stranahan's gift, and the corpus of the foundation was added to existing funds of the Fort Lauderdale Historical Society. The combined total was sufficient to purchase the property from the Seventh Day Adventist Church, and a deed was recorded in February 1975.[36]

The trustees of the Fort Lauderdale Historical Society began plans to restore the Stranahan property, a project to begin after the Blackwell's restaurant lease expired. In 1980 the Fort Lauderdale Board of Realtors entered into a joint venture with the historical society to restore the Stranahan House. Prominent restoration architect Herschel Sheppard, whose projects included renovation of the Old Florida State Capitol in Tallahassee, supervised the more than $500,000 project. In 1973 the Stranahan home was placed on the National Register of Historic Places. Stranahan House, Inc., became an independent corporation with its own board of trustees in 1981. Following completion of the renovation in 1984, the house was opened for guided tours and educational programs. The facility is also a popular venue for weddings, receptions, and other social gatherings. Thus the wishes of Frank and Ivy Stranahan that their house be maintained as a historical site became a reality—although Ivy would probably be appalled that alcoholic beverages are occasionally served on the property!

Stranahan House is located on three-quarters of an acre fronting the New River, just off Las Olas Boulevard in the heart of downtown Fort Lauderdale. To the east is the New River Tunnel, while the Hyde Park Market occupied land on the west and north sides of the residence. For many years supporters of Stranahan House sought without success to purchase the supermarket property. With the renovation of Stranahan House in 1980, there was renewed interest in acquiring the adjoining property as a way to save the historic house from falling in the shadow of high-rise development. In 1998 the commercial property adjoining Stranahan

House was purchased by a development corporation; the following spring it revealed plans for a thirty-eight-story building with an eight-story parking garage to be placed just eighty feet from the historic house. An anonymous gift of $2 million from a long-time Stranahan House supporter was intended to help realize the dream of acquiring the property and creating a park. In October 1999, the developer's project was submitted to the development review committee of the city of Fort Lauderdale, where evaluation of several development requirements prevented approval for the project to go forward. Meanwhile, a petition drive headed by the historical society and Stranahan House trustees garnered over 13,000 signatures and forced the city to place the issue on the March ballot. The petition called for the city "to take all necessary steps, including condemnation if necessary to acquire the Hyde Park property."[37] The city commission placed a bond issue on the March ballot, setting a maximum burden on the city taxpayers of $8 million, less than fifty cents per month for the average homeowner. On March 14, 2000, the bond issue passed with 56 percent voter support. However, the developer claimed that the land that he purchased for $2 million was now worth $36 million, so the property is currently tied up in an eminent-domain action between the city of Fort Lauderdale and the developer.

On September 15, 2000, during a ceremony at the Stranahan House, James E. Billie, chairman of the Seminole Tribe of Florida, pledged $3 million to build a community park on the land next to Stranahan House.[38] None of the Seminole gift will be used to purchase the property, but once the land is secured, the park will be developed where the Hyde Park Market on Las Olas Boulevard stands empty. The city commission passed a resolution accepting the donation with two stipulations. First, the park is to be named Seminole Park at Stranahan House; and second, it will feature the history of the tribe and city pioneers Frank and Ivy Stranahan. Chairman Billie, whose tribe has become wealthy on proceeds from bingo and other enterprises, noted, "Ivy Stranahan was a good friend to our tribe. We're back to help out as much as we can."[39]

The Stranahan name remains a permanent legacy in the city of Fort Lauderdale. A high school and numerous other public places bear the family name—although if the couple returned today, the only recognizable landmark would be their restored house. The Reverend Robert Stranahan stressed the importance of history and civic virtue to his son, and the lesson was not lost. Frank and Ivy were private people who always retained a keen sense of their public role in the community. No doubt they would be gratified to know that the citizens of Fort Lauderdale and the Seminole Tribe have insured that Stranahan House, which celebrated its centennial in 2001, will forever remain a part of New River history.

10

Epilogue

One humid summer day in 1968 I found myself driving slowly along Las Olas Boulevard in downtown Fort Lauderdale, on the way to interview the city's matriarch, Ivy Cromartie Stranahan. It was difficult to imagine what the place had looked like some seventy-five years earlier, when Frank Stranahan first settled on the New River. Although a native Floridian and quite familiar with the state's history, I nevertheless associated Fort Lauderdale with sun-baked beaches, glistening yachts, beach-blanket movies, and that icon of my generation: college spring break. As I turned off bustling Las Olas into a small parking lot behind the big two-story ramshackle frame building, a fading sign reminded me that the Pioneer House Restaurant now occupied the lower floor of the house. Here winter tourists enjoyed views of the New River that once belonged only to Frank Stranahan and his Seminole clientele. The small, overgrown garden, with its huge palms, philodendrons, and a gnarled old purple bougainvillea climbing up to the second floor, recalled better times when the house's occupants had taken great pride in their garden. And now the structure itself was in a sad state; it badly needed fresh paint, and the second-floor porch overlooking the river sagged at precarious angles.

It was certainly not the setting in which one expected to encounter the grand dame of Fort Lauderdale. Little did I suspect that within a decade the Fort Lauderdale Historical Society would enlist me as part of a restoration team that returned the house to its former glory.

Climbing the steep stairs, I noticed they were flanked by an electric seat lift. Ivy Stranahan at age eighty-seven was in rapidly failing health, yet her letters responding to my requests for a meeting displayed a clear, firm handwriting. When I announced myself at the screen door, a soft voice invited me in, and I met a small, slim woman in a plain housedress, her hair pulled back and held with combs, and wearing thick tinted "cataract glasses." We settled ourselves in a small sunlit sitting room with a view of the river, and for the next two enchanting hours Ivy Stranahan spun the tale of her life on the New River, from young schoolteacher to wife of the Indian trader Frank Stranahan and, after his death, her involvement with a broad range of civic activities.

Because my research interest was the Indian trade in Florida, the interview explored her vast knowledge of the Seminoles. Most of what she had to say was not new, for her story had been recounted in countless newspaper and magazine profiles over the years. Yet it was incredibly exciting hearing the story from the woman herself. As we chatted she kept staring out at the New River, but I knew she was not observing the yachts and commercial boats moving along that crowded waterway. In her mind she saw those Seminole families moving down the river and landing their canoes at Stranahan's store. She saw the powerful Henry M. Flagler, founder of the Florida East Coast Railway, standing in a corner of the store watching Seminoles trade with her husband, totally ignored by the Indians, who had no idea who he was and no interest in the man. She saw the small Indian children who had the run of her house trying on her Merry Widow hats and high-heeled shoes and learning their letters on her front-porch school. We talked about many people, Indian and white, most long dead but still alive to a woman who had matured through one of the most interesting periods of Florida's history. Now, thanks to her, I also saw the era in a different way.

When we parted, I promised to return for more long talks, but it was not to be. Although we spoke by telephone a number of times, that proved to be my last visit with a very gracious lady. Then it was 1971, and she was gone—the only link with a special era. In subsequent years Ivy Stranahan's story has occupied a prominent place in my books on the Florida Seminoles, while her contributions in the fight for women's suffrage, public education, and other causes have become better understood. Now the magnificently restored Stranahan House stands as a permanent memorial to a unique pioneer family. I hope this work adequately reflects a community's appreciation of the legacy that Frank and Ivy Stranahan left for all Floridians.

Appendix A

Fort Lauderdale, Florida
October 13th, 1925
TO THE HONORABLE CITY COMMISSIONERS,
Fort Lauderdale, Florida.
Gentlemen:

I wish to submit a tentative proposition to you on properties owned by me in the City of Fort Lauderdale for city purposes; this proposition being as follows:

I will lease to the City for Ninety-nine (99) years, with an option to purchase by the city after the first period of ten years of said lease:

> Block "I" of Stranahan's Subdivision of part of the South half (S H) of Block Fourteen (14), and other lands, the river front boundary of said property to contain the same description and boundary as is contained in deed dated June 4th, 1894, and being lands conveyed to Frank Stranahan by William and Mary Brickell, which property is known as the Home Place, less that certain strip commencing at the Southwest corner of Block "I," and running thence North along the West boundary of said Block "I," twenty-eight (28) feet; thence Easterly fifty-six (56) feet, more or less, to the Northeast outside corner of a certain boat slip; thence in a Southerly direction twenty-one (21) feet, more or less, to the waters of New River. And also less the Northwest corner of Block "I," after Las Olas Boulevard and Stranahan Avenue, are widened and improved as is herein specified and described, said Northwest corner being described as, "commencing at the Northwest corner of Block 'I,' and running thence along the North boundary of said Block 'I' in a Easterly direction one hundred twenty (120) feet, thence South ninety (90) feet; thence West one

hundred twenty (120) feet, thence North along Stranahan Avenue and on the west boundary of said Block 'I' one hundred twenty (120) feet to point of beginning."

The valuation on the above described property, together with other property herein described and included, shall be SIX HUNDRED THOUSAND ($600,000.00) DOLLARS, and the rental to be based on an amount equal to four per cent (4%) of Six Hundred thousand ($600,000.00) Dollars for the first three years of said lease; four and a half per cent (4H%) for the second three years; five per cent (5%) for the third three years, and five and a half per cent (5H%) for the remainder of said term of ninety-nine (99) years; said rental to be paid semi-annually.

It is to be understood that sufficient land on the North side of Block "I" is to be used to widen Las Olas Boulevard to a width of not less than fifty (50) feet from curb to curb, and also sufficient land on the West boundary of said Block "I," as called for in lease, is to be used and taken to widen Stranahan Avenue to a width of not less than forty-two (42) feet from curb to curb, provided, the trees on Stranahan Avenue are not removed, molested and destroyed in the widening of Stranahan Avenue, unless it is agreed by all parties that to permit said trees to remain would cause traffic to become dangerous on said Avenue.

The Northwest corner of Block "I," described as:

commencing at the Northwest corner of said Block and running thence along the North boundary of said Block "I" in an Easterly direction one hundred and twenty (120) feet, thence South ninety (90) feet; thence West one hundred and twenty (120) feet; thence North along Stranahan Avenue and on the West boundary of said Block "I" one hundred and twenty (120) feet to point of beginning is to be deeded by me to the Woman's Club of Fort Lauderdale, if acceptable to said Club, for a Woman's Club building and public library, and it shall be deeded to said club exclusively for said purposes, with reservation to the effect that should said Woman's Club use or attempt to use said lands for any other purposes other than a Woman's Club or public library, the title thereto shall revert to me.

I am also to reserve from Block "I" for personal use, a five-year old Royal Palm Tree; fifty (50) Coconut trees and twenty-five (25) lime trees, to be removed by me at the time of giving possession of said property pursuant to said ninety-nine (99) year lease.

I am to give possession of said Block "I," as aforesaid, not earlier than May 1st, 1926. This proposition also includes the South two hundred and eighty-five (285) feet, more or less, of Lot One (1), Block Sixty (60), of Knollton's survey of the Town of Fort Lauderdale, to be used by the City for public park purposes, or public buildings, provided, the City shall purchase the South side school property adjoining the said South two hundred and eighty-five (285) feet, more or less, of Lot One (1), Block Sixty (60) for public park purposes or for public buildings.

This offer is also made with the express understanding and on the condition that the city shall purchase the Woman's Club building and property situated on Andrews Avenue, to be used as a public park or public building.

If this proposition is accepted, and as a part thereof, we agree to deed to the city of Fort Lauderdale, that part of Block "F" of Stranahan's Subdivision of part of the South half (S H) of Block Fourteen (14); and other lands, lying East of the center line of Stranahan Avenue, and South Himmarshe Canal, known as Stranahan Field, less the East fifteen (15) feet of said property which is to be used to widen East Avenue, and less the Southeast corner of said property, after East Avenue is widened,

> Beginning at said Southeast corner of said property, and running thence along the South boundary thereof, one hundred (100) feet; thence North one hundred and forty (140) feet; thence East one hundred (100) feet, thence South along the East boundary of said property one hundred and forty (140) feet to point of beginning.

In agreeing to lease or sell the last above described property, we do so with the understanding and upon the express condition that the city of Fort Lauderdale shall maintain, control and keep up in good order and repair said property as a baseball diamond, track, tennis courts and other courts, or play ground, or fixtures, as is usually and generally found in parks and play grounds; and it shall be included in the lease or deed of conveyance that should the city fail or refuse to control, keep up in good order and repair the property as last set forth, for the purposes mentioned aforesaid, the title thereto shall revert to me.

The city is to assume and pay all State, County and city taxes and all assessments that may exist or be created against said property subsequent to the year 1925.

In the foregoing proposition, each and every condition therein set forth is dependent upon the proposition as a whole, and the non-compliance of one shall mean a rejection of this offer.

Should this offer be accepted by the city, the city shall assume and pay all expenses of abstracts, transfers, surveys, attorneys fees, and all other expenses necessary and incidental to the lease and transfer of said property, which I might have to pay.

This proposition is also made subject to the approval of Mrs. Stranahan, and should Mrs. Stranahan approve of this offer, it is understood that all covenants and agreements to be contained in said lease, are to be agreed upon between us, as well as the time when said lease shall commence to run.

Respectfully submitted,

[*Note: This carbon copy of the proposal has no signature.*]

Appendix B

Fort Lauderdale, Fla.
June 18, 1963
To Whom it May Concern:
This is to certify that I, Ivy J. Stranahan, (Mrs. Frank Stranahan) has received check No. 1317 in the amt of 39,845.00 as her portion of School Board of Broward County settelment of "Public Purpose" clause on portion of Old Fort Lauderdale High School property.

I do this day deposit above amt. in First Federal Savings Bank of Fort Lauderdale trustee revocable when a permanent and Satisfactory trust agreement has been prepared directing interest or income to Fort Lauderdale Historical Society.

Certain deductions as income tax & est to [?] considered as yet.
Signed by Ivy J. Stranahan
Signed June 18, 1963
/s/ Harriet T. True
/s/ DeWitt T. Cromartie
;30 [sic] P.M. June 18, 1963

Appendix 1

Notes

Abbreviations

BIACF   Bureau of Indian Affairs Central Files
BIACOF Bureau of Indian Affairs, Commissioner's Office Files
FEC   Florida East Coast Railway
FLHS   Fort Lauderdale Historical Society
NA   National Archives, Washington DC
SCFLHS Stranahan Collection, Fort Lauderdale Historical Society
SPOHP Samuel Proctor Oral History Program
WPUM Willson Papers, University of Miami

Chapter 1. The New River Mystique

1. True, "The Freducci Map of 1514–1515: What It Discloses of Early Florida History," 50–55, and "Some Early Maps Relating to Florida," 79–80; Milanich and Milanich, "Revisiting the Freducci Map: A Description of Ponce DeLeon's 1513 Florida Voyage?" 319–28; Scisco, "The Track of Ponce De Leon in 1513," 721–35.

2. Kirk, "Broward County Geography before Drainage and Reclamation," 1.

3. *America Septemtrionalis*, 1631; identified in "A Selected Atlas of Fort Lauderdale," 4 (author unknown).

4. Cumming, *The Southeast in Early Maps*, plate 56.

5. Marcellus Williams Survey Diary, December 7, 1870, Fort Lauderdale Historical Society (FLHS), History Files: Geography and Land Development, Mackay and Williams Surveys.

6. Pierce, *Pioneer Life in Southeast Florida*, 158–59.

7. Kirk, "Foundations of Broward County Waterways," 2–4.

8. DeVorsey, *DeBrahm's Report of the General Survey in the Southern District of North America*, 208; Corse, "De Brahm's Report on East Florida, 1773," 219–26.

9. Romans, *A Concise Natural History of East and West Florida*, 22 in appendix.

10. Whitaker, *Documents Relating to the Commercial Policy of Spain in the Floridas*, 131, quoted in Kirk, "Broward County Geography," 1.

11. Wright, *William Augustus Bowles, Director General of the Creek Nation*.

12. Murdoch, "Documents Concerning a Voyage to the Miami Region in 1793," 16–32.

13. Ibid., 26.

14. Abstract of Title, Frankee Lewis Donation, FLHS: History Files: Geography and Land Development.

15. Ibid.

16. Ibid.

17. The location of the "Lewis Place" or Frankee Lewis Donation, as it came to be known, is easily identified today: the northwest corner is at the intersection of Broward Boulevard and U.S. Highway 1, in Fort Lauderdale.

18. Straight, "Odet Philippe: Friend of Napoleon, Naval Surgeon, and Pinellas Pioneer," 1–7.

19. Kirk, "William Cooley: Broward Legend," 12–13.

20. Richard Fitzpatrick to John Simonton, October 1, 1832, quoted in Kirk, "William Cooley," 14–15.

21. Clubbs, "Stephen R. Mallory," 241.

22. Kirk, "William Cooley," 18.

23. Buker, *Swamp Sailors: Riverine Warfare in the Everglades, 1835–1842*, 17.

24. Mahon, *History of the Second Seminole War, 1835–1842*, 87–113.

25. Kirk, *William Lauderdale, General Andrew Jackson's Warrior*, 1–10.

26. Buker, *Swamp Sailors*, 66.

27. Motte, *Journey into Wilderness*, 222.

28. Hammond, "Dr. Stroebel Reports on Southeast Florida, 1836," 65–75.

29. Motte, *Journey into Wilderness*, 199.

30. 1st Lt. Christopher Tompkins to Lt. Col. William Gates, August 7, 1839, quoted in Megna, "New River Chronicle," 19.

31. Ibid.

32. Motte, *Journey into Wilderness*, 226.

33. Today a historical marker at the Bahia Mar Hotel and Yachting Center in Fort Lauderdale identifies the site of "Indian Haulover."

34. Ramsey, "Abner Doubleday and the Third Seminole War," 318.

35. Ibid., 332–33.

36. Ibid., 333.

37. Peters, *Biscayne Bay Country, 1870–1926*, 7–9.

38. Abstract of Title, Frankee Lewis Donation, FLHS.

39. Henshall, *Camping and Cruising in Florida*.

40. Cory, *Hunting and Fishing in Florida*.

41. West, "Seminoles in Broward County: The Pine Island Legacy," 4–11.

42. Henshall, *Camping and Cruising in Florida*, 162.

43. Cory, *Hunting and Fishing in Florida*, 96–97.

Chapter 2. The Buckeye Connection

1. W. R. Hawkins to Franklin Benjamin Stranahan, February 27, 1876, File 66, Stranahan Collection, Fort Lauderdale Historical Society (SCFLHS). This is the only reference to "Franklin Benjamin Stranahan" in SCFLHS.

2. Will Stranahan to Frank Stranahan, June 1, 1883, ibid.
3. Ibid., August 12, 1883.
4. Ibid., March 23, 1884.
5. Allen Stranahan to Frank Stranahan, February 9, 1886, ibid.
6. Robert Stranahan to Frank Stranahan, February 19, 1886, ibid.
7. Will Stranahan to Frank Stranahan, April 6, 1886, ibid.
8. Robert Stranahan to Frank Stranahan, June 3, 1886, ibid.
9. Will Stranahan to Frank Stranahan, February 5, 1887, ibid.
10. *Florida Star*, February 2, 1887.
11. *East Coast Advocate*, October 31, 1891.
12. *Florida Star*, March 3, 1887.
13. Ibid., April 7, 1887.
14. Ibid., August 4, 1887.
15. Ibid., October 27, 1887.
16. Ibid., November 24, 1887.
17. Frank Stranahan to Robert Stranahan, March 20, 1889, File 66, SCFLHS.
18. Curl, *Palm Beach County: An Illustrated History*, 32.
19. Ibid.
20. *East Coast Advocate*, March 27, 1891.
21. *Tropical Sun*, September 29, 1892.
22. Minutes of the Dade County Commission, Minute Book A, November 14, 1892.
23. Ibid., March 20, 1893.
24. Mary Brickell to Dade County Commissioners, April 13, 1893, ibid., May 1, 1893.
25. Minutes of the Dade County Commission, Minute Book A, July 5, 1893.
26. Ibid., November 2, 1891.
27. *Indian River Advocate*, April 15, 1892.
28. Martin, *Florida's Flagler*, 138.
29. Akin, *Flagler: Rockefeller Partner and Florida Land Baron*, 141–42.
30. *Indian River Advocate*, January 20, 1893.
31. Ibid., January 6, 1893.
32. A. E. Lyman receipt, January 21, 1893, File 56, SCFLHS.
33. E. P. Branch letter, January 21, 1893, ibid.
34. E. C. Thomas and Company letter, January 21, 1893, ibid.

Chapter 3. The New River Camp

1. According to the *Florida Star* of February 24, 1887, Dennis "O'Neil" served as the Dade County deputy sheriff during at least part of that year. O'Neill had purchased land before 1892 that was less than three-quarters of a mile south of the original site of the New River camp.

2. Valentine lived near the ocean in the area now known as Harbor Beach. Be-

fore 1892 he bought additional land within a half-mile north of the site at which the county road crossed New River.

3. On February 23, 1893, W. C. Collier entered into an agreement with Albert W. Robert, Palm Beach agent in Dade County for the Florida Coast Line Canal and Transportation Company and Florida Atlantic Coast Land Company. He agreed to pay $365.75 for 71.35 acres in Lot 4, and 19 acres in Lot 5 of Section 26, Township 49 South, Range 42 East—about $5.00 per acre.

4. Frank Stranahan to Will Stranahan, January 31, 1893, File 56, SCFLHS.
5. *Florida Times-Union*, February 21, 1893.
6. *Tropical Sun*, April 9, 1893.
7. Ibid.
8. Peters, *Lemon City: Pioneering on Biscayne Bay, 1850–1925*, 108.
9. Ibid., 109.
10. *Tropical Sun*, November 29, 1894.
11. Peters, *Lemon City*, 96.
12. Minutes of the Dade County Commission, Minute Book A, May 1, 1893.
13. Ibid., August 9, 1893.
14. Ibid., April 3, 1894.
15. Peters, *Lemon City*, 144.
16. Banyan was a small community in Brevard County. It appears that Welles already had a business there similar to the one he and Stranahan planned for New River.
17. F. M. Welles to Frank Stranahan, May 3, 1893, File 57, SCFLHS.
18. Ibid., June 2, 1893.
19. Ibid.
20. Ibid., June 3, 1893.
21. Ibid., June 29, 1893.
22. Ibid., June 30, 1893.
23. Ibid.
24. Ibid., June [?], 1893. Guy Metcalf married Edith Augusta Lacey in Niles, Michigan, on June 12, 1893. She was the cousin of E. N. Dimick, a pioneer Lake Worth resident (*Florida Times-Union*, June 5, 1893).
25. F. M. Welles to Frank Stranahan, July 18, 1893, File 57, SCFLHS.
26. Martin, *Florida's Flagler*, 256–57.
27. F. M. Welles to Frank Stranahan, August 17, 1893, File 57, SCFLHS. Stranahan's check for $300, written to Welles on the Indian River State Bank, is dated August 2, 1893.
28. Ibid., July 18, 1893.
29. Ibid., August 17, 1893.
30. Ibid., January 8, 1894.
31. Ibid., March 4, 1894.
32. Ibid., April 6, 1894.

33. Robert Stranahan to Frank Stranahan, August 21, 1893, File 57, SCFLHS.

34. Robbins, Graham, and Chillingworth to Frank Stranahan, November 29, 1894, File 56, SCFLHS.

Chapter 4. Stranahan & Co., 1894–1911

1. Greater Miami Genealogical Society, *1896 Directory*, 54.

2. Akin, *Flagler*, 160–61.

3. Henry M. Flagler to Julia Tuttle, April 22, 1895, History Files: Transportation, Railroads, FEC, FLHS; copied from Flagler/Tuttle correspondence, Flagler Archives, Flagler Museum, Palm Beach.

4. Greater Miami Genealogical Society, *1896 Directory*, 70.

5. Weidling and Burghard, *Checkered Sunshine: The Story of Fort Lauderdale, 1793–1955*, 56–59; Riparian Rights Lawsuit File, FLHS.

6. *Tropical Sun*, October 28, 1897.

7. Ibid., November 18, 1897.

8. Ibid.

9. Peters, *Lemon City*, 90.

10. Ibid., 89.

11. Ivy Stranahan interview, October 25, 1970, Samuel Proctor Oral History Archive (SPOHA), SEM 1, 13.

12. Frank Stranahan to Ivy Cromartie, May 4, 1900, File 67, SCFLHS.

13. Ibid., May 15, 1900.

14. Ibid., May 4, 1900.

15. Ibid., May 31, 1900.

16. Ibid., August 10, 1900.

17. Peters, *Lemon City*, 157.

18. Frank Stranahan to J. E. Ingraham, November 21, 1900, History Files: Transportation, Railroads, FEC, FLHS.

19. George L. Bahl to J. E. Ingraham, November 22, 1900, quoted in Megna, "New River Chronicle," 98–99.

20. J. R. Parrott to J. E. Ingraham, November 21, 1900, quoted ibid., 99.

21. Frank Stranahan to Robert Stranahan, November 7, 1909, File 68, SCFLHS.

22. Craig and McJunkin, "Stranahan's: Last of the Seminole Trading Posts," 48.

23. Kersey, *Pelts, Plumes and Hides: White Traders among the Seminole Indians, 1870–1930*, 133–34.

24. Will Stranahan to Robert Stranahan, May 26, 1902, File 67, SCFLHS.

25. Ibid., September 4, 1902.

26. Ibid., October 26, 1902.

27. *Free Press*, May 22, 1936.

28. J. R. Parrott to Frank Stranahan, March 1, 1905, File 69, SCFLHS.

29. *Fort Lauderdale Herald*, clipping c. 1910, History Files: Business, Community and Industry, Trading Post, FLHS.

Chapter 5. Stranahan: Land Agent, Banker, and Promoter

1. E. C. Parker to Frank Stranahan, August 24, 1912, File 92, SCFLHS.
2. Ibid.
3. Ibid.
4. E. E. Rogers to Frank Stranahan, September 15, 1912, File 92, SCFLHS.
5. Allen Stranahan to Frank Stranahan, August 10, 1913, File 92, SCFLHS.
6. Osky's to Frank Stranahan, April 13, 1914, File 51, SCFLHS.
7. Tony Tommie to Frank Stranahan, October 4, 1916, letter in collection of Harry A. Kersey, Jr.
8. Kersey, "The Tony Tommie Letter, 1916: A Transitional Seminole Document," 301–14.
9. Mary Brickell to Frank Stranahan, October 9, 1908, File 70, SCFLHS.
10. Ibid., September 3, 1914.
11. Hugh T. Birch to Frank Stranahan, June 2, 1922, Birch File, FLHS.
12. *Fort Lauderdale News*, February 17, 1956.
13. U.S. Department of Agriculture, Bureau of Soils, "Soil Survey of the Fort Lauderdale Area, Florida," 8.
14. Nash, "Survey of the Seminole Indians of Florida," 72.
15. G. B. Lamar to Frank Stranahan, May 5, 1910, File 69, SCFLHS.
16. Ibid., February 3, 1911.
17. Ibid., March 29, 1911.
18. Frank Stranahan to G. C. Varney, February 24, 1923, File 95, SCFLHS.
19. Robert Hall interview, August 22, 1979 (typescript), FLHS, 15–16.
20. Ibid.
21. Davis, "D. C. Alexander, Pioneer and Developer of Las Olas Beach," FLHS, 1–2.

Chapter 6. Stranahan: Civic Leader and Politician

1. Bridge Petition and Pledge, File 54, Stranahan Collection, SCFLHS.
2. Allen Stranahan to Frank Stranahan, October 24, 1915, File 68, SCFLHS. When the riparian rights case involving downtown New River frontage was ultimately decided, Stranahan's property was not affected although others on the riverfront were. Judge Drake remained in town and took a prominent role in promoting the development of Port Everglades.
3. Ibid.
4. Ivy Stranahan to Frank Stranahan, May 30, 1916, File 52, SCFLHS.
5. Ibid.
6. Ibid., June 7, 1916.
7. Allen Stranahan to Frank Stranahan, April 3, 1916, File 68, SCFLHS.
8. Ibid., June 16, 1916.

9. Ivy Stranahan to Frank Stranahan, June 20, 1916, File 52, SCFLHS.

10. Certified copy, certificate of death for Guy Irwin Metcalf, February 7, 1918, Palm Beach County, Florida. The certificate lists his occupation as "Superintendent of Public Instruction" and the cause of death as "Suicide, shooting."

11. C. G. Rodes to Frank Stranahan, August 23, 1927, File 84, SCFLHS.

12. "A Resident" to Frank Stranahan, September 26, 1927, File 85, SCFLHS.

13. W. E. Rasey to Frank Stranahan, September 29, 1927, File 84, SCFLHS.

14. Letter to "Mr. Commissioner," c. 1927, ibid.

15. Glenn E. Turner to Frank Stranahan, August 16, 1928, ibid.

16. Ibid.

17. A. W. Erkins to City Commission, October 26, 1928, ibid.

18. Glenn E. Turner to Ivy Stranahan, May 23, 1929, File 159, SCFLHS.

19. Weidling and Burghard, *Checkered Sunshine*, 60.

20. Articles of agreement, File 109, SCFLHS.

21. D. B. Sharp to Frank Stranahan, October 20, 1922, File 84, SCFLHS.

Chapter 7. Ivy Stranahan, Civic Activist

1. Craig and McJunkin, "Stranahan's," 45, 49.

2. Ibid., 48.

3. Peters, *Lemon City*, 109, 124, 163; Pierce, *Pioneer Life*, 92, 96, 149, 164, 199–201.

4. McIver, "Plume Hunt on Cypress Creek," 21.

5. Weidling and Burghard, *Checkered Sunshine*, 36.

6. Van Howe, "The Women's Suffrage Movement in Broward County and Florida," 37.

7. Danese, "Disenfranchisement, Women's Suffrage and the Failure of Florida's Grandfather Clause," 117–31. This clause was a political device used in southern states to deny voting rights to anyone whose grandfather had not had the legal right to vote, thus disenfranchizing Negroes.

8. Douglas, *Voice of the River*, 108–9.

9. Johnson, "The Woman Suffrage Movement in Florida," 211.

10. Ibid., 218.

11. Ibid., 219.

12. Weatherford, "Last Instead of First," 20; Danese, "Disenfranchisement," 131.

13. Ivy Stranahan to May Mann Jennings, July 7, 1917, quoted in Johnson, "Woman Suffrage," 242.

14. *Fort Lauderdale Sentinel*, July 15, 1917.

15. Johnson, "Woman Suffrage," 249.

16. Ibid., 114.

17. Ibid., 115.

18. Ibid., 79. Also quoted in Van Howe, "The Women's Suffrage Movement," 38.

19. American Red Cross, File 116; American Red Cross 1917–51, File 165; American Red Cross, 1923–40, File 224, SCFLHS.

20. *Fort Lauderdale News*, May 21, 1958.

21. Near East Relief, 1921, File 157, SCFLHS.

22. Red Cross, 1940–51, File 165; World War II and British War Relief, File 186, SCFLHS.

23. American Social Hygiene Association and World War II, File 133, SCFLHS.

24. Broward County Welfare, File 62; Welfare Records, 1935–41, File 187; Welfare, 1912–1963, File 188; Ivy Stranahan 1938 welfare notes, File 212; all SCFLHS.

25. *Fort Lauderdale Sun-Sentinel*, September 9, 1967.

26. Colored Medical Relief, Colored Sanitarium, Files 62, 63; Provident Hospital 1938–1941, Files 89, 90; Accounts Receivable 1938, 1939, 1940, File 209; Dr. Sistrunk Hospital 1942–1943, Files 97, 98; all SCFLHS.

27. *Fort Lauderdale News*, May 28, 1929.

28. File on damage to Stranahan House, File 158, SCFLHS.

29. *Fort Lauderdale News*, January 28, 1968.

30. Governor's proclamation, February 8, 1968, SCFLHS.

31. *Miami Herald*, May 22, 1956.

32. Ibid., August 13, 1967.

Chapter 8. Ivy Stranahan and the Indian Reform Movement

1. Kersey, *Pelts, Plumes and Hides*, 52.

2. Ivy Stranahan interview, SPOHA, 25.

3. Kersey, and Goldman, "The Dania Indian School, 1927–1936," 42–53; Alice Cromartie Simpson interview, April 3, 1980 (tape and typescript), FLHS, 15.

4. Burghard, *Watchie-Esta/Hutrie* (The little white mother). Dr. William Sturtevant of the Smithsonian Institution has challenged the accuracy of this translation. In a conversation with Susan Gillis he indicated that the "Creek name should be *Wace este-hutke*. *Wace* means mother; *esta-hutke* means white. *Cotuske* means little person. It seems likely that Ivy just misheard the *K* in *hutke*. And the diminutive 'little' may have been thrown in by Tony Tommie." Correspondence with Susan Gillis, February 1, 2003.

5. Sturtevant, "A Seminole Personal Document," 55–75.

6. Kersey, "Educating the Seminole Indians of Florida, 1879–1970," 16–35.

7. Kersey, "The Tony Tommie Letter," 301–14.

8. West, "The Miami Tourist Attractions: A History and Analysis of a Transitional Seminole Environment," 200–224; West, *The Enduring Seminoles: From Alligator Wrestling to Ecotourism*, 72.

9. Kersey, "The 'Friends of the Florida Seminoles' Society: 1899–1926," 3–20.

10. Kersey, "Private Societies and the Maintenance of Seminole Tribal Integrity, 1899–1957," 297–316.

11. May Mann Jennings to Minnie Moore-Willson, May 12, 1915, Willson Papers, University of Miami (WPUM).
12. Ivy Stranahan to Minnie Moore-Willson, December 27, 1916, ibid.
13. Minnie Moore-Willson to Ivy Stranahan, January 7, 1917, ibid.
14. Kersey and Pullease, "Bishop William Crane Gray's Mission to the Seminole Indians in Florida, 1893–1914," 257–73.
15. Ivy Stranahan interview, SPOHA, 37–38.
16. Nash, "Survey of the Seminole Indians," 72.
17. Jumper and West, *A Seminole Legend: The Life of Betty Mae Tiger Jumper*, 50.
18. Glenn, *My Work among the Florida Seminoles*.
19. MacCauley, "The Seminole Indians of Florida."
20. Nash, "Survey of the Seminole Indians," 54.
21. U.S. Congress, Senate. Subcommittee of the Committee on Indian Affairs, *Survey of Conditions of the Indians of the United States*, 7603–14.
22. Ivy Stranahan to John Collier, March 25, 1935, Record Group (RG) 75, Bureau of Indian Affairs Commissioner's Office Files, National Archives, Washington, D.C. (BIACOF, NA).
23. Kersey, "Federal Schools and Acculturation among the Florida Seminoles, 1927–1954," 165–81.
24. "Billy Osceola's House," File 31, SCFLHS.
25. Kersey, *An Assumption of Sovereignty*, 23–50.
26. Friends of the Seminoles Correspondence, File 14, SCFLHS; Kersey and Kushin, "Ivy Stranahan and the 'Friends of the Seminoles,' 1899–1971."
27. Glenn L. Emmons to Ivy Stranahan, December 17, 1953, File 82; George A. Smathers to Ivy Stranahan, December 13, 1953, File 29; both SCFLHS.
28. U.S. Congress, *Termination of Federal Supervision over Certain Tribes of Indians*, 1126.
29. Ibid., 1131.
30. Spessard L. Holland to Ivy Stranahan, October 24, 1954, File 29, SCFLHS.
31. U.S. Congress, House, *Hearings before the Subcommittee on Indian Affairs of the Committee on Interior and Insular Affairs, Seminole Indians, Florida*, 74.
32. 1954 Report of Congressional Committee of Friends of the Seminoles of Florida, File 163–1955–Seminole-050, Part I, RG75, BIACF, NA.
33. *Miami Herald*, December 4, 1962.
34. Jumper and West, *A Seminole Legend*, 119–30.
35. Kirk and Cunningham, "The Seminoles Today: An Oral History Interview with Betty Mae Jumper," *Broward Legacy* 4 (Winter–Spring 1981): 43.
36. *Fort Lauderdale Sun-Sentinel*, September 1, 1971.

Chapter 9. Public Lives, Private People

1. Alice Cromartie Simpson interview, SCFLHS, 11.
2. Ogle and Korb, *Stranahan's People*, 17–18.
3. Ibid.

4. Alice Cromartie Simpson interview, SCFLHS, 16.
5. Ibid., 1.
6. Robert Hall interview, FLHS, 26–27.
7. Ibid., 16–17.
8. Helen Howard Woodruff to Marjorie D. Parsons, April 22, 1983, letter in collection of Marjorie D. Parsons.
9. Alice Cromartie Simpson interview, SCFLHS, 1.
10. See Appendix A.
11. Margaret Oliver Crews interview, October 29, 1982 (tape), FLHS.
12. Ivy Stranahan interview, SPOHA, 25.
13. Robert Hall interview, FLHS, 13.
14. Ibid., 14.
15. Ibid.
16. Cutler, *History of Florida Past and Present: Historical and Biographical*, 2: 239.
17. Allen Stranahan to Frank Stranahan, June 17, 1924, SCFLHS.
18. *Free Press*, May 22, 1936.
19. Ogle and Korb, *Stranahan's People*, 12.
20. Ibid.
21. *Miami Herald*, September 2, 1925.
22. Cutler, *History of Florida*, 239.
23. Income tax return of Frank Stranahan, 1928, File 161, SCFLHS.
24. W. C. Kyle to Bank of Biscayne, March 22, 1929, File 104, SCFLHS.
25. Ibid., March 27, 1929.
26. Ibid., May 20, 1929.
27. Frank Stranahan's notebook, April 9, 1929, File 198, SCFLHS.
28. Robert Hall interview, FLHS, 21–23.
29. An older sister of Frank Stranahan, Ida Thompson, reportedly took her own life in Ohio in 1915. Frank Stranahan's notebook, 1916, File 212, SCFLHS.
30. Alice Cromartie Simpson interview, FLHS, 12–13.
31. Robert Hall interview, FLHS, 24.
32. *Fort Lauderdale City Directory, 1936–1937*.
33. Alice Cromartie Simpson interview, FLHS, 24.
34. *Fort Lauderdale News* (undated clipping), File 197, SCFLHS.
35. Ibid., April 18, 1964.
36. History File: Stranahan House Acquisition, FLHS.
37. *The Trading Post* (Winter 2001): 8.
38. Ibid., 9.
39. Ibid., 3.

Bibliography

Document Collections and Abbreviations

BIACF   Bureau of Indian Affairs Central Files, Record Group 75, National Archives (RG75, BIACF, NA)
BIACOF   Bureau of Indian Affairs, Commissioner's Office Files, Record Group 75, National Archives (RG75, BIACOF, NA)
FLHS   Fort Lauderdale Historical Society
SCFLHS   Stranahan Collection, Fort Lauderdale Historical Society
SPOHA   Samuel Proctor Oral History Archives, University of Florida, Gainesville
WPUM   Minnie Moore-Willson Papers, University of Miami

Published Works

Akin, Edward N. *Flagler: Rockefeller Partner and Florida Land Baron*. Kent, Ohio: Kent State University Press, 1988. Reprint, Gainesville: University Press of Florida, 1992.
Buker, George E. *Swamp Sailors: Riverine Warfare in the Everglades, 1835–1842*. Gainesville: University Presses of Florida, 1975.
Burghard, August. *Watchie-Esta/Hutrie* (The little white mother). Fort Lauderdale: published by the author, 1968.
Clubbs, Occie. "Stephen R. Mallory." *Florida Historical Quarterly* 25 (October 1946): 221–45.
Corse, Carita Doggett. "De Brahm's Report on East Florida, 1773." *Florida Historical Quarterly* 17 (1939): 219–26.
Cory, Charles B. *Hunting and Fishing in Florida*. Boston: Estes and Lauriat, 1896.
Craig, Alan K., and David McJunkin. "Stranahan's: Last of the Seminole Trading Posts." *Florida Anthropologist* 24 (June 1971): 45–49.
Cumming, William P. *The Southeast in Early Maps*. Chapel Hill: University of North Carolina Press, 1965.
Curl, Donald W. *Palm Beach County: An Illustrated History*. Northridge, Calif.:

Windsor Publications, 1986.
Cutler, Harry G. *History of Florida Past and Present: Historical and Biographical.* Vol. 2. New York: Lewis Publishing Co., 1923.
Danese, Tracy E. "Disenfranchisement, Women's Suffrage and the Failure of Florida's Grandfather Clause." *Florida Historical Quarterly* 74 (Fall 1995): 117–31.
Davis, Betty Lou. "D. C. Alexander, Pioneer and Developer of Las Olas Beach." *New River News* 10 (January 1972): 1–5.
DeFoor, J. Allison II. *Odet Philippe: Peninsular Pioneer.* Safety Harbor, Fla.: Safety Harbor Museum of Regional History, 1997.
DeVorsey, Louis, Jr., ed. *DeBrahm's Report of the General Survey in the Southern District of North America.* Columbia: University of South Carolina Press, 1971.
Dillon, Rodney E., and Joe Knetsch. "Forgotten Pioneer: The Legacy of Capt. William C. Valentine." *Broward Legacy* 17 (Winter/Spring 1994): 39–41.
Douglas, Marjorie Stoneman. *Voice of the River.* Englewood, Fla.: Pineapple Press, 1987.
Durkin, Joseph T. *Confederate Navy Chief: Stephen R. Mallory.* Chapel Hill: University of North Carolina Press, 1954.
Glenn, James L. *My Work among the Florida Seminoles*, ed. Harry A. Kersey, Jr. Gainesville: University Presses of Florida, 1982.
Greater Miami Genealogical Society. *1896 Directory, Guide and History of Dade County, Florida.* Facsimile edition. West Palm Beach: C. M. Gardner and C. F. Kennedy, 1996.
Hammond, E. A., ed. "Dr. Stroebel Reports on Southeast Florida, 1836." *Tequesta* 21 (1961): 65–75.
Henshall, James A. *Camping and Cruising in Florida.* Cincinnati: Clark and Co., 1884.
Johnson, Henry E. III. "The Many Faces of Guy I. Metcalf." *Broward Legacy* 9 (Summer/Fall 1986): 2–11.
Johnson, Kenneth Ray. "The Woman Suffrage Movement in Florida." Ph.D. diss., Florida State University, 1966.
Jumper, Betty Mae Tiger, and Patsy West. *A Seminole Legend: The Life of Betty Mae Tiger Jumper.* Gainesville: University Press of Florida, 2001.
Kersey, Harry A., Jr. *An Assumption of Sovereignty: Social and Political Transformation among the Florida Seminoles, 1953–1979.* Lincoln: University of Nebraska Press, 1996.
———. "Educating the Seminole Indians of Florida, 1879–1970." *Florida Historical Quarterly* 49 (July 1970): 16–35.
———. "Federal Schools and Acculturation among the Florida Seminoles, 1927–1954." *Florida Historical Quarterly* 64 (October 1980): 165–81.
———. *The Florida Seminoles and the New Deal, 1933–1942.* Gainesville: University Presses of Florida, 1989.

———. "The 'Friends of the Florida Seminoles' Society: 1899–1926." *Tequesta* 34 (1974): 3–20.

———. *Pelts, Plumes and Hides: White Traders among the Seminole Indians, 1870–1930*. Gainesville: University Presses of Florida, 1975.

———. "Private Societies and the Maintenance of Seminole Tribal Integrity, 1899–1957." *Florida Historical Quarterly* 61 (January 1978): 297–316.

———. "The Tony Tommie Letter, 1916: A Transitional Seminole Document." *Florida Historical Quarterly* 64 (January 1986): 301–14.

Kersey, Harry A., Jr., and Mark S. Goldman. "The Dania Indian School, 1927–1936." *Tequesta* 39 (1979): 42–53.

Kersey, Harry A., Jr., and Rochelle Kushin. "Ivy Stranahan and the 'Friends of the Seminoles,' 1899–1971." *Broward Legacy* 1, no. 1 (October 1976): 6–11.

Kersey, Harry A., Jr., and Donald E. Pullease. "Bishop William Crane Gray's Mission to the Seminole Indians in Florida, 1893–1914." *Historical Magazine of the Protestant Episcopal Church* 42 (September 1973): 257–73.

Kirk, Cooper C. "Broward County Geography before Drainage and Reclamation." *New River News* 14 (October 1975): 1.

———. "Foundations of Broward County Waterways." *Broward Legacy* 8 (Winter/Spring 1985): 2–4.

———. "William Cooley: Broward Legend." *Broward Legacy* 1 (October 1976): 12–13.

———. *William Lauderdale: General Andrew Jackson's Warrior*. Fort Lauderdale: Manatee Books, 1982.

Kirk, Cooper C., and Pat Cunningham. "The Seminoles Today: An Oral History Interview with Betty Mae Jumper." *Broward Legacy* 4 (Winter–Spring 1981): 30–44.

MacCauley, Clay. "The Seminole Indians of Florida." In Smithsonian Institution, Bureau of American Ethnology, *Fifth Annual Report, 1883–1884*, 469–531. Washington, D.C.: Government Printing Office, 1887.

Mahon, John K. *History of the Second Seminole War, 1835–1842*. Gainesville: University Presses of Florida, 1967; rev. ed., 1985.

Martin, Sidney Walter. *Florida's Flagler*. Athens: University of Georgia Press, 1949.

McIver, Stuart. "Plume Hunt on Cypress Creek." *Broward Legacy* 1 (October 1976): 21–26.

Megna, Ralph J., ed. "New River Chronicle: A Documentary History of Life in the Fort Lauderdale Region, 1765 to 1911." Typescript, Fort Lauderdale Historical Society, 1978.

Milanich, Jerald T., and Nara B. Milanich. "Revisiting the Freducci Map: A Description of Ponce DeLeon's 1513 Florida Voyage?" *Florida Historical Quarterly* 64 (Winter 1996): 319–28.

Motte, Jacob Rhett. *Journey into Wilderness: An Army Surgeon's Account of Life in Camp and Field during the Creek and Seminole Wars, 1836–1838*, ed. James F.

Sunderman. Gainesville: University of Florida Press, 1953.

Murdoch, Richard K. "Documents Concerning a Voyage to the Miami Region in 1793." *Florida Historical Quarterly* 31 (July 1952): 16–32.

Nash, Roy. "Survey of the Seminole Indians of Florida." 71st Cong., 3d sess., February 28, 1931. S. Doc. 314. Washington: Government Printing Office, 1931.

Ogle, Boyd, and Wally Korb, eds. *Stranahan's People*. Fort Lauderdale: Stranahan High School, 1975.

Peters, Thelma. *Biscayne Bay Country, 1870–1926*. Miami: Banyan Books, 1981.

———. *Lemon City: Pioneering on Biscayne Bay, 1850–1925*. Miami: Banyan Books, 1976.

Pierce, Charles W. *Pioneer Life in Southeast Florida*, ed. Donald W. Curl. Miami: University of Miami Press, 1970.

Ramsey, David, ed. "Abner Doubleday and the Third Seminole War." *Florida Historical Quarterly* 59 (January 1981): 318–35.

Romans, Bernard. *A Concise Natural History of East and West Florida*. A facsimile reproduction of the 1775 edition, with introduction by Rembert W. Patrick. Gainesville: University of Florida Press, 1962.

Scisco, Louis D. "The Track of Ponce De Leon in 1513." *Bulletin of the American Geographical Society* 45 (1913): 721–35.

"A Selected Atlas of Fort Lauderdale." *New River News* 21 (Fall 1982): 4.

Straight, William M. "Odet Philippe: Friend of Napoleon, Naval Surgeon and Pinellas Pioneer." *New River News* 9 (April 1970): 1–7.

Sturtevant, William C. "A Seminole Personal Document." *Tequesta* 16 (1956): 55–75.

Tiger, Buffalo, and Harry A. Kersey, Jr. *Buffalo Tiger: A Life in the Everglades*. Lincoln: University of Nebraska Press, 2002.

True, David O. "The Freducci Map of 1514–1515: What It Discloses of Early Florida History." *Tequesta* 4 (1944): 50–55.

———. "Some Early Maps Relating to Florida." *Imago Mundi* 11 (1955): 79–80.

U.S. Congress. *Termination of Federal Supervision over Certain Tribes of Indians*. Joint Hearings before the Subcommittees of the Committee of the Interior and Insular Affairs, on S. 2747 and H.R. 7321, Part 8, Seminole Indians, Florida. 83d Cong., 2d sess., March 1–2, 1954. Washington: Government Printing Office, 1954.

———. House. *Hearings before the Subcommittee on Indian Affairs of the Committee on Interior and Insular Affairs, Seminole Indians, Florida*, Pursuant to H. Res. 30, April 6–7, 1955. Serial no. 8, 84th Cong. Washington: Government Printing Office, 1955.

———. Senate. Committee on Indian Affairs. *Survey of Conditions of the Indians of the United States*. Hearing Pursuant to Senate Resolution 79 and Senate Resolution 308, Part 16, 71st Cong., 3d sess., March 31, 1930. Washington: Government Printing Office, 1931.

U.S. Department of Agriculture. Bureau of Soils. "Soil Survey of the Fort Lauderdale Area, Florida," by Mark Baldwin and E. W. Hawker. Washington: Government Printing Office, 1915.

Vance, Linda D. "May Mann Jennings." *Forum: Magazine of the Florida Humanities Council* 18 (Winter 1995–96): 10–15.

———. *May Mann Jennings: Florida's Genteel Activist.* Gainesville: University Presses of Florida, 1985.

Van Howe, Annette. "The Women's Suffrage Movement in Broward County and Florida." *Broward Legacy* 14 (Summer–Fall 1991): 37–42.

Weatherford, Doris. *A History of the American Suffragist Movement.* Santa Barbara, Calif.: ABC-CLIO, 1997.

———. "Last Instead of First." *Forum: The Magazine of the Florida Humanities Council* 18 (Winter 1995–96): 16–21.

Weidling, Philip J., and August Burghard. *Checkered Sunshine: The Story of Fort Lauderdale, 1793–1955.* Gainesville: University of Florida Press, 1966.

West, Patsy. *The Enduring Seminoles: From Alligator Wrestling to Ecotourism.* Gainesville: University Press of Florida, 1998.

———. "The Miami Tourist Attractions: A History and Analysis of a Transitional Seminole Environment." *Florida Anthropologist* 34 (December 1981): 200–224.

———. "Seminoles in Broward County: The Pine Island Legacy." *New River News* 23 (Fall 1985): 4–11.

Whitaker, Arthur Preston, ed. and trans. *Documents Relating to the Commercial Policy of Spain in the Floridas.* Deland: Florida State Historical Society, 1931.

Wright, J. Leitch, Jr. *William Augustus Bowles, Director General of the Creek Nation.* Athens: University of Georgia Press, 1967.

Interviews

Crews, Margaret Oliver. Taped interview, October 29, 1982. Fort Lauderdale Historical Society.

Hall, Robert. Taped interview and typescript, August 22, 1979. Fort Lauderdale Historical Society.

Simpson, Alice Cromartie. Taped interview and typescript, April 3, 1980. Fort Lauderdale Historical Society.

Stranahan, Ivy Cromartie. Taped interview and typescript, October 25, 1970. Samuel Proctor Oral History Archive, University of Florida, SEM 1.

Index

Note: Page number in *italics* indicate photos.

Abbey, Erma, 140, 142
Addison, John, 13
Agriculture: development of, 70; produce, for Stranahan and Company, 71, 77; produce, shipment of, 90–91; truck gardening, 91; winter freezes, 70
Alcohol: Pioneer House and, 161–62; Seminoles and, 137; I. Stranahan views on, 115–16
Alexander, D. C., 96
Alligator hide, 77
Alligators, baby, 77, 85
American Indian Defense Association, 138
American Red Cross, 125
America Septemtrionalis map, 1
Archibald, J. W., 42, 43, 44
Arredondo, Antonio de, 1
Atlantic, Okeechobee, and Gulf Railway, 98

Bahl, George L., 75–76
Banking business, 91–95
Bank of Bay Biscayne, 155
Barrett, Fred, 96
Baseley, Edward, 13
Baxter, Maxwell, 153, 158
Beach road, construction of, 96–97
Beck, Annie, 119, 128
Berryhill, Ivy, 149, 152
Berryhill, W. O., 76, 77, 79–80, 82, 101, 152

Billard, F. C., 106
Billie, Agnes, *62*
Billie, James E., 163
Billingsley, J. L., 101
Birch, Hugh Taylor, 87–88
Bird life, conservation of, 116–17
Blackwell, E. J., 158–59, 161–62
Blank, R. J., 150
Bolles, Richard J., 90
Bond issue, 106–8
Boston and Florida Atlantic Coast Land Company, 68, 86
Bowles, William August, 4
Bradley, Guy, 117
Branch, E. P., 31–32
Brantley, J. N., 37, 72
Brickell, Mary and William B., Sr.: county road and, 26–27; land agent business and, 85–86; landholdings of, 17; location of overnight camp and, 46; move to Florida, 14; railroad and, 68; sale of property to Stranahan, 47–48; survey for town site, 69
Bridges: over New River, 80, 100–101; over Tarpon River, 47
Brook, A. H., 150
Broward, Annie, 119
Broward, N. B., 81, 102
Broward County: beach access in, 96; creation of, 102; homestead exemption law, 125–26; property in, 89
Broward General Hospital, 126
Broward State Bank, 93
Brown, H. T., 104

192 · Index

Brown, John, 13
Bryan, Mary Elizabeth, 119–21
Bryan, P. N., 88, 96, 101
Bryan, Reed A., 88, 96, 100–101
Bryan, Susie M., 82
Bryan, Tom M., 105
Bryan, William Jennings, 119–20
Buker, George, 8
Burnham, Edith, 94, 155, 158

Camp, overnight, 52; location of, 46; renovation of, 71; reputation of, 69–70
Camp Fire Girls, 128
Camping and Cruising in Florida (Henshall), 15
Canals: completion of, 81; construction of, 28–29; Fitzpatrick and, 6–7; Florida East Coast Canal, 68, 69; North New River Canal, 83, 90–91
Champion Bridge Company, 96–97
Chevelier, Jean, 117
City commission, 105–6, 108, 126–27
City council, 101, 105, 122
City manager position and salary, 108–9
City politics, 102–5
Civil War, 13, 18
Colee, James L., 17, 68
Collier, John, 138, 139
Collier, W. C., 33, 146
Coman, C. W., 89
Cooley, William, 6, 7–8
Coontie, 6, 9, 77
Cory, Charles B., *Hunting and Fishing in Florida*, 15, 16
Crews, Margaret Oliver, 149–50
Cromartie, Augustus Whitfield, 72, 147
Cromartie, Bloxham, 74, 80, 82, 157
Cromartie, DeWitt T., 160
Cromartie, Ivy Julia. *See* Stranahan, Ivy Julia Cromartie
Cromartie, Sarah, 126
Cunningham, P. A., 41, 42–43, 44
Curl, Donald, 25
Curtis, A. H., 69–70

D. N. *Reynolds*, 41
Dade, Francis L., 8

Dade County: county seat of, 24–25; ferry tolls and, 37–38; military activity in, 71; roads in, 25–27
Dade County Bank, 93
Dade County Real Estate and Abstract of Title Company, 31
Dade Massacre, 8
Daly, Eugenia, 39
Daly, Lucette, 39
Dania, Florida, 96
Dania Seminole Reservation, 134–37
Davie, Florida, 96
Davis, C. M., 101
De Brahm, William Gerard, 3
Deep-water harbor, 97–98
Deep Water Harbor Company, 97
Dimick, E. N., 178n.24
Doubleday, Abner, 12–13, 27
Douglas, Marjorie Stoneman, 120
Drake, S. L., 104
Driver, Sara Elizabeth, 72
Dunlap, Charles, 20, 46
Dunlap, Grace, 20, 76, 150
Dunlap, Lucy Stranahan, 20, 46

East and South Florida Canal Company, 7
Education issues, 111–13, 131–33, 136–37, 139
Edwards, Scott, 113
Edwick, Geo. R., 38
Emmons, Glenn, 142
English, George W., Jr., 154–55, 160
English, Harriet, 11, 14
English, William F., 11–12
Erkins, A. W., 109
Estate, settlement of, 157–58
Everglades. *See* Florida Everglades
Everglades Lumber Company, 98
Everglades Telephone Company, 98

F. M. Welles and Company, 45
Family backgrounds, 147
Family planning, 126
Farrow, J. G., 37, 88, 101
Fatio, Francis, 3–4
FEC. *See* Florida East Coast Railway Company (FEC)

Ferry across New River: Metcalf and, 38; public reaction to, 38; sale of, 37; Stranahan and, 66, 80
FESA. *See* Florida Equal Suffrage Association (FESA)
FFWC. *See* Florida Federation of Women's Clubs (FFWC)
First National Bank, 160
First National Bank of Saint Augustine, 90, 91–93, 94
Fisher, F. T., 101
"Fishhouse," 76
Fitzpatrick, Richard, 5, 6–7, 11
Flagler, Henry Morrison, 27–28, 44, 67–68, 69, 130–31
Fletcher, Duncan U., 106, 138
Florida: admission to Union, 12; climate of, 10, 15; Great Britain and, 3; reputation of, 3–4; seat of government of, 6; Spain and, 4; visitor reactions to, 17
Florida Atlantic Coast Land Company, 178n.3
Florida Coast Line Canal and Transportation Company, 17, 29, 86, 178n.3
Florida East Coast Canal and Transportation Company, 68
Florida East Coast Railway Company (FEC), 68, 75, 76, 81, 86
Florida Equal Suffrage Association (FESA), 119, 122–24
Florida Everglades: drainage project in, 81, 90; New River and, 2; Pine Island, 16
Florida Federation of Women's Clubs (FFWC), 118, 123, 133
Florida Fiber Company, 17
Florida Tropical Fruit Propagating and Land Improvement Company, 15
Fort Lauderdale: Andrews Avenue, 83–84; bank, first, 82; beach road, construction of, 96–97; board of trade, 82, 101; city program, *62*; deep-water harbor for, 97–98; disagreement with Brickells over, 85–86; farms in, 91; financial affairs of, 109–10, 154–55; fire in, 83; growth of, in 1920s, 94; incorporation of, 82, 101; location of, 9, 13; naming of, 8–9; population of, 83, 101; reports of soldiers from, 9–13; school in, 72; social life in, 73–74; store, first, 48; Stranahan name in, 89, 100, 163; survey for, 69; "Tuskegee Park," 89–90; work camp in, 17
Fort Lauderdale Bank and Trust Company, 94–95, 155
Fort Lauderdale Baseball Club, 111
Fort Lauderdale Garden Club, 128
Fort Lauderdale Historical Society, xvii, 128, 160, 161, 162
Fort Lauderdale Mutual Loan and Building Association, 98
Fort Lauderdale Securities Company, 98–99
Fort Lauderdale State Bank, 92, 93
Fort Lauderdale Woman's Club, 111, 117–18, 154
"Frankee Lewis Donation." *See* "Lewis Place"
Frederick S. Morse, 86–87
Freducci map, 1
French and Indian War, 3
Friends of the Florida Seminoles, 133–34
Friends of the Seminoles, 139, 142
Friends of the Seminoles, Florida Foundation, Inc., 139–40
Fritz, C. E., 108
Frost, W. J., 104–5

"Gala Week" fairs at Jacksonville, 75
Gate City Transportation Company, 98
Gil Blas, 8
Gilchrist, Albert W., 90
Glenn, James L., 137, 138–39
Gopher, Jimmy, wife of, 55
Gray, William Crane, 134

Hack line: agent for, 65; camp location, 46–47; camp manager for, 31–32, 48–49; description of, 33–34, 68–69; drivers for, 37; mail and, 35; origins of, 29; problems of, 43–44; promotion of, 30–31, 36; sportsmen and, 36; tent camp of, 34–35
Haley, James A., 141, 144

Hall, George W., 95–96, 101
Hall, Isaiah, 13
Hall, M. Lewis, 154
Hall, Robert (Bob): on F. Stranahan, 95–96, 149, 150–51, 156–57; on I. Stranahan, 150, 158; on trading post, 111
Hanson, W. Stanley, 138–39
Harper, F. W., 105
"Harvest Home Picnic and Barbecue at Seminole Park, New River," 88–89, 90
Hawkins, W. R., 19
Hazelton, Ohio, 19
Health problems of F. Stranahan, 151–53, 155
Heloise, 80–81
Henshall, James A., *Camping and Cruising in Florida*, 15, 16
Heyser, A. E., 25, 31
Hiaasen, Carl, 149
Hinton, J. S., 153
Holding, J. M., 104, 105
Holland, C. G., 101
Holland, Spessard, 143
Horne, B. J., 106, 108
Horton, R. A., 98
Hubbell, E. P., 106
Hunting and Fishing in Florida (Cory), 15
Hurricane: of 1895, 66; of 1926, 94, 96, 105–6

"Indian Haulover," 11
Indian Rights Association, 134
Indian River Advocate, 27
Indian River State Bank of Titusville, 41, 42
Infinger, Francis, 13
Ingraham, James E., 68, 75
Ives map, 11

Jacksonville, Saint Augustine, and Halifax River Railway, 28
Jenkins, Joseph, 13
Jenkins, Josiah, 13
Jenkins, Washington, 13, 14, 89
Jennings, May Mann, 119, 121, 122–23, 125, 133
Jennings, William S., 119
Jesup, Thomas, 8
Johnson, Kenneth, 121
Juan Nepomuceno, 4
Jumper, Betty Mae Tiger. *See* Tiger, Betty Mae
Jumper, Frank, 75
Jumper, Willy, 135
Juno, Florida, 25

Key West, Florida, 6
King, E. T., 73, 74, 76
Kirk, Claude, 128
Knight, May, 13
Knowlton, A. L., 69
Kuhn, Alfred G., 113
Kunti. See *coontie*
Kyle, W. C., 93–94, 96, 98, 99, 106, 155

Lacey, Edith Augusts, 178n.24
Lamar, G. B., 92, 93
Land agent business, 85–89
Land boom, Florida: collapse of, 105–6; Seminoles and, 134; stalling of, 94
Las Olas Beach, pavilion on, 95–96
Las Olas Bridge Company, 96–97
Lauderdale, William, 8–9
Lauderdale Amusement Company, 98–99
Lauderdale Angler's Club, 150
Lawrence, Malinda J., 96
Lemon City, 27
Lewis, Frankee, 5
Lewis, Jonathan, 4–5
Lewis, Polly, 4–5
Lewis, Surla, 4
Lewis, Walter B., 137
"Lewis Place": Brickell purchase of, 14; claims on, 5; county road and, 26–27; sale of, 6; survey of, 12
Liberty Loan drive, 122, 125
Library, personal, 147–48, 161
Life-saving stations, 14, 124–25. *See also* Station No. 4
Lindenville, Ohio, 20
Lochrie, John, 94
Lyman, A. E., 31

Lyman, B., 48
Lyman, George, 65
Lyman, Morris Benson, 65

MacCauley, Clay, 137
Mallory, Stephen R., 7, 11
Marshall, J. W., 72
Marshall, Mrs. John, 136
Marshall, Mrs. W. H., 111
Marshall, W. H., 84, 90, 97, 101
Martin, Sidney, 44
McFadden, Jennie Leah, 18–19
McKay, George, 12
Mecca Oil Company, 98
Melbourne, Florida, 22, 29–30
Melbourne News, 22–23
Merritt, Ada, 72
Merritt, Zachary T., 72
Metcalf, Guy Irwin: birth of, 18–19; business interests of, 27, 31, 43–44; death of, 105, 157; as editor of *Melbourne News*, 22–23; ferry and, 38; health problems of, 21–22; in Juno, 25; marriage of, 43, 178n.24; in Melbourne, 30; road building and, 25–26; A. Stranahan on, 102; F. Stranahan and, 48–49; I. Stranahan on, 105. *See also* hack line
Metcalf, William Irwin, 19, 22–23, 25, 27, 31
Miami, Florida, railroad to, 67–68
Miccosukee Tribe of Indians of Florida, 144–45
Millinery industry, 116–17
Mizell, Von D., 126
Model Land Company, 86
Moffat, Ed, 37, 44
Moore-Willson, Minnie, 133
Mortgage Security Corporation of America, 98
Motte, Jacob Rhett, 10, 11
Munroe, Kirk, 117
Munroe, Mary Barr, 103, 117

Nash, Roy, 91, 137
National Audubon Society, 116–17
National Register of Historic Places, 162

National Society Daughters of the American Revolution, 128, 140
Near East Relief, 125
Needham property, 106
New River: bridge over, 80, 100–101; crossing of, 12–13; deep-water harbor and, 97; early settlers on, 4–7; image of, 1; inlet of, 2–3, 10–11; Lewis family tracts on, 4–5; location of crossing for, 26–27; mariners and, 11; military operations and, 8; name of, 1–2; opening of area for development, 13–14; outdoorsmen and, 15; population of, 7, 13, 14–15; riparian rights, 69; survey for town site, 69. *See also* Ferry across New River
New River tunnel, 127
The Ney, 5
Niles, Garry, 37
1919 Study Club, 128
Nineteenth Amendment, 124
North New River Canal, 83, 90–91
Nugent, Florence, 66
Nugent, James L., 66

Oliver, D. D., 150
Oliver, Eva Bryan (Mrs. Frank), 79, 118, 149–50, 152
Oliver, Frank R., 80, 92, 93, 96
Oliver, J. D., 93, 96
Oliver Brothers, 82, 92–93
O'Neill, Dennis, 33, 66, 89, 146
Osceola, Robert, 75
Osky's, 85
Otter pelt, 54, 76–77

Palm Beach wheelchairs, 57, 147
Parker, Agnes, 150
Parker, E. C., 83–84
Parker, Mary, 62, 150
Parrott, Joseph R., 68, 76, 81
Peacock, Charles, 14
Peacock, J. T., 14
Pent, W. T., 37
Peters, Thelma, 37, 38
Philippe, Odet, 5, 8

Pierce, Charles, 2
Pine Island, 16
Pioneer families in South Florida, xvi–xvii
Pioneer House, 116, 158–59, 161–62
Pitts, N. W., 26
Planning and zoning board, 126
Plant, Henry B., 27–28
Plume trade, 116–17
Pompano, Florida, 96
Produce: shipment of, 90–91; for Stranahan and Company, 71, 77; winter freezes, 70
Property: in Broward County, 89–90; as collateral, 65; commercial, adjoining Stranahan House, 162–63; financing of, 90; "Home Place" proposal, 153–54, 169–72; for hospital, 113; on New River, 47–48; for Salvation Army, 113–14; school board and, 111–13, 159–60, 173; of W. Stranahan, 78, 79; of Stranahan and Company, 80; Stranahan Park, 113; for Women's Club of Fort Lauderdale, 111
Provident Hospital, 126
Pynchon, Genevieve, 127

Railroad development, 27–28, 67, 70
Rasey, W. E., 107
Real estate. *See* Land agent business; Land boom; Property
Rickard, C. E., 106
Rickards, James S., 105
Riley, James Whitcomb, 118
Roads: to beach, construction of, 96–97; Dade county, 25–27
Robbins, Graham, and Chillingworth, 49
Robbins, Joseph, 4
Robert, Albert W., 178n.3
Rockefeller, John D., 28
Rodes, C. G., 107
Rogers, Dwight L., 126, 142
Rogers, E. E., 84
Roller-skating rink, 98–99
Romans, Bernard, 3

Saint Augustine, Florida, 28
Salvation Army, 113–14

Scott, Bertram, 143
Second Seminole War, 7–8, 9
Seminole Indian Association, 138–39
Seminoles: alcohol and, 137; in City of Fort Lauderdale program, 62; coexistence with settlers by, 15–16; Dania Reservation, 134–37; education of children of, 131–33, 136–37, 139; in 1845, 12; Flagler and, 130–31; "Gala Week" fairs and, 75–76; hunting and trapping methods of, 16; otter pelts and, 54; Pine Island camp, 16; reservation for, 133–34; sale of liquor to, 116; Second Seminole War, 7–8, 9; termination of tribe, 140–44; Third Seminole War, 11, 12; trading post and, 53, 55, 66–67, 76–77, 82
The Seminoles of Florida (Moore-Willson), 133
Seminole Tribe of Florida, Inc., 144, 163
Seventh Day Adventist Church, 127–28, 161
Sheppard, Herschel, 162
Simpson, Alice Cromartie, 132, 147
Sistrunk, James, 126
Smathers, George, 142, 144
Snyder, Solomon, 5
Social and personal lives, 148–50
Spanish-American War, 71
Spencer, Lucien A., 134–35
Spencer, Melville, 25
Station No. 4, 14, 33, 66
Stewart, Billy, wife of, 55
Stranahan, Alice, 84
Stranahan, Allen, 20, 46, 84, 102, 104, 152
Stranahan, Frank, 51, 57, 63; arrival at New River, 33; assets of, 154; birth of, 18; death of, 155–57; early life of, 19; letters to Ivy, 73–74; letter to Will, 33–35; marriage of, 74, 147; in Melbourne, 23–24, 29–30; move to Florida, 21, 23; move to New River, 31–32; as reclusive, 146; travels of, 20; visit to Ohio, 71, 83, 84. *See also* Hack line
Stranahan, Ivy Julia Cromartie, 56, 57, 59, 64; birth and education of, 72; death of, 161; death of Frank and, 156, 159;

on her activism, 129; interview with, 165, 166; letters to Frank, 102–4, 105; marriage of, 74, 147; recognition for, 128–29; on Seminole tribe termination, 142–43, 144; as teacher, 72, 73; on trip to reservation land, 135–36
Stranahan, John, 18
Stranahan, Rachel, 18
Stranahan, Robert, 18, 20, 84, 147
Stranahan, Sarah McFadden, 18, *59*
Stranahan, Will, 19–21, 46, *54*, 74–75, 78, 79
Stranahan and Company: activities of, 78–79; building for, 48, 66, 76, 80; employees of, 76; financial backing for, 66; goods in store, 77–78, 82; incorporation of, 79–80; license for, 71, 81–82; location of, *58*; produce for, 71, 77; sale of, 82, 83, 90; Seminoles and, 76–77
Stranahan Building Company, 155
Stranahan home, *60*, *61*; death of I. Stranahan and, 161; furnishings of, 80; New River tunnel construction and, 127; renovation from store into residence, 80; restoration of, 162, 165; seawall and, 81. *See also* Pioneer House
Stranahan House, Inc., 162
Strobel, Benjamin B., 9
Sunset Investment Company, 109

Taravella, J. P., 91
Tarpon River bridge, 47
Taxpayer revolt, 107–8
TenBrook, Frances (Mrs. D. C.), 118, 119, 122
Termination of Seminole tribe, 140–44
Third Seminole War, 11, 12
Tidball, John W., 153
Tiger, Ada, 136
Tiger, Betty Mae, *62*, 136–37, 144, 150
Tiger, Buffalo, 144
Tiger, Howard, *62*
Tiger, Tom, 75
Tommie, Annie, 132, 135
Tommie, Doctor, 132
Tommie, Howard, 145

Tommie, Mary, *62*, 150
Tommie, Tony, 85, 132–33
Tompkins, Christopher, 10–11
Tortugas, 43
Trading post: in 1896, *50*; Seminoles and, 66–67; social activities in, 110–11; Welles and, 39–43, 44. *See also* Stranahan and Company
Tropical Real Estate Exchange, 25
Tropical Sun, 25, 27
True, Harriet T., 160
Turner, Glenn E., 108–9
Tuttle, Julia D., 67–68

U.S. Coast Guard, 14, 124
U.S. Senate Subcommittee of the Committee on Indian Affairs, 138

Valentine, W. C., 33, 146
Varney, G. C., 86–87, 94
Verezaluze, Sebastian, 4
Vienna, Ohio, 18, 19

Ward, Mrs. Miller, 158
Watchie Esta/Hutrie, 132
Watson, Thomas E., 87
Welles, F. M., 39–43, 44–46, 85
Wheeler, H. G., 101
Wheeler, Mrs. H. G., 118
Whidden, W., 38
Williams, Arthur T., 15
Williams, Marcellus, 2, 13
Wilson, Lake, 55
Winter freezes, 70
Women's Christian Temperance Union, 115, 118
Women's Civic Improvement Association, 117
Women's suffrage, 118–24
World War I, 124–25
Wrecking business, 6
Wright, James, 7

Young, Joseph W., 97

Zamia integrifolia, 9

Harry A. Kersey, Jr. (1935–2021), was professor emeritus of history at Florida Atlantic University. He is the author of several books, including *The Florida Seminoles and the New Deal, 1933–1942*, and *Pelts, Plumes, and Hides: White Traders among the Seminole Indians, 1870–1930*, and the co-author of *Buffalo Tiger: A Life in the Everglades*.

The Florida History and Culture Series
Edited by Raymond Arsenault and Gary R. Mormino

Al Burt's Florida: Snowbirds, Sand Castles, and Self-Rising Crackers, by Al Burt (1997)
Black Miami in the Twentieth Century, by Marvin Dunn (1997; first paperback edition, 2016)
Gladesmen: Gator Hunters, Moonshiners, and Skiffers, by Glen Simmons and Laura Ogden (1998)
"Come to My Sunland": Letters of Julia Daniels Moseley from the Florida Frontier, 1882–1886, edited by Julia Winifred Moseley and Betty Powers Crislip (1998; first paperback edition, 2020)
The Enduring Seminoles: From Alligator Wrestling to Ecotourism, by Patsy West (1998)
Government in the Sunshine State: Florida Since Statehood, by David R. Colburn and Lance deHaven-Smith (1999)
The Everglades: An Environmental History, by David McCally (1999; first paperback edition, 2000)
Beechers, Stowes, and Yankee Strangers: The Transformation of Florida, by John T. Foster Jr. and Sarah Whitmer Foster (1999)
The Tropic of Cracker, by Al Burt (1999; first paperback edition, 2009)
Balancing Evils Judiciously: The Proslavery Writings of Zephaniah Kingsley, edited and annotated by Daniel W. Stowell (2000)
Hitler's Soldiers in the Sunshine State: German POWs in Florida, by Robert D. Billinger Jr. (2000; first paperback edition, 2009)
Cassadaga: The South's Oldest Spiritualist Community, edited by John J. Guthrie Jr., Phillip Charles Lucas, and Gary Monroe (2000)
Claude Pepper and Ed Ball: Politics, Purpose, and Power, by Tracy E. Danese (2000)
Pensacola during the Civil War: A Thorn in the Side of the Confederacy, by George F. Pearce (2000; first paperback edition, 2008)
Castles in the Sand: The Life and Times of Carl Graham Fisher, by Mark S. Foster (2000)
Miami, U.S.A., by Helen Muir (2000)
Politics and Growth in Twentieth-Century Tampa, by Robert Kerstein (2001)
The Invisible Empire: The Ku Klux Klan in Florida, by Michael Newton (2001)
The Wide Brim: Early Poems and Ponderings of Marjory Stoneman Douglas, edited by Jack E. Davis (2002)
The Architecture of Leisure: The Florida Resort Hotels of Henry Flagler and Henry Plant, by Susan R. Braden (2002)
Florida's Space Coast: The Impact of NASA on the Sunshine State, by William Barnaby Faherty, S.J. (2002)
In the Eye of Hurricane Andrew, by Eugene F. Provenzo Jr. and Asterie Baker Provenzo (2002)
Florida's Farmworkers in the Twenty-first Century, text by Nano Riley and photographs by Davida Johns (2003)
Making Waves: Female Activists in Twentieth-Century Florida, edited by Jack E. Davis and Kari Frederickson (2003; first paperback edition, 2003)
Orange Journalism: Voices from Florida Newspapers, by Julian M. Pleasants (2003)
The Stranahans of Fort Lauderdale: A Pioneer Family of New River, by Harry A. Kersey Jr. (2003; first paperback edition, 2022)
Death in the Everglades: The Murder of Guy Bradley, America's First Martyr to Environmental-

ism, by Stuart B. McIver (2003; first paperback edition, 2009)
Jacksonville: The Consolidation Story, from Civil Rights to the Jaguars, by James B. Crooks (2004; first paperback edition, 2019)
The Seminole Wars: America's Longest Indian Conflict, by John and Mary Lou Missall (2004; first paperback edition, 2016)
The Mosquito Wars: A History of Mosquito Control in Florida, by Gordon Patterson (2004)
Seasons of Real Florida, by Jeff Klinkenberg (2004; first paperback edition, 2009)
Land of Sunshine, State of Dreams: A Social History of Modern Florida, by Gary R. Mormino (2005; first paperback edition, 2008)
Paradise Lost? The Environmental History of Florida, edited by Jack E. Davis and Raymond Arsenault (2005; first paperback edition, 2005)
Frolicking Bears, Wet Vultures, and Other Oddities: A New York City Journalist in Nineteenth-Century Florida, edited by Jerald T. Milanich (2005)
Waters Less Traveled: Exploring Florida's Big Bend Coast, by Doug Alderson (2005)
Saving South Beach, by M. Barron Stofik (2005; first paperback edition, 2012)
Losing It All to Sprawl: How Progress Ate My Cracker Landscape, by Bill Belleville (2006; first paperback edition, 2010)
Voices of the Apalachicola, compiled and edited by Faith Eidse (2006)
Floridian of His Century: The Courage of Governor LeRoy Collins, by Martin A. Dyckman (2006)
America's Fortress: A History of Fort Jefferson, Dry Tortugas, Florida, by Thomas Reid (2006)
Weeki Wachee, City of Mermaids: A History of One of Florida's Oldest Roadside Attractions, by Lu Vickers (2007)
City of Intrigue, Nest of Revolution: A Documentary History of Key West in the Nineteenth Century, by Consuelo E. Stebbins (2007)
The New Deal in South Florida: Design, Policy, and Community Building, 1933–1940, edited by John A. Stuart and John F. Stack Jr. (2008)
The Enduring Seminoles: From Alligator Wrestling to Casino Gaming, Revised and Expanded Edition, by Patsy West (2008)
Pilgrim in the Land of Alligators: More Stories about Real Florida, by Jeff Klinkenberg (2008; first paperback edition, 2011)
A Most Disorderly Court: Scandal and Reform in the Florida Judiciary, by Martin A. Dyckman (2008)
A Journey into Florida Railroad History, by Gregg M. Turner (2008; first paperback edition, 2012)
Sandspurs: Notes from a Coastal Columnist, by Mark Lane (2008)
Paving Paradise: Florida's Vanishing Wetlands and the Failure of No Net Loss, by Craig Pittman and Matthew Waite (2009; first paperback edition, 2010)
Embry-Riddle at War: Aviation Training during World War II, by Stephen G. Craft (2009)
The Columbia Restaurant: Celebrating a Century of History, Culture, and Cuisine, by Andrew T. Huse, with recipes and memories from Richard Gonzmart and the Columbia restaurant family (2009)
Ditch of Dreams: The Cross Florida Barge Canal and the Struggle for Florida's Future, by Steven Noll and David Tegeder (2009; first paperback edition, 2015)
Manatee Insanity: Inside the War over Florida's Most Famous Endangered Species, by Craig Pittman (2010; first paperback edition, 2022)
Frank Lloyd Wright's Florida Southern College, by Dale Allen Gyure (2010)

Sunshine Paradise: A History of Florida Tourism, by Tracy J. Revels (2011; first paperback edition, 2020)
Hidden Seminoles: Julian Dimock's Historic Florida Photographs, by Jerald T. Milanich and Nina J. Root (2011)
Treasures of the Panhandle: A Journey through West Florida, by Brian R. Rucker (2011)
Key West on the Edge: Inventing the Conch Republic, by Robert Kerstein (2012)
The Scent of Scandal: Greed, Betrayal, and the World's Most Beautiful Orchid, by Craig Pittman (2012; first paperback edition, 2014)
Backcountry Lawman: True Stories from a Florida Game Warden, by Bob H. Lee (2013; first paperback edition, 2015)
Alligators in B-Flat: Improbable Tales from the Files of Real Florida, by Jeff Klinkenberg (2013; first paperback edition, 2015)

www.ingramcontent.com/pod-product-compliance
Lightning Source LLC
Chambersburg PA
CBHW031436160426
43195CB00010BB/753